D1539139

DATE DUE

ORGANIZATIONS AS THEATRE: A SOCIAL PSYCHOLOGY OF DRAMATIC APPEARANCES

ORGANIZATIONS AS THEATRE: A SOCIAL PSYCHOLOGY OF DRAMATIC APPEARANCES

Iain L. Mangham

*Centre for the Study of
Organizational Change
and Development
University of Bath*

Michael A. Overington

*Department of Sociology
Saint Mary's University
Halifax
Nova Scotia*

John Wiley & Sons

Chichester · New York · Brisbane · Toronto · Singapore

Library of Congress Cataloging in Publication Data:

Mangham, I. L.
  Organizations as theatre.
  Bibliography: p.
  Includes index.
  1. Organizational behavior.   2. Social psychology.
1. Overington, Michael A.   II. Title.
HD58.7.M365   1987   302.3'5   86–19199

ISBN 0 471 90892 4

British Library Cataloguing in Publication Data:

Mangham, Iain
  Organizations as theatre: a social
psychology of dramatic appearances.
  1. Social psychology
  I. Title   II. Overington, Michael A.
  302   HM251

ISBN 0 471 90892 4

Printed and bound in Great Britain

Contents

Introduction

Comedy is not a drama with the addition of laughs. It is a world of its own
. . . when we leave it again, it can have given the world of action we rejoin
something of a new cast. (Christopher Fry, 1952)

Introductions are often the most interesting part of a book and perhaps that
is because they have been fun to write. They offer a chance at the end of all
the writing to step back a little, get some distance and talk rather more directly
to readers about the book just finished. We come to this point at the end of
our efforts: you are just beginning to find out what we have been up to. Here
is a moment for us to look back and recognize that this book is not the one
which we began — they never are; to show a little more humility about our
work than a text can support if it is to be convincing; to reflect on four years
of transatlantic collaboration and wonder how we managed it. It is also,
concretely, an occasion to talk frankly about our objectives here, to say for
whom we wrote this, to identify our intellectual friends and defy our enemies,
to guide readers into the book, and finally to say a few words of thanks to
those who helped us get as far as these self-congratulations.

As social psychologists we have long been interested in the application of
a theatrical metaphor to social life, particularly as that is found in the workplace. When we sat down in 1981 to talk about doing a joint book, our first,
crucial agreement was that there was no need for another partial application of
a theatrical analogy to some aspect of the social world. While a dramaturgical
approach to social science has been attractive, 'theatre' has not been developed
as a general conceptual model for social scientific analysis. We decided to
attempt this. We decided then, because of our interest in what women and
men do at work, to develop an account of 'theatre' which would serve as a
conceptual model for discussing people and organizations. We are satisfied
that we have done this. Yet we too play before a public and it will have to
decide how adequate is our performance.

Our emphasis has been threefold. We have tried to establish an understanding of theatre, in its broadest sense as a performing art, in order to use
this as a general model for social action. We have attempted to indicate that

1

such a model has deep historical roots and can draw legitimately on a mass of both classic and contemporary work in social science. Finally, we have thought in a meditative way about the application of this model to organizational life, *particularly to interactions among senior managers*. Modesty requires that we acknowledge the incompleteness of these efforts. Our model is internally consistent and intends to be conceptually exhaustive, but it is only partially enunciated; our reportage of its historical roots and social scientific resources is suggestive; and the application of the model to organizations draws upon no more than a part of our own enunciation. More importantly, perhaps, in applying the theatrical model to organizations, we have restricted ourselves to showing how this can be accomplished: we have not tried to press the metaphor at its limits to see what it cannot achieve. In that sense, we are proffering an invitation to think about organizations with this metaphor, unfettered by too many considerations for its formal adequacy. In our judgements, students of organizations are currently in more need of flexibility in their thinking than in further restrictions on such creativity, however they be justified.

As we wrote this volume, we had a broad variety of 'students' in mind. We have tried to present our argument in such a way that it would appeal to almost anyone with any curiosity about organizations, theatre and human conduct. Of course, some chapters take up issues that might be of more interest to social scientists and others deal with matters that are likely to be more attractive to practising managers; but, in general, we have written in order to address people interested in our ideas, whether or not they would consider themselves 'prepared'. In particular, this means that we have in mind both senior and junior managers, that we have considered undergraduates in management, commerce and the social sciences, and finally we have tried to throw in enough novelty to give practising social scientists a moment or two's thought. Naturally, we think that there is originality in our work; but we have tried very hard not to make a 'song and dance' about that. Our object is to attract responses from organizational practitioners that will affect social conduct in their organization and to stimulate critical extension and application of our conceptual model among social scientists. In bridging that difference between practice and analysis, we have opted for a simplicity of presentation that is 'po-faced' about any difficulties which could be raised, in order to encourage individual managers to do something with all this. We are committed to the simplicity of a theatrical metaphor, to its ease of application and to the importance of its use in practice. As academics, we too enjoy picking away at the nagging difficulties of any perspective, our own not excluded; but here those are peripheral matters which we have assigned to off-hand comments and to the notes.

Yet surely there is something puzzling in this talk of metaphors *and* social science. Whatever happened to good ol' facts and figures? The short answer is that nothing happened to them; they continue to have a place in efforts to understand people and organizations. Balance-sheets do offer the tough figures which can tell us key facts about an enterprise. Measures of profitability, debt to earnings ratios, reports of capital investment and the like are vital information about any enterprise. They are not, however, quite the 'facts' and 'figures' which a simple economic framework would suggest. Balance-sheets, time and motion studies, systems analyses, traffic flow reports and so on — the facts of organizational life — all have to be made sense of, have to be given a context in which they mean 'this' rather than 'that'. It is these contexts, frameworks, viewpoints, intellectual positions which operate as metaphors, as ways of grasping some things in terms of others. Indeed there are no 'facts' apart from some interpretation of them. They are mute numbers, words on a page, unless and until they are drawn into some context of human meaning. In that sense, metaphors, and their more developed form — models — are not simply true or false. They offer us sets of concepts which enable us to ask questions about some social reality, like an organization. Such realities, however, are whatever they are; our concepts can only organize understanding with respect to what they suggest about such a reality.

All of this, of course, applies to the theatrical metaphor or model. No more and no less than any other approach, it provides a perspective on organizational life. Yet, because the playful imagery it calls up runs counter to the more usual, much more 'serious' notions of organizations, it does perhaps require some recommendation on our part. Paramountly, an approach to organizations through the conceptual framing of a theatrical model allows us to use all that theatre, as a performing art, implies. It allows us to think about creativity, to consider the craft of actors playing characterizations, it provides considerations of tragedy and comedy, it suggests all the constraints of situation and history which affect any live performance, it allows for inquiry about the link between performance and what goes on backstage. In short, it offers a general model for social life that is self-consistently complete with respect to all and any aspect of organizations which have been considered by managers, analysts or consultants. Whether one is interested in creativity or constraint, it is available in the model without the eclectic in-gathering of disjunct concepts that all too frequently marks organizational thinking.

The theatrical analogy is not a fresh image. From Plato to the present day it surfaces again and again in the work of philosophers, social thinkers, novelists, playwrights and social scientists. Its aptness has clearly varied; in some ages the metaphor is a commonplace of everyday talk, in others it hardly receives a mention. The late twentieth century is one of those moments in human history when the comparison of life to theatre is once more especially pertinent. Once again, the theatre is reflecting on the nature of human identity in everyday life. And in the mundane world, people experience themselves in the ever-growing cities as caught in a web of interactions that call for such differences in conduct as to make them all too aware of their own theatricality.

None the less, to advocate a theatrical model as apt for understanding organizations in this modern world is not simply to accept non-reflectively that the alienated social actor created by late capitalism is the normal form of human nature. For a theatrical model, human nature is that of an actor playing characters and alienation is an issue raised by twentieth-century playwrights and directors. The notion that one might step outside history and recognize from that position historically determined forms of thought, such as bourgeois capitalism, sits poorly with a theatrical model. Yet the model can offer a *history* of theatre in many *cultures* as the basis for a broadly comparative approach to organizations. In particular, it provides, within itself, analytic devices for standing back from a situation in order not to be drawn unknowingly into the play of events. The first of these, comedic distance — the ability to recognize that things are not what they seem — is found in the nature of comedy as a profound reservation about authoritative claims of all kinds. The second, which was created by Brecht in this century, is a technique for revealing during performance the constructed nature of play-acting itself. The last of these, which may in fact be the most profound, is a recognition that any performance results from laborious preparation and choices about direction, text, actors and interpretation that the presentation itself mystifies and conceals. The theatrical model as applied to organizational life is, essentially, a device for uncovering and demystifying the constructed nature of action. Yet for all that, it is on no particular side: heroes and villains are found in surprising places and this model commits one only to a careful acknowledgement of their presence and a recognition of the choices which have made such a participation possible.

However, even as we claim this book to be a first, contemporary attempt to use the theatrical model as a general conceptual resource for understanding social interaction in organizations, we are obviously not without influences. Our performance of authority and understanding is itself greatly in need of demystification. Few in science are totally original; even the most creative work at problems which they find in their intellectual tradition. Our tradition goes by the name of *symbolic interactionism*. We have drawn upon it for support in formulating questions and in recognizing what should be allowed to stand as answers. More importantly, we have taken its philosophical roots for granted. For those who would care, this means that we are students of George Herbert Mead and have used his work to find a comfortable place from which to start our inquiries. None the less, little of this is visible in the book itself. Our more obvious and most important influences are Kenneth Burke and his student, Hugh Duncan. It is their recognition of drama as the key trope for explaining social life which is the foundation of our understanding of the theatrical metaphor. Yet, unlike them and R. S. Perinbanayagam, we do not take drama as a literal model of social life. Drama, for us, is a *metaphor* that allows a specific, detailed conceptual address of social action, and our work fits more comfortably against the efforts of people like Elizabeth Burns (1972), Paul Hare (1985), Brisset and Edgley (1975) and Combs and Mansfield (1976); or for the philosophy orientated, Bruce Wilshire (1982).

Yet neither of us comes to the work herein as a novice. Both of us hold academic posts where, for some years, we have shared our perspective with undergraduate and graduate students. Iain Mangham has taught theatre, produced, directed and acted both student and amateur theatre; he has also done research in the professional theatre in the United Kingdom. With this as a background, or an interference, he has worked as a senior manager in a large pharmaceutical enterprise and as a consultant to a variety of organizations. Michael Overington watches television when he has time and stands second to none in his devotion to Kenneth Burke, Hugh Duncan and real ale. In this volume, original information about senior managers and the performing arts is extracted from a number of studies conducted through the Centre for the Study of Organizational Change and Development, University of Bath. As director of that centre, Iain Mangham is largely responsible for this work and its results which appear here in the form of transcripts and other, more vagrant, observations.

We have chosen an order of presentation for this volume which allows us to lead readers gently into the perspective which the book elaborates. Thus, we begin with a discussion of metaphor and conceptualization, conceptualization in the social sciences and metaphors of organization before looking at some of the historically rich linkages between an explicit theatricality in everyday life and a conception of theatre as 'reflective' of life. This historical density to our metaphor established, we turn to a detailed justification for our viewpoint that is rooted in an analysis of the way in which people become aware of themselves when confronting a problem arising in the recurrent processes of everyday life. With the image of a 'theatrical' awareness in the midst of ritual process established, we explore the utility of reading modern social science, or some parts of it, with a theatrical metaphor, before coming to Chapters 5 and 6 which are the hub around which the book turns. In the first, we elaborate a conceptual model of 'theatre' which is then mirrored in the narrative form of Chapter 6 where organizations are treated as the expressive performance of social relationships in which status and feeling are the key issues. With this general outline of organizations as theatre accomplished, we devote the next four chapters to a systematic meditation on aspects of organizational conduct as one can understand them within this model. We talk about organizational settings, spaces and the clothing of people in them; we look at 'flat' and 'rounded' characterizations; we draw these themes together in order to display the interpretative form of organizational life and our own efforts to make some sense of that; finally, we conclude with some discussion of the nature of organizational texts and those who proffer particular readings of them so as to direct the choices that social actors make in their conduct at work.

Like any performance, this work is best taken, in our view, from curtain-up to its denouement, and in that order. We suggest the notes as intellectual asides that can be left until later. However, we do recognize that some people never get into their seats until after the first act; that others only come for the ballet which begins the second act; that some are merely waiting for the actors to take a blunder; that yet others have come to see if the show will run and so on. If such be you, do not miss Chapters 3, 5 and 6. For those who would take our recommendations, the following outline can serve as a programme guide.

In Chapter 1 we hope to persuade readers that one cannot produce analyses of the social world — including organizations — without using metaphors, or their elaborated form models. This argument is essentially made in terms of the metaphoric character of conceptualization, be that commonplace or scientific. To establish this we begin by dealing with the everyday nature of conceptualization, the way in which from childhood people experience their world through a faceted vision provided by society. To make this point clear for our purposes, we continue with a short account of the leading metaphors in organizational analysis and conclude by emphasizing that we choose models because of the reality they promise to create and not for the relative adequacy of their truth claims.

In Chapter 2 we document the way in which a metaphor of theatre fulfils the transitivity of any trope, allowing us to experience both life as like theatre and theatre as an image of life. Although this tendency to move both ways along the line of metaphoric tension which binds 'theatre' and 'life' together stretches from Plato to the present day, we have restricted our discussion. In particular we limit our illustrations of the overlap of theatre and life to some periods of the English stage, before taking up a number of episodes of everyday theatricality. Yet the theatricality of life has most frequently been encouraged by social thinkers to the élite, such as Ralegh and Machiavelli, and the vignettes — Venice of the Doges, Versailles under Louis XIV, Bath under Beau Nash, Bali in the nineteenth century, the dramatic pomp of Nazi Germany — are anything but 'everyday'. In a tacit way, we are encouraging the use of a dramaturgical framing of social life for the demystification of hierarchical orders.

Chapter 3 deserves particular attention because we have tried to lay out in it all the twists and turns of our reasoning on behalf of a theatrical model of human action in organizations. Our roots in symbolic interactionism are here more apparent and we have tried to develop the argument in terms that link a notion of dramaturgy quite directly to George Herbert Mead's thinking. In particular, we offer a way of handling both recurrent events in the social process and the less common moments in which self-awareness emerges to handle problematic situations; we find a way of talking about social reality and appearance that fits into such a dialectical process; and we suggest that the conditions for human self-awareness are precisely the formal conditions for dramatic performance. Then we push beyond Mead's interests to argue that the emergence of self-awareness in the ritual spaces of recurrent activity is directly parallel with the historical emergence of drama from ritual. This justifies our view that human self-awareness is, indeed, a theatrical conscious-ness and allows us to ask some further questions about the nature of reality and appearance in 'theatre' such that it can be a conceptual resource for understanding organizational life.

Chapter 4 is a chapter which seems to have book-length ambitions. However, it only deals with some matters in social psychology, anthropology, social survey research and Burkean dramaturgical sociology. We have tried to suggest some further resources that are available when one applies a theatrical metaphor to the social sciences. Here, we are considering work that is ongoing and, with the exception of the Burkean material, unaware of its dramaturgical qualities. There are four parts to this chapter which are connected only by our reading of them from a dramaturgical perspective. In the first, we examine social experimentation by psychologists as research by dramatic staging. The second looks at the use of 'performance' and 'text' images in the work of social anthropologists. In the next part, we suggest that the subjective meaning of survey researchers' data is only available through the use of an unacknowledged and commonplace dramaturgical perspective. To conclude, we survey work produced by sociologists working in the intellectual debt of Kenneth Burke and thus sneak in Erving Goffman and ourselves.

Chapter 5 was, in some ways, the most difficult chapter to write: what does one say about the theatre in a single chapter? Obviously one does not say much that is original in the face of the centuries of scholarship. Instead, we have written about the theatre as might any interactionist doing observational research on a somewhat closed social world. We enter the theatre, as would any member of an audience, in order to attend a performance. Here we establish what is socially required for a play to be taken for granted as dramatic reality; then, we move behind the scenes to discover what social arrangements have made a staging of reality possible. Our narrative tries to show how the naturalness of performance is accomplished; first, by the audience's framing of the play as theatrical reality; and, second, as a result of the choices made about plays, directors, actors, interpretations and so on. We have written this account in such a way as to contrast the naturalness of theatrical action with the choices and resultant constraints from which this is created. By this, we hope to offer our understanding of 'theatre' as a general model of social action, both for the givenness of the recurrent patterns of everyday life and for the constraints from which these emerge.

This is a chapter to which people will want to return when thinking about using dramaturgical concepts analytically. Although we have sought to develop a general model of social action, with a very deliberate interplay between choice, constraint and the accomplished mystification of performance, it is by no means completely enunciated. An acceptable test of this acclaimed generality would be the invention of further concepts using the framework we have offered.

Chapter 6 outlines the form of organizational life as a mingling of ritual performance with times of rehearsal-like awareness. Obviously, the alternation of these kinds of action will vary in terms of the organizational level one examines; it is more obvious in our illustrations drawn largely from interactions among senior managers. This chapter takes pains to deal with the crucial issues of appearance and reality in organizations and tries to draw a general map of action in organizations with the model of theatre as a guide.

Chapter 7 treats the expressive aspects of space, setting and clothing as semiotic of persons and their positions. We take space and setting in organizations as frames around the characters who act within them: they are aspects of situations useful when gathering information about persons and their likely characterizations. In much the same way, and surely familiar to those interested in 'power dressing' for 'power lunches', we suggest that clothes do much more than provide social modesty. They express character and social rank, they suggest an individual's likely attitude towards certain social conduct, they are a claim on audiences' credence for particular social characterizations.

Chapter 8 shifts attention to issues of actors and characterizations, to the human actors and the organizational parts which they rehearse and perform in order to maintain themselves on that 'stage'. We approach this by an examination of the stereotypic, 'flat' character in contrast to the 'rounded' human as these are presented in the work of a number of writers about managerial conduct. We also consider the importance of 'types' of persons in organizations and the ease these offer in ritual performance. Yet, all characterizations on stage or in organizations are the creation of actors before audiences; it is only some persons in an organization whose conduct allows one access to the richness of actorial technique, to the possibilities which are within reach of that technique.

In the next chapter, Chapter 9, we come to grips with the way in which the interpretation of social action, for those participant or those merely observing, is the key factor in making sense. Here we try to reassemble the disassociated parts of organizational conduct in order to show, however incompletely, that it is only through bringing a general model of action to bear on any action episode that we and the participants can make sense of it. Interpretation is the core of social action and for students of that process it is doubly so — making scientific sense of what is 'common sense'. We have to use a theatrical model holistically, as do theatrical audiences striving to understand a play, if it is to offer a sensible interpretation of organizational conduct. We may treat aspects of that model separately in our exposition, but that is not the way in which to employ the model as manager, consultant or analyst.

In our final chapter we yield to an audience's desire to see the playwright, to know who provided a text *for* interpretation. In organizations one cannot easily find the playwright unless one is looking at a founder and owner. More frequently one is dealing with a long-established organization, whether that be an enterprise or no. In such cases, with the author long dead, our authority, both for the text which is played and for the sub-textual interpretation, will be found among the senior management. Of course, there are any number of organizational writers who claim to have privileged knowledge about successful subtexts; but they are no more convincing than such recommendations among interpreters of drama. The key figure in giving sense to organizations, to providing convincing sub-texts, is the director. Organizations, like the theatre, are currently the interpretive arenas of directors. Success and failure depend on directorial choices of action and interpretation; but lurking behind them are the choices which make such persons the sub-textual inspirations for their organization. And that is, perhaps, the announcement of another volume!

As with any other project that takes up four years of life, we have incurred a number of personal and intellectual debts. It is the usual pretension of acknowledgements that these are discharged with a few kind words; that just is not the case. Moreover, with a book that is a joint effort we each have our separate thanks to make.

Iain Mangham was assisted by funds from the Social Science Research Council (now renamed the Economic and Social Research Council in a piece of characteristic inanity perpetrated by the Secretary of State for Education and Science) and has been given considerable support by his immediate colleagues — Colin Eden, Steve Fineman, Adrian McLean, Judi Marshall, Peter Reason and David Sims — throughout this period. Bob Cooper from Lancaster, John Hayes from Leeds and Albert Natchkirk of Sussex have been less immediate but important critics of some of the ideas which have eventually found their way into this work, as have two generations of students. Olive, Alasdair, Catriona and the dogs have been — as always — understanding of the demands that writing can make on a household and ever ready to share tea and sympathy. Finally, much of what has gone into this book began nearly twenty years ago in work stimulated by Dorrie and Galvin Whittaker (both then of the University of Leeds). I owe them a great deal; I trust they will find in these pages echoes of some of the things we talked about.

Michael Overington was assisted with funds from the Social Science and Humanities Research Council of Canada and the Senate Research Committee of Saint Mary's University. Kirby Abbott, Paul Bate, Peter Case, Ian Colville, Annie Pye, Peter Ryan and Valerie Sloane have either been forbearing in their reading of parts of the work or have put their time at my disposal as I wrestled with what seemed insoluble problems. And they bought their share of the beer. Barbara Overington, despite her Bostonian origins, has little time for pragmatic philosophy and less for a theatrical metaphor. There is nothing like living with firm scepticism to remind you, when you say that dramaturgy is only a perspective, that you really know what you are saying. Catherine Watson has simply been the best and most thorough critic one could hope for; I still think she appreciates more about what we are trying here than do we. Finally without the support provided by my late friend, Ken Morris, my ambitions for the book would never have come to fruition. Ken was my first boss when I went to work in a public library at age sixteen. For the next thirty years, until his premature death, we maintained all the contact we could, all the intimacy his fierce spirit could tolerate. His generosity buoyed me both practically and spiritually. My contribution here is dedicated to his memory.

We know that we should not have got this far without Joan Budge's selfless efforts. Situated at the University of Bath, she has been our nexus over the years of transatlantic collaboration. For the occasional gin and tonic and an infrequent kind word she has smoothed journeys, accommodation and the complex communications that have made this book a truly joint effort.

I.L.M.
M.A.O.   Bath, August 1985.

Chapter 1

Organizing Metaphors

Metaphor is a device for saying something in terms of something else. It brings out the thisness of a that, or the thatness of a this. (Burke, 1969a)

What do you do when reality is an empty space? You can make things happen — and conjure up, with all the risks, a little token Here and Now; you can drink and be merry and forget what your sober mind tells you. Or, like the Cricks who out of their watery toils could always dredge up a tale or two, you can tell stories. (Swift, 1983)

Monsieur Jourdain, that innocent snob in Molière's *Le Bourgeois Gentilhomme*, has won renown through the years with his amazing discovery that if there are only two ways of expressing oneself — prose and verse, then: 'Good Heavens! I have been speaking prose for more than forty years without knowing it'. This same naïvety, without the snobbery, could well characterize most of us when it comes to the position of metaphors.[1] We have all heard metaphors — 'He drinks *like a fish*', 'She's a *bright* child', 'Their marriage is *on the rocks*', 'That's an *empty* comment' — and assumed them to be part of the way in which we enliven expression. Metaphors are generally regarded as stylistic devices which bring variety and richness to our speaking and writing. They beautify poems, they elevate political speeches, they help out the limping sermon, they assist the frustrated lover, they provide an optimistic conclusion to managerial reports. They are embellishments on plain language; good like chocolate in small amounts but cloying and bad for you in large quantities. This is the innocent view which we should like to change in order to suggest that, far from being stylistic decoration, metaphors are fundamental to our speaking, to our writing and to our understanding.

Of course, many expressions which we use in everyday life seem merely literal. 'Here's the cup', 'Jessica has chicken-pox', 'I'm going to church on Sunday', 'What time is the train for London? are statements and questions that are determinedly matter-of-fact — no allusions, no fanciful images, no stylized embellishments. They are not, however, 'typical' of human discourse. It is little more than a philosophic snobbery which has tried to establish such utterances as the only acceptable form of meaningful speech; and while that might satisfy the interests which limit any kind of prejudice, it is out of sympathy with the world in which most of us speak and write. Clearly, people intend to write and speak both literally and metaphorically. Both kinds of expression have their place, and little practical distinction is made between them. None the less, in this book we shall treat metaphorical expressions and the conceptions which they create as the typical case of human language and consider literal expression, therefore, as a special and limited kind of utterance. From this perspective, metaphors provide the possibility of literal expression.

Perhaps we can best present what must seem an unusual point of view through an account of the way in which people experience their world. We encounter our world — people, places, things — through concepts, through categories which organize perceptions into regular and patterned experience. Our bodies may have sensations, our skin may react to heat, our eyeballs to light, our ear-drums to sound: but we, as human persons, encounter all such sensation only in a particular conceptual form. We do not, in other words, make sense of *the* world directly: we experience it as sensible through a framework of concepts that yields it up as *our* world. This world comes not on its own terms, but on the conceptual terms which our society, our time and place, allow.

This is not to say that we sit, each isolated in our own little world, inventing concepts with which to constitute a meaningful life. Experience is *not* ultimately subjective: experience is given meaning with the collectively shared concepts that our culture produces. We acquire the concepts which shape our experience in relationships with other people, notably in family settings where we first encounter language and the objects which it indicates. There, we discover not only 'Mamma' and 'Dadda'; we also find 'Teddy Bear', 'spinach' and 'chocolate'. The conceptual objects which children uncover in the language use of their home life are eminently commonplace and recognizable to other members of the same culture. A paradigm illustration of this process is the acquisition of the concept of the negative — as in such commands as 'No, Sarah!' Before we learn our names, or can readily identify 'Mamma', we have been introduced to the moral imperatives of our home, to those things which are permitted and those things which are forbidden.

Modern experts in child-rearing tell us how important is this process, but warn that it is difficult for a small child to make sense of the negative concept if there are too many items to which it can be attached. They tell us to provide our children with an environment in which to wander freely and safely and to introduce into this, one object at a time, things which fit into the category of the forbidden. Typically, we are teaching the one-year-old, not the Ninth Commandment, but specific prohibitions about some plant, pot, fork, picture or whatever. It is these objects that introduce the child to the negative and it will be about such familiar items that the child will inquire when seeking to evaluate the full meaning of this category. They will wander about touching things quizzically, saying 'No?' as they touch them, in order to interrogate us as to whether or not this item or that falls under our negative ban. Children understand — whether or not we know it — that the negative is a category which *we* create for them. Their forbidden object will often be our most cherished possession.

Learning what objects cannot be touched, understanding in that process some of the elementary dimensions of the concept of the negative, is achieved through the child's application of what it knows about one object or category of objects to another object or category. Children make the great step of moving from what they *do* know about the stove, the aspirin bottle, the African violets — that they are '*not* for touching' — to another object that they are also scolded for touching. Recognizing that the negative applies to this new thing — say, the iron — they know *what* this means by experiencing the new, forbidden object through their previous experience with other members of that category — minimally, that they may be spanked if they *do* touch it!

Even if the moral order of the world is created through a concept of the negative, and we do first encounter the negative as a moral concept, our world is not just composed of things that we should not touch, or actions we should not take. It is made up of all the objects of experience. It is constituted from material objects like chairs, buses and trees; of social objects such as parents, families and laws; of cognitive objects such as beauty, God and truth. All of these are required as objects in our experience in the same way, through reference to something which we already know. Past experience, taken as a whole, is the frame within which we encounter the present. Our previous experiences act as metaphorical frameworks within which we come to understand the new, be that the totally novel or simply a new instance of an earlier experience.

To this point, we have been making the very general claim that humans experience their world through frameworks of concepts which organize an understanding of people, events and objects on lines that compare the present with past experience. We have called this metaphorical framing. It is so, however, only in the broad way that metaphors involve us understanding one thing in terms of something else. In that sense, we can hardly help encountering a present moment in terms of something else — we have never been there before and, hence, have to draw on what we do know from past activities. Nor, in so far as we encounter the things of this world through cultural symbols, can we experience them as other than they are — most things are not themselves symbolic and yet we are forced to understand them through language, art, music, mathematics or whatever.

Of course, this is an immodest claim that sets aside as 'snobbery' philosophic views which would argue for the normalcy of literal — determinate — expressions. Moreover, it discards by implication a tradition in philosophy which treats the world as composed of objects whose qualities and relations are independent of our understanding of them. We are led to this view less by philosophic conviction than by our belief as social scientists that we should acknowledge the evidence which students of everyday life find in their studies of the way in which people organize their experience. Metaphors are everywhere. They dot our conversations; they fill the stories which we tell each other; they occupy the mass media to which we attend with such devotion. They flood the memos, reports, discussions, meetings and so on that make up so much of managerial activity in organizations. They even penetrate the writing of social scientists. Making sense together depends on the use of metaphors.

Metaphorical expressions are everywhere in the form of simile, analogy, metonymy and so on. We are constantly involved in treating one thing as another, in terms of another. 'She's as *cold as ice*', 'That's a *dead* issue', 'He has a *long row to hoe* with those children', 'I have never heard such an *obsolete* notion', are all easily recognized metaphorical expressions that can stand as illustrations for our point. However, we are not interested here in categorizing the many kinds of metaphors or figures of speech that the everyday world offers. To do so would only reinforce the common view that such expressions are stylistic *embellishments* of language to be studied by scholars whose concern is more style than substance. We, on the other hand, are more concerned to present metaphors as *organizing* forms through which we experience our life in the world. They serve as perspectives through which we are able to make sense of experience: we frame our world with concepts that select both *what* we can know and *how* we can know it. In the work of Lakoff and Johnson (1980) we find this argument made in some detail. One fine chapter, particularly, reveals the extent of metaphorical expression, offering a number of illustrations of their position 'that metaphors partially structure our everyday concepts and . . . this structure is reflected in our literal language'. Among their examples, one of the more captivating is the extended array of metaphors through which we talk about, and hence, experience 'love'.

From the time that a notion of 'love' entered the vocabulary as an emotion that could be felt between humans, there have been metaphors to express what sort of experience it was or was to be like. Indeed, one could track the meaning of love as a human experience through the changing arrays of metaphor in which it has been addressed. Metaphors change and with them will change the quality and character of that which they express. Any contemporary usage, then, is just that: it is the way in which we are accustomed to express the emotion *now*. Lakoff and Johnson (1980) offer a selection from among current metaphors for 'love' that includes: 'Love is a physical force', 'Love is a patient', 'Love is magic', 'Love is madness', 'Love is war'. Such expressions as: 'There is incredible energy in their relationship', 'I could feel the electricity between us', 'This is a sick relationship', 'They have a healthy marriage', 'She has me in a trance', 'He's crazy about her', 'She fought to retain his affections', serve, then, to display their conviction that there are systematic metaphorical forms in which such emotions as 'love' (or any other experience, for that matter) are presented as meaningful organizations of essentially inchoate moments of life.

To extend their illustration just a little, we can add another image which is modish at the moment — 'Love is a drug'. Expressions such as 'I'm hooked on her', 'I get a rush whenever I see him', 'We're really wired on each other', 'She's high on him', suggest a metaphoric link between the sensation of using drugs and being in love, and because of the transitive character of metaphors, between the sensations of being in love and using drugs. Of course, it is only meaningful to compare 'love' to drug experiences if there are enough people around who can refer to an experience with drugs as a way of understanding the encounter between people as 'love', and vice versa. This would not have been the case only a few years ago. It is in this shifting of metaphors that we are able to locate a way in which human life can take on different meanings. One can fight for another's affections, one can put warlike energy into such a struggle, *only* if love is seen as like war: if, on the other hand, it is like a drug, one may have to find strategies for detoxifying the infatuated.

However, in organizations little love is lost; they are serious places and if there are warlike images they are more likely to be about *work* than leisure pastime. Yet even a word as commonplace as 'work' has taken its metaphoric flights: the kind of experiences which are said to be 'work' and the nature of those experiences has not been particularly stable. 'Work as toil', 'work as vocation', 'work as gainful employment', 'work as punishment for original sin', 'work as manual labour', and the sinister slogan *'Arbeit macht frei'* that stood over the gates of Auschwitz, are all images which have communicated what work is or is like. Management and workers are often in dispute over the stretching and shrinking of the metaphoric frame which 'work' offers. Arguments about whether breaks and cleaning-up time should be paid depend upon their falling into the category of work; the labyrinthine struggles about jurisdiction among trades have all dealt with the expansion and contraction of the meaning of craft work; and the difference between salaries and wages has monetarized a distinction between work as a calling and work as toil — only for the latter do you pay overtime.

Of course, while concepts do structure experience, not all concepts are plainly metaphoric; nor does the scope of any metaphorical expression necessarily extend to all those concepts which could be teased out of it. Many aspects of metaphors go unused as Lytton Strachey points out offhandedly in his biography of Florence Nightingale (1942). There, he comments on her proof for the existence of God that was based upon the metaphoric conception of natural, logical and social patterns *as laws* for which it was obvious, to her, that there had to be a 'lawgiver'.

> Clearly, if we are to trust the analogy of human institutions, we must remember that laws are, as a matter of fact, not dispensed by lawgivers, but passed by Act of Parliament. Miss Nightingale . . . never stopped to consider the question whether God might not be a Limited Monarch. (Strachey, 1942)

However, even in this acerbic extension of a metaphor into images that were largely neglected, we can see that they do pattern conceptualization.

Metaphors are organizing principles which permit us to judge the effectiveness of conceptual expressions. Argument and counter-argument, statement and counter-statement, illustration and counter-example are reliant upon metaphors as tacit principles for shaping the meaning and relevance of the concepts with which we express ourselves and the nature of experience. If 'life' is to be understood, then it has to be formulated as conceptually of this or that category: if it is expressed *as* journey, discovery, exile, struggle or whatever, then it is those metaphors which will guide our explorations of the *meaning* of life.

Turning to the world of organizational life does not somehow put us beyond the reach of the metaphoric: the government bureaucrat, the hard-nosed business man, the union leader are no less users of metaphors than the rest of us. The idea of organizational life as a highly rational process conducted by tough-minded people might seem at first blush to predicate a literal world without time for the luxury of style and decoration. But organizing metaphors are not simply embellishments to the literal, as we have argued; they are the tacit forms of our conceptualization. Thus, even if organizational life were taken as rational, it would still offer a host of metaphors: life in organizations is no different from other social worlds in that metaphoric expression constitutes its modes of experience. There are, of course, specific and typical organizational events and figures, and to that extent one will find metaphors in and about organizations that particularly address such experiences.

For example, the growth of enterprises through merger and take-over has been characteristic of larger organizations for many years. Occasionally, there has been a flurry in this growth and the issue of take-overs has come to occupy a central place in the concerns of many business people. At such times there have been efforts to organize experiences of this process with metaphors offering current appeal in the lives of those involved. A brief but fascinating discussion of the take-over process (Hirsch and Andrews, 1983, but see also Mangham, 1973/74) suggests that, if the normal language of the business world is accounting, the appeal to popular cultures such as the Western or Romance in discussing take-overs is evidence that these are *not* a taken-for-granted part of business practice. They assume that metaphors of courtship, warfare and the Wild West — as ways of organizing the experience of more *or* less friendly take-overs — are *special* devices for handling a process that violates many expectations about the way in which enterprises relate to each other. Treating the friendlier kind of take-over as a form of courtship allows the experience to be organized by such images as 'wooing', 'dancing', 'studs' and 'afterglow', thus pulling into one framework activities as varied as friendly negotiations, prospective partners and the limited post-merger euphoria. Likewise, conceiving a forced take-over as organized by such images as 'summer soldier', 'flak', 'hot pursuit' and the like, allows the acquiescent executive, the various obstacles thrown up to thwart the acquisition and the aggressive acquirer to be considered as parts of the same hostile process.

The eruption of take-over activities into a mundane world of business practice demands a freshness of metaphor in order to allow for the conceptualization of events that are hard to emplace in a literal scheme of things. But we should be wrong if we then concluded that the accepted use of the rational language of accounting in organizations — as a key illustration — was not *also* metaphoric in many of its uses. While we often forget the metaphoric framing which the accepted extension of some conceptualization provides, as in financial imagery for personnel considerations, this represents more of a victory for commonplace literalism than it does the erosion of metaphor. We notice the colourful imagery of take-overs because it is novel and unexpected, allowing us to think about this process creatively and bring it within our experience in terms that have made sense of more familiar regions of life. We do not 'see' the everyday metaphors of accounting because they have become the commonplace expressive form within which organizational activities are framed.

Research, production, marketing and personnel are all separable functions of enterprise; increasingly, however, these activities are being expressed in financial terms. The expert skill of engineers, for example, which might once have been presented in terms of craft, exactness, superiority of design and quality of assembly is all too likely to be now qualified by a cost/benefit terminology. Thus, an advertising campaign for a new car promoted it as: 'The *affordable* German engineered road sedan' (emphasis added) and elaborated this message about the financial advantages of such engineering with a stylistically balanced claim: 'Rather than driving a German engineered road sedan that tells people how much money you earn, now you can drive a German engineered road sedan that tells people how much money you've saved.' Even in government and non-profit organizations, where one might anticipate finding a language of service as a framing for activity, the terminology of finance has grown in dominance. No longer is it the *unquestioned* right of a psychiatric nurse, say, to report on her work with anorexics in terms of their weight stabilization, their 'contracts' to stay above a particular minimum weight, their control of compulsive behaviour and so on. Rather, she must also talk about the number of visits, the proportion of time spent with these patients in comparison to others, vehicle expenses to provide visitation and so on. All of this allows for a financial framework — an accounting metaphor — to be extended to incorporate activities that were once assumed to be matters of medical practice.

The fact that we infrequently notice this monetarization of organizational life, that we take 'the bottom line' as a literal expression, is a measure of the normalization of a financial framework. Ironically, this acceptance of a particular terminological framework as 'natural' leads us to take what was once both metaphoric and conceptually creative as both literal and matter-of-fact. The 'normalization' of metaphors, then, is a cause of their downfall as sources of insight: where they initially clarified through the provision of a different perspective, they later obscure through their semblance to literal facticity. Of course, this is so not only for the metaphors used *in* organizations but also for the metaphors which are used, particularly by social scientists, *about* organizations. Thus, social scientific frames for the analysis of organizations become, through usage and acceptance, less devices for thinking about organizations than literal descriptions of what they are. It is our general view that this acceptance of social scientific frameworks, either by people in organizations or by social scientists analysing them, is *not* a good thing. It transforms a way of thinking creatively into a way of describing literally: it makes a metaphor into a myth.

At this point, then, we want to offer a brief account of some of these social scientific frames that have been proposed for organizational analysis in order to remember them as they once were — inventive metaphoric frameworks that created ways of thinking about organizations.[2] Of course, it would have been simple to set these approaches up for critical comment in order to show off the merits of our metaphor — *organizations as theatre*. We have chosen not to do that because this strategy is all too often tied into a view of social science which expects metaphors (usually called models and theories in this notion of 'science') to be something which they are not. Such criticisms will allege that a view lacks this or that, has this or that bias; that it neglects the crucial part of economic factors, or that it fails to allow for individuals and their choices and so on. In so doing, however, these comments misunderstand the limited character of organizing metaphors: they are, after all, only perspectives on organizations and not literal descriptions. One may prefer one perspective over another, as do we; but that preference does not eliminate the selectivity of the metaphor.

The notion of *organizations as system* is not only the best known of these frameworks, it is also the most widely accepted among both analysts and organizational people themselves. Simply understood, a 'system' is a set of interrelated parts which function as elements of a single whole. The first images of what such a set of interrelated parts might be as a whole were derived from living organisms — plants, animals and humans. 'System', then, was a unifying image for thinking about an organizing principle which would constitute the difference between the living and the inorganic. In some sense, the search for the 'vital principle' which would explain how life and non-life were different, led to the careful investigation of plant, animal and human physiology and uncovered a connectedness of their parts that was grasped in terms of functional contributions to the organism as a whole. Therefore, 'system' carried a burden of organic imagery when it was originally proposed as a way of thinking about organization — organizations as living things — and allowed us to consider how the various parts of an organization contribute to its survival.

Organizations as 'living' systems, then, will clearly have *needs* which they must satisfy if they are to survive. A key question will become, therefore, what does each part of an organization contribute to the survival of the whole? This allows one to consider the interconnectedness of the various parts as given in the particular contributions which each makes to overall survival. It also indicates that no single part is somehow dispensable or indispensable in itself: each gives and receives as part of the whole. Taking this image of an organic system, analysts have been able to think about organizations as complex wholes which live or die, in so far as they are able to satisfy their survival needs. They have been able to consider organizations as self-adjusting processes that have a life of their own, their own capacity for change and adjustment, and are more or less effective in dealing with the contingencies that condition survival.

However, if organizations are like living things, they will live in *environments* and cannot simply be thought about as functioning systems that are self-contained and explicable as such. This later extension of the metaphor opened up all kinds of questions about the interchange between organizations and their environments, about the nature of such environments, about the kind of organizational system that is taken as 'open' to an environment and so on. Yet, as the image of system became more familiar and more generalized, it was easier to think about systems as *sub*-systems, systems *within* systems, about the systemic character of organizational environments. At this point, then, all the world's a system and the simple image of system *as organism* was replaced by the more complex and abstract 'general' systems approach that regards organizations as only one form in which the systematic character of *organization* makes itself apparent. Something of an organic character has still persisted in the metaphor, particularly in the way in which some analysts discuss the ecological relations of organization and environment, but one is more likely to read of 'inputs', 'outputs' and 'throughputs' as the image of system is now offered in cybernetic terms.

Whether as living organism or as computer, the image of organizations as systematic processes allows us to think about them as things which have patterns of relationship among their parts, which follow 'laws' of structure and process, which do things, independent of the actions and intentions of the people who work in them. 'System' allows an approach to these large impersonal social entities which respects our experience that there is some kind of 'reality' which looms behind and above the individual with which we have to deal when getting our driving licence, our groceries or our teeth filled. The metaphor also captures our sense that organizations are all of a piece, that they hang together in such a way that what happens in one part will affect the rest of it.

As will be plain by now, the notion of 'system' as an organizing metaphor cannot be communicated without resorting to still other metaphoric forms that draw upon images that are not kin to the 'system' image. Metaphors nest one within another precisely because language is non-literal. Thus, to discuss a systems framework, we have had to use any number of other metaphors and, in the same way, one can find metaphors which use a systems terminology in order to grasp organization, for example, as a process of social order or social conflict. If we consider *organizations as arenas of conflict*, then this image offers a very direct contrast to the insights which the organic image of systems gives into the stability and balance of organizations. This metaphor suggests inquiry about the nature of conflict and its protagonists; it provokes questions about the differing contexts of organizational struggle; it fosters a view of conflict as normal — even beneficial — within and between organizations. Organizational conflict, as in hostile take-overs, might be figured as war or a Wild West shoot-out; more frequently, conflict is taken as a struggle over access to scarce resources. Organizational conflict in general, therefore, is not to be seen as an aberration — like war or the Western shoot-out; it is a normal, understandable struggle to get a share of resources that are both limited and valued.

This struggle can be featured by analysts as part of the competition among groups and individuals *or* as the operation of system processes in organizations. Clearly, following out the systemic nature of conflict leads to a sense of inevitable recurrence in which the scarcity of resources and the competition therefore are taken as part of the very nature of organization. On the other hand, considering conflict as generated by and among people would suggest that, while conflict might be inevitable and recurrent, this has to do with *people* and not with the organizations in which they struggle. People come into conflict as their interests differ. It is people and groups of varying power who struggle for position, control and resources. One finds among some analysts, then, a fascination with power struggles in organizations whether they be in the executive offices, between workers and management, or more mundanely over the award of prestige markers among those whose position is between the shop floor and the top floor.

Yet here, a metaphor of conflict has begun to emerge through an image of *organizations as the sum of individual action*, and the interweaving of metaphoric images which characterizes the way we conceptualize experience becomes more obvious. Thus, we find that an understanding of conflict as essential *and* interest created can direct us to contrasting approaches. One way leads to a study of *organizations as social controls*: the other takes conflict as the product of misunderstanding in human relations and leads to the study of *organizations as humane work environments*. In both cases, however, we are looking at images of individuals in the struggle and harmony of the workplace.

'Control' is a metaphoric frame for organizational processes which guides us in thinking about organizations as achieving their ends through authoritative dominance. An image of 'control', then, suggests that we look at organizations in terms of authority and obedience — in the light of the hierarchy of ranks down which such authority proceeds — from the viewpoint of the forms of *effective* authority. In other words, conflict is checked and limited by effective forms of social control that allow organizations to operate without disruptive struggle. The management of the shop floor, in particular, has been a site where analysts have sought to understand how obedience is routinely achieved and what forms of authority are most effective. For that reason, it has also been a place where other analysts have searched to understand resistance to authority and the alienation of individuals from themselves and their work.

20

Like most metaphors of organizational life, the image of control fosters inquiry which both celebrates *and* criticizes the very viewpoint that it sustains.

The shop floor, then, can be understood as a *humane* place when framed as the outcome of reasonable compromise between the interests of workers and management. Conflict and struggle are not inevitable; nor is control and obedience a central concern in the humane environment of the organization. Certainly, misunderstandings will arise from time to time, but this has nothing to do with a clash of interests. Rather, it results from individuals who do not understand their parts in the organizational process, who have been failed by those required to exercise leadership and as a result suffer from low job morale. The *humane* organization has to be concerned to provide conditions under which people do know the importance of their positions; it has to construct workplaces that recognize the effects of workers' attitudes on their work, as it is supported by their peers; it has to hire and train managers who can exercise democratic leadership. With this image of the organization, it is the management of individuals *by* individuals which attracts the fullest attention and by metaphoric extension leads to the notion of *organizations as defence mechanisms*.

If organizations are the results of individual action, then we might ask, how do they deal with the besetting problem of anxiety? One answer to this would suggest that the process of organizing provides some kind of defence mechanisms which individuals create for themselves. In so far as any organization creates anxiety in its members through the routines of its everyday activities, it will also develop (or individuals will collectively develop) mechanisms that protect them from this anxiety. In this sense, many of the forms of organizational life are little more than neurotic defences which individuals use against the chronic anxiety that working in the organization creates. 'Projection', as one individual defence mechanism, allows individuals to place on others the blame or guilt that they themselves would otherwise experience. In organizations, 'projection' allows for forms of interaction to develop which 'systematically' place blame on some individuals or groups while deflecting it from yet others. Thus, one might find that anxiety about keeping one's job during a recession is projectively handled by placing the blame for this concern on the recently hired female employees, who are required to bear the blame *as women*. When any such projected defences are institutionalized — accepted as patterns of organizational interaction and passed on from one generation to another — we can talk about organizing as a defence mechanism.

And so we could go on with other images of organizations, *as cultures, as rational activities, as processes of exchange* and the like; but it is precisely these kinds of metaphoric frameworks which have become taken for granted as literal descriptions of organizations. They are acceptable, well known; some are routinely used as the accurate view of organizational experiences! Less and less have people been inclined to understand them as creative tales, as metaphoric reconstructions of experience, and this has been all the more so because they are presented as *scientific* frameworks for organizational analysis. After all, one might argue, scientific frames are not the same as the commonplace metaphors of everyday life: minimally, they are the basis for the models and theories through which we gain access to the real character of organizations. In that sense, it is easy to take them for granted and regard them as literal descriptions. There is, however, another way of thinking about scientific models and theories which concentrates on commonalities they share with the conceptual frameworks of everyday life and, thus, upon the ultimately metaphoric character of all knowledge, whether that be common or scientific sense.[3]

Certainly the metaphoric images of organizations that we have been discussing are not scientific models, any more than they are scientific theories. We too can recognize a distinction between the broad sweep of a metaphoric expression and the more rigorous specifications of a model: we would have no more difficulty in seeing a difference between a metaphoric framework and a theory. None the less, without entering a discussion on the nature of models and theories in the social sciences — whether they are the same as models and theories in the natural sciences, whether there is an acceptable definition of a model or a theory about which all social scientists agree — we can still defend the view that the metaphoric nature of all concepts, scientific and otherwise, is quite fundamental. Thus, social scientific metaphors, models and theories are always representations of the domain that they describe. Whatever the nature of organizations, it is plain that they are not merely words: the various metaphors, models and theories which we entertain about them cannot literally be the same as any organization. Models and theories are forms of conceptual discourse; as such, they are rooted in that metaphoric ground which sustains all human talking and writing. Yet for all that, we do recognize that scientific theories and models are quite different in some ways from other forms of human conceptualization — theories of electricity, molecular structure or coalition formation are just not the same as discussions about a failed love affair.

Simply and typically, models and theories in science have been understood as ways of more or less carefully setting out the factors and conditions under which one can expect to make some particular observation. Models provide a kind of visualizable picture of the general domain under investigation, and theories carefully specify, in terms that can be checked by observation, the nature and form of relationships among contingently linked factors. Thus, one model of social inequality which is used among social scientists, 'stratification', is visualized by analogy with the bedding plains of sedimentary rocks. This model produces a sense of solid facticity in the social layers which are taken to constitute complex society, treating them as sitting rock-like, immobile one upon the other. Social theories which are based in this model are concerned for such things as the constellation of factors which constitute the style of life of particular strata, the relative homogeneity of human relationships in terms of social strata or the relative permeability of barriers between strata.

For most people, however, theories and models are all about data and facts; all about making sense of the data and getting the facts straight. Science and common sense, hence scientific and commonplace concepts, are different because of this concern for rigorous justification by reference to observable facts. There is a general tendency to think of science as marked by this disciplined obsession with factual justification: images of scientific instrumentation, laboratories and massive banks of computers are likely to float in our heads when we consider any form of scientific endeavour. In other words, it is commonly 'known' that scientific concepts are different from the 'merely' metaphoric images of everyday life because of the way in which they are proved out. This view, however, is only partially correct.

There are distinctive styles of justifying statements that various kinds of scientists acknowledge as their practice. These styles *are* different in some respects from commonplace forms of evidence production used in everyday life; if only because scientific reasoning presumes a specially selected and trained public. However, these practices are just part of science; they deal only with the processes of justification — the practices of evidence creation and presentation which are acceptable as techniques of validation. They are crucial in that they do provide grounds for accepting scientific imagination, hence it is right to accept the common-sense image of science; they do not, however, provide for that imagination itself, hence we would be wrong in taking science to be essentially its methods of validation. Science is a blend of imagination *and* the techniques which evaluate the products of these insights. The common-sense view of science as only a body of facts and fact-finding techniques has been encouraged by our society's utilitarian fascination with outcomes and the attention which most recent philosophers of science have paid to those parts of scientific inquiry which they can construe as 'rational'. None the less, this widely shared view has blocked our ability to take full account of the imaginative, inventive elements of scientific practice and, as a result, hidden the creative part that metaphor plays in scientific discovery.

Metaphors allow us to think rigorously about novel experiences by drawing imaginative parallels between one conceptual domain and another. In proposing these links, we invent the meaningful forms that we expect in the new domain. This was the case when electricity was constructed as an *hydraulic* process, when the atom was grasped as like a miniature solar system, when light was understood as being like a wave, when society is understood as rational economic exchange, when the family is taken as a struggle for power among shifting coalitions, when rumours are thought to spread in the same way as contagious disease and so on. Metaphors are the conceptual power which provide for a scientific 'logic' of discovery: it is they which give systematic form to the inventive thinking which leads, ultimately, to scientific discovery. They do this, more easily, when elaborated into the form of a model.

There are, of course, various kinds of metaphors and models employed in the social sciences: only some of these are interesting when it comes to the development of fresh insights. Following the helpful distinction made by Richard Brown (1977) between 'iconic' and 'analogic' models, we can understand models to be elaborated metaphors — metaphors blending into models as they become increasingly developed. *Iconic* models are efforts to visualize what things are through a description of the way in which various parts of the model are interrelated. Thus, a functional model of organization is iconic in that it explains the working of some particular part in terms of its position and contribution to the whole organization. The extension of such iconic models, then, is by developing a fuller understanding of the links among elements of that model. On the other hand, *analogic* models are attempts to portray what things are through a comparison to some other domain. These models seek for descriptive and explanatory adequacy by means of comparison and contrast: they are efforts to discover the nature of something that is not known or understood by comparison to something which *is* known or understood. Most of the metaphors which we have outlined as dealing with organizations are, when elaborated, analogic models. It is fair to note, however, that there are few pure types of either iconic or analogic models; most are mixed as they become more and more elaborated.

Employing an analogic model — as we shall in this volume — to frame our questions, in order to develop a way of thinking about the domain of the organization, involves one in first making a choice among such models. Obviously, we have no grounds for preferring one metaphor or model because it is closer to some absolute reality. We have given up such a possibility in accepting the metaphoric foundation of all knowledge, accepting that reality is a symbolic construct available to us only through the concepts which constitute our metaphors and models whether these are common-sense or scientific. To prefer one model over another, therefore, cannot be the accomplishment of some procedures of justification in which one takes the valid over the invalid; validity is a criterion that can only be assessed within models in terms of relevant sense-making procedures. Mechanistic and systems models suggest one set of procedures; cultural models suggest something quite different. There is no distinct realm of 'brute facts' where social scientists can test the adequacy of all and any models: it is models themselves which allow us to discover a range of information that can be treated as 'brute facts'. Thus, to make choices among models, one has to establish what one wants of such an approach, what range of facts are important, what questions are crucial and what secondary, what is the relative generality, economy and cogency of invention promised by a model and so on. Scientific models and metaphors, then, have their different virtues and vices, advantages and disadvantages, insights and their obscurities; they reveal and conceal each in their own particular fashion.

None the less, social scientists' preferences among models more often exhibit the conventional practices of their training — the range of questions they have learned to be important, the justificational procedures that have become most widely accepted — than ever they do a concern for the inventional possibilities of any particular approach. In fact, many social scientists have become captivated by the sway of particular justificational procedures. Their interests have been diverted more to convincing others that the statements that they make about organizations are justified than persuading their various publics, both lay and scientific, that the insights which their analytic approaches provide are important enough to justify detailed investigation. To use Kuhn's (1970) perceptive, if now hackneyed, distinction between 'normal' and 'revolutionary' science, social scientists are more generally concerned for the routine exploration of the details of models taken as iconic than they are with the formulation of novel analogic metaphors and models.

In this book, we have opted to place matters of justification second to our concern for elaborating a particular analogic model of organizations. Rigorous discussions of the techniques of inquiry and validation are not lacking in the social scientific literature on organizations: self-reflective developments of a logic of discovery through particular analogic models is more uncommon. In our view, the field of organizational study stands now in more need of exemplars of thinking creatively than ever it does of another illustration of the painstaking application of rigorous techniques of inquiry to models whose presentation has made them literal and mythically descriptive.

We have chosen here to offer a detailed presentation of a model of organizations that is based on the metaphor of *organizations as theatre*. This particular image preserves the essential 'as if' quality of analogic models — we all know the image of life as theatre and few take it literally. Moreover, there is an historical density to this image in which the crucial transitivity of metaphors is represented; both the notion of life as theatre and the opposite of this, theatre as life, have been lively views informing popular and scholarly talk over the centuries. Clearly, 'theatre' as an analytic framework permits a humanistic, artistic and creatively playful approach to organizations which offers a resistance to heavy-handed models of systematic rationality that are 'thoughtlessly' tragic in portraying people in organizations as the victims of forces they do not understand and cannot control. Taking organizations as theatre allows us to ask about the *staging* of tragedy and the possibility of the liberation of spirit and person that is achieved in high comedy. It permits this through the ability of the model to allow considerations about individual action at the same time as it highlights the constraints of social contingency. In other words, this analogic model provides possibilities for demystifying the conditions of organizational life, as these are directly or analytically experienced, while it resists being itself turned into a literal myth.

Our choice to elaborate this metaphor of life as theatre into an analogic model, then, is based on our sense that it offers a general framework for understanding conduct in organizations which can grasp both individual and group conduct, which can locate the situational constraints on joint action and can achieve this without resort to *ad hoc* additions from other metaphoric frameworks. Further, this approach allows us to inquire into the symbolic construction of meaning with research techniques that presume only the same practised skill which theatre-goers bring to their appreciation of the drama. The final justification for our choice of this perspective — as must be the ultimate justification for any such choice — results from a principled view of human life. This model fosters the kind of approach to organizations, and to human action in organizations, that promises to equip people working in organizations, and people studying them, with a way of acting which frees them from the absurd belief that our world is made by forces over which we humans exercise no control. Humans write the plays, humans characterize the parts and humans sit in the audiences. This is our world. The organizations which promise us life and death are the products of human action: we want a perspective which forcibly makes that point and allows us a part as moral actors to do what we can to work for life and against death, to give the world high comedy and not great tragedy.

Chapter 2

Life and Theatre

I could wish this tragic scene were over, but I hope to go through with it with becoming dignity. (Dying words of Quin, the actor)

Metaphors, as we said in the previous chapter, are transitive. So that if a change in social status occurs for the better and we are 'elevated', 'raised up', 'given a higher position' and so on, talking about 'rising', 'elevation', 'higher', 'up' and the like can suggest an improvement in status whether or not that be explicit in the verbal context. Naturally, the ease of shifting backward and forward along the line of tension between the parts of a conceptual metaphor is quite variable. The clarity of image which comparing one's love to a 'red, red rose' achieves is not so easily found when one attempts to reverse this and treat the 'red, red rose' as an image of one's sweetheart.

One important reason for the durability of the theatrical metaphor is plainly the ease with which one can shift between a view of theatre as like life to its reverse, in which life is taken as theatre. This facility and the consequent persistence of the image has turned it into a commonplace of speech in which the metaphorical roots are obscured. We *dress up* and *make up* to go out; we *play roles*; we *stage* parties; we *entertain* friends; we *upstage* political opponents; we *prompt* nervous candidates in interviews; we *perform* our marital duties; we *act out* our emotional difficulties; and so on and on. And we do all these things with little sense that we are speaking metaphorically. At the same time, we do use the notion of 'theatricality' more deliberately in the everyday world as a way of framing persons and their conduct in a fashion which separates the theatrical in life from what is taken as simply living. We say things like: that make-up is rather theatrical; his leaving the party so early was a stagy bit of business; what a clown that man is; she's such an actress; our rehearsal for the wedding went off very smoothly; we are raising the curtain on our new product today; and so forth. Today, therefore, a dramatic metaphor is employed both in some commonplace, unreflective forms of speech and as an assertion that some aspects of everyday life are 'theatrical', and perhaps unnecessarily so.

If we take a more historical perspective on the theatrical metaphor, its transitive nature is all the more apparent. It is not difficult to look back over the history of British theatre to locate times when there was a specific emphasis on the theatre as being a reflection, a mirror of life; but it is hard to keep that vision of the theatre from becoming entangled in notions of the theatricality of the everyday. There has been a continuing tendency to experience theatre as like life as well as to grasp life as like theatre which has resulted from a metaphoric link that is made between the two concepts of 'theatre' and 'life'.

It is possible, then, to illustrate moments when the theatre is effectively a mirror to life, when one can find theatre as being like life; and it does seem equally the case that this is so most often when life is most theatricalized. However, we are more interested here in examining systematic efforts to make the comparison between life and theatre, in presenting some illustrations of what we want to take as a tradition of such a viewpoint that is both reflective and practical. Which is to say that many writers have taken up this metaphor before we did, that many time periods have grasped their style of life as theatricalized, that cultures have variously concentrated themselves on social expressions. We want to locate all these as a 'tradition' to which our work makes some contribution.[1]

Once we recognize that theatre imitates life, it is not too great a step to claim that life is like theatre. Sequences such as the following, taken from the Towneley Cycle of Mystery Plays, reveal the growth of a strong secular aspect to what had previously been regarded as liturgical theatre. The farcical nature of the substitution of a sheep for the infant Jesus and the worldly comments of some of the characters in the Second Shepherd's Play from the Wakefield (or Towneley) Cycle are a long way from simple celebration:

3RD SHEPHERD: Give me leave him to kiss, and once lift him out.
What the devil is this? He has a long snout!
1ST SHEPHERD: He is marked amiss. Come, best meddle nowt.
2ND SHEPHERD: The ill-spun weft is ever foully turned out.
Quit talk!
He is like to our sheep.
3RD SHEPHERD: How, Gib! May I peep?
1ST SHEPHERD: Aye, cunning will creep
Where it may not walk.
2ND SHEPHERD: A ruse to record, and craftily cast.
It was a fine fraud.
3RD SHEPHERD: And prettily passed.
Let's burn this bawd and bind her fast.
This shrew with a cord will be hanged at last.
So shalt thou.
Will you see how they swaddle
His four feet in the middle.
Saw I never in a cradle
A horned lad ere now.
(Rose, 1961)

Although eventually disowned by the church authorities, this kind of entertainment provoked little comment about the nature of art and reality. The butchers, bakers and candlestick-makers, apparently, were not much exercised by issues of identity, of play-acting and dissembling. Three generations or so later, their successors were:

What is our life? A play of passion,
Our mirth the music of division;
Our mother's wombs the tiring houses be,
Where we are dressed for this short comedy;
Heaven the judicious sharp spectator is
That sits and marks still who doth act amiss;
Our graves that hide us from the searching sun
Are like drawn curtains when the play is done.
Thus march we playing to our latest rest,
Only we die in earnest, that's no jest.

Sir Walter Ralegh's epigram reminds us that by Elizabethan times in England, at least, the metaphor of life as theatre had become a literary cliché. Ralegh is a rich source of such allusions reminding us, for example, in the preface to his *History of the World* that God is 'the author of all tragedies', who 'hath written out for us, and appointed us all the parts we are to play. . . . Certainly there is no other account to be made of this ridiculous world than to resolve that the change of fortune on the great theatre is but as the change of garments on the less. . . .' Later in the same passage he refers to 'the false and dureless pleasures of this stage-play world'.

All such uses of the metaphor serve to highlight a sense of individual alienation from allotted roles and convey a sense of distance, of watching rather than fully participating in the pageants and rituals of everyday life. Robert Nye's (1982) splendid fictional account of the life of Ralegh, *The Voyage of the Destiny*, from which the opening quotation is taken, admirably illustrates the *courtier* as player; a man of high intelligence and introspection taking part in, but not committed to, the elaborate rituals and charades of the court. The widespread use of the theatrical metaphor expresses a more general concern about the gap between actor and performance which, Anne Righter (1962) points out, indicates a world characterized by a 'sense of futility, of the vanity or folly of human ambition, [that] is characteristic of all meditative Elizabethan comparisons of the world to a stage. Even at their most cheerful, such descriptions manage to mock the seriousness of man's pursuits, to point out the somehow ludicrous nature of his perpetual activity.'

Although it is far too simplistic to assume that the Elizabethans were suffering from a surfeit of Machiavelli, it is worth noting that much of their drama is influenced by him. In late-sixteenth-century English drama, *the* villain is Machiavellian: he is conceived of as possessing quite exceptional powers of dissembling — 'Men should be what they seem', declared of all people by Iago. Machiavelli was responsible in large part for the popularity of the image — the conception of human behaviour as intensely theatrical, through his book *The Prince*. In it he urges that the ruler control through appearances. Such appearances may or may not correspond to the truth about himself — what matters is that they serve tactical ends. The image is the reality. He advises the ruler to combine the strength of the lion with the cunning of the fox; what is more he is to disguise the fox's slyness with the appearance of innocence. The skills of acting are at a premium, it helps to be 'a great feigner and dissembler; and men are so simple and so ready to obey present necessities, that one who deceives will always find those who allow themselves to be deceived'. The main thing is not actually to possess virtues, but to *seem* to possess them. 'For men in general judge more by the eyes than by the hands, for every one can see, but very few have to feel. Everybody sees what you appear to be, few feel what you are.' The would-be ruler, if he is to be effective, must pursue a theatrical approach to rule, must become a master mummer, an expert in pageant, spectacle and appearance. The prince is forever and inevitably an actor; any man who would succeed in the world, it is implied, must do likewise. An ethic of deceit, perhaps, but one which feeds directly into the Elizabethan world picture:

Why, I can smile, and murder whiles I smile,
And cry 'Content!' to that which grieves my heart,
And wet my cheeks with artificial tears,
And frame my face to all occasions
. . . I can add colours to the chameleon,
Change shapes with Proteus for advantages
And set the murderous Machiavel to school.
Can I do this, and cannot get a crown?
Tut, were it farther off, I'll pluck it down.
(Richard in Shakespeare's *Henry VI, Part III*)

Machiavelli's dictums seem to have been thoroughly assimilated by those responsible for court spectacle in the Jacobean era. Masques of this time combine the most elaborate spectacle, the finest music, the most clever poetry and drawing to embody and celebrate the magnificence of the king and his retainers. It is wrong to assume that they represent little more than extravagance, 'mere show', or a crude demonstration of conspicuous consumption. Certainly as far as Ben Jonson, one of the key figures in the design and execution of masques was concerned, this form of drama combined both celebration and moral education. Indeed, within many of his masques is the notion of the philosopher-king and his court as a repository of virtue. In these spectacular productions, members of the court saw themselves as reflecting an ideal, 'a kind of mimetic magic on a sophisticated level, the attempt to secure social health and tranquillity for the realm by miming it in front of its chief figure' as Barish (1983) has put it.

Jonson sits squarely in the long tradition of poets who saw it as part of their function to educate and reform. His expressed intention was to present philosophical truths delightfully and to encourage change. The masque, for Jonson, highlighted and celebrated the power of the king to change society, restore current custom and practice, to be almost divine in right and power. In one such spectacle, *The Vision of Delight* (1617), Wonder asks:

> What better change appears?
> Whence is it that the air so suddenly clears,
> And all things in a moment turn so mild?

Fantasy replies:

> Behold a king
> Whose presence maketh this perpetual spring,
> The glories of which spring grow in that bower
> And are the marks and beauties of his power.
> (Quoted in Briggs, 1983)

Such representations of absolute power — to change winter to summer — could well have had a profound influence upon James's son, the young Charles I. It is certain that his years of rule were marked by ever more elaborate pageants wherein he played 'himself' — the philosopher-king — and culminated in his starring role as royal martyr.

> . . . thence the *Royal Actor* born
> The *Tragick Scaffold* might adorn;
> While round the Armed Bands
> Did clap their bloody hands;
> *He* nothing common did or mean
> Upon that memorable Scene:
> But with his keener Eye
> The Axes edge did try:
> Nor call'd the *Gods* with vulgar spight
> To vindicate his helpless Right,
> But bow'd his comely Head
> Down, as upon a Bed.
> (Andrew Marvell, in Orgel, 1975)

The tragic end to that king put paid not only to that notion of monarchy, it also destroyed a link between theatre and life during the period of the Commonwealth. Not only were the theatres closed, but most aspects of theatricality in the everyday world were vigorously censored and persecuted. It took the Restoration of Charles II to provide a court style which could again be mirrored in the theatre. Thus, the plays of the latter part of this century addressed themselves to a mirroring of the styles and manners, the intrigues and escapades, the follies and foibles of a society which attended the playhouse to see itself there portrayed.

On 12 March 1700, Lady Marow wrote to Arthur Kay, comparing two recent visits to the theatre:

> I have been at a play, 'The Island Princes', which is mighty fine. 'The Way of the World', Congreve's new play, doth not answer expectation, there being no plot in it but many witty things to ridicule the Chocolate House, and the fantastical part of the world. (Holland, 1979)

Arguably *The Way of the World*, although lacking in an immediately transparent plot, mirrors life beyond the Chocolate House. The audience, as Holland notes, feels itself in 'a world as confusing as the real one', where small pieces of information provoke premature and unwise judgements on the part of both characters and audience and, as a result, cause both to think. In this respect Congreve plays with the audience, depriving them of their omniscience, putting them on a par with many of the characters, to be duped and gulled along with them. He signals, as do a number of other Restoration dramatists, that he is presenting '. . . some new Thought; Some Humour too, no farce . . .' but that he is presenting it in a form which mirrors life. The play, like life in form and feature, poses itself as an enigma. The audience, notwithstanding Lady Marow, will have to work at it if it is to benefit. Restoration and eighteenth-century dramatists are just as likely to play with the notion of life as theatre, theatre as life, in form and content as any of their predecessors.

The theatre itself — the physical structure — was commented upon at the time by one of Goldsmith's correspondents, a Chinese, Lien Chi Altangi, who described Drury Lane:

> The rich in general were placed in the lowest seats, and the poor rose above them in degrees proportional to their poverty. The order of precedence seemed here inverted; those who were undermost all day now enjoyed a temporary eminence, and became masters of the ceremonies. It was they who called for the music, indulging every noisy freedom, and testifying all the insolence of beggary in exultation. (Fieldman, 1966)

The confusion about who was performing what for whom was considerable; one went to the theatre to perform as well as to watch a performance. Goldsmith's correspondent found the aristocrats particularly interesting: 'I could not avoid considering them as acting parts in dumb show, not a curtsey, or nod, that was not the result of art.' Garrick depicts such a patron in *Lethe*:

> I dress in the evening and go generally behind the scenes of both play houses; not, you may imagine, to be diverted with the play but to intrigue and show myself. I stand upon the stage, talk loud and stare about, which confounds the actors and disturbs the audience. Upon which the galleries, who hate the apearance of one of us, begin to hiss and cry 'Off, off!' while I, undaunted, stamp

my foot so, loll with my shoulders thus, take snuff with my right hand and smile scornfully thus.

The transitive nature of the theatrical metaphor is thus displayed upon the stage and within the theatre; as in Shakespeare's time, the image was a commonplace: 'stage and scene are by common use grown as familiar to us, when we speak of life in general, as when we confine ourselves to dramatic performances: and when transactions behind the curtain are mentioned, St James's is more likely to occur to our thoughts than Drury Lane' (*Tom Jones*). Unlike the Elizabethans who, as we have seen, evince a kind of weariness, a sense of futility covering the necessity to play roles, and unlike the Jacobeans who appear to seek to influence events through enactment, the patrons of the drama in the eighteenth century accept and utilize the image of man-as-actor readily and knowingly. To perform on the stage and to perform in public, as Lord Chesterfield remarks, a 'man of the world must, like the chameleon, be able to take every different hue; which is by no means a criminal or abject, but a necessary complaisance; for it relates only to manners and not to morals'.

Finally, to skip over more than a little time, if we turn to the twentieth century we find a growing difficulty for playwrights in crafting dramatic work that is straightforward theatre, that entertains, that offers productions in which famous actors declaim magnificent speeches. Pirandello revealed all the machinery of drama in the drama itself and for this century has made it difficult for others to write and stage plays that operate as if unknowing about this very staging process. The urban world in which we experience the multiple possibilities of social roles has made us more like actors than perhaps ever before. Identity for Pirandello, as for so many playwrights of this century, is a mask that people assume for specific purposes. 'But man? Always wearing a mask, unwillingly, unwittingly — a mask of what he, in all good faith, believes himself to be: handsome, honourable, elegant, unsuccessful, etc. . . . He cannot ever stop posing and attitudinising over the most trifling events and details — even with himself. And he invents so much and creates so many parts for himself which he needs to believe in and take seriously. . . .' (Bassnett-McGuire, 1983). The audience to this kind of theatre brings a precarious consciousness of its own reality to the staging of any drama and this is mirrored back to them by playwrights concerned with the meaning of self, with the staged nature of theatre, with the ultimately absurd, i.e. humanly constructed, form of life's meaning:

THE IRRITATED SPECTATOR: Why can't we ever come to a first night of a Pirandello play without there being a fight?
THE GOOD-TEMPERED SPECTATOR: Let's hope nobody gets hurt.
SOMEONE WHO LIES THE PLAY: It's a fine state of affairs, though. When you
come to other writer's plays, you can settle down in your seat and be prepared
to accept the illusion that the stage creates for you — if it manages to create
one at all. But when you come to a Pirandello play, you have to hang on to

the back of your seat with both hands — like this, and put your head down —
like this — ready to butt back everything the writer tries to shove at you. . . .
(Pirandello, *Each in his Own Way*)

There are, of course, genre dramas presented on television and in the
cinema that presume a different audience. The various soap operas that glossily
portray a life-style shared by almost none of those watching illustrate this
well: but at the same time, and for the same public there is an enormous
production of magazines and such that treats the real lives of the actors who
play these melodramatic characters. Even in this situation the staged character
of the genre is a topic for enormous interest among its audience. The life
which contemporary theatre presents to us, then, is a vision of it as essentially
theatricalized. Indeed, one wonders in the face of such enormous attention to
media, particularly visual media, what any longer counts as a spontaneous
act, what counts as an action that has no precedent in a media image?

The twentieth century being, we are told, the era of the common man, it
is hardly surprising to find his position also being theatricalized. For the most
part, theatre and spectacle have served to dramatize and reinforce social order.
As we noted in both Jacobean and Restoration times, the masques and the
plays were expressions of celebrations of the prevailing order. However, it is
not only in the court of James I and Charles I that masques are used to
communicate the realities of rule as seen by the ruler, we can also find
examples of this in such places as the Republic of Venice where Muir (1981)
has argued that 'One can best see the hierarchic conception of the republic in
an analysis of the ducal procession.'

Processions were of importance in Venice and elsewhere as theatricalizations
of the ordering of society. To these, citizens might turn for information about
the status rankings of the court, who was in and who out of favour, the
positions of influence held by different noble familes and so on. In Venice,
for instance, there was a ducal procession on specific festivals and holy days,
and for the observer from abroad this was characterized by the strictness of the
ordering of the magistrates following the doge himself. One such observer, a
Milanese, compared the strict pairwise ordering of the magistrates with the
more usual rush for a favourable position that marked other places and
processions (Muir, 1981). In this perfection of order, there was mystified the
serene character of the republic that fostered a contrast with the more conflic-
tive aspects of other states.

Of course, not even Venice was this orderly all the time. There were
incidents in which a struggle for precedence in a procession did take place.
There was also an important carnival season in which public theatricality told
a story of order through disorderly conduct. As with many societies that are
rigid in their social hierarchies, Venice experienced and benefited from the
reversals of social position that carnival permitted. Here the young portrayed
the old, men acted as women, the poor dressed up as aristocrats, the nobles
appeared as peasants and so on. But order and its inversion were both dramati-

zations of the form of society that communicated directly to the populace and to the rulers the authority of that kind of social organization. Theatricality was the order of the day.

Nowhere, perhaps, was such a dramatization of élites carried to such lengths as at the court of Louis XIV of France. Versailles in the mid to late seventeenth century was an enormous stage on which Louis and his courtiers displayed the absolute central authority of his rulership of France. The principle of absolute and divinely justified monarchy was here enacted in so complete a fashion as to make the Jacobean court, by comparison, seem uninterested in matters of theatrical communication. However, as in England, the theatricality of *le roi soleil* and his court was devoted to the celebration of a social order which had the monarch at its apex. All action was to express the centrality of the king both as a personage and as a position, to impose a social ordering on the life of the court which plainly declared the absolute dependence of all upon the monarch's actions. In this, Louis was more successful than was Charles I. Courtiers banished from Versailles did express themselves as cut off from the only life which counted, and nobility too poor to support themselves in the magnificence of the court, condemned as it were to live in the provinces, were held in contempt.

Being a king was a matter not only of holding the position but of acting the way a king should act, as Machiavelli had earlier claimed. It was to this public life of acting as a monarch that Louis XIV devoted himself so that all his conduct should communicate a regal character. Of course, there was a private life, but more of this than we can easily imagine was conducted in public. Louis did sleep in his own or some lady's bed at night, but his rising in the morning was a ceremonial conducted in a state bedroom. Thus to rise in the morning he had first to get up from where he had slept in order to be installed in the state bed from which he could officially rise in the presence of the court. Nor, indeed, was his retiring to bed in the evening a less elaborate affair:

> The King, wishing to retire, went and fed his dogs; then said good night, passed into his chamber to the *ruelle* of his bed, where he said his prayer, as in the morning, then undressed. He said good night with an inclination of the head, and while everybody was leaving the room stood at the corner of the mantle-piece, where he gave the order to the colonel of the guards alone. Then commenced what was called the *petit coucher*, at which only the specially privileged remained. That was short. They did not leave until he got into bed. (Saint-Simon, 1901)

Yet it is not only in the ceremonials that we find a theatrical quality to the court of Louis, it is also in the whole deportment of the king as he moves around the palace. With a set of assumptions about the way in which the body and its demeanour communicated the character of a person, Louis scrutinized his own and others' conduct in order to note not only that a certain person was actually present, but also to know what to make of that individual's conduct. He would have known, for example, that 'A person with a good voice is often bold, wise, and speaks well with persons. . . . A loud voice in a woman is a very bad sign. A person who moves about when he speaks and whose voice breaks is envious and simple-minded, drunken and very badly brought up', and he would surely have applied himself in particular to the notion that 'A person who speaks moderately without moving is of great and perfect understanding and of very genteel station, and gives loyal advice' (Ranum and Ranum, 1972). This widely accepted vision of the character of persons as available in their appearance and deportment, published at that time, licenses our understanding of the theatricality of the court of Versailles and further illuminates the observations of someone like Saint-Simon on the courtesy which Louis displayed to all around:

> These various levels were clearly marked . . . age, merit and rank . . . in his manner of greeting and of receiving bows, when people departed or arrived. . . . But above all nothing equalled him in respect to women. Before ladies, he removed his hat completely, but to a greater or lesser degree; to titled persons, half off, and held it in the air or near his ear for a few more or less prolonged instants; before lords, real ones, he merely put his hand to his hat; for princes of the blood, he removed it as he did before ladies; if he approached ladies, to put on his hat only after having left them. All this only was true outside; for in the house he never wore a hat. (Ranum and Ranum, 1972)

The social reality of kingship was, thus, available in every detail of the public conduct of this monarch, and from the standards which were established in his theatricalization of everyday living there developed models for courtly behaviour. Louis's life, indeed, was given to the *performance* of the duties of kingship.

The theatricality of the court in seventeenth-century France became of less importance in the following century as the focus of social life shifted to the streets, cafés and theatres of Paris. Here, the social intimacy of persons at the court, where people were known to each other, was replaced by public spaces filled with strangers whose appearances had to communicate all that one needed to know about them in order to facilitate social relationships. In this situation, Richard Sennett (1974) argues that the conventions of theatrical communication become the conventions of everyday life. All that one knows about a particular characterization is available in what an actor says and does in the part: one does not have, nor need to have, a biographical sketch of a character in order to be able to make sense of it. Just so, in the public areas of the city, all that was needed for social intercourse was available in the expressive conduct of the persons who frequented them. One did not require a personal history from people before engaging them in conversation; one did not expect to understand them only by securing detailed information about their inner thoughts. As on the stage, motives were public and explicit — what you saw and heard was all there was to know.

Nor was it only in France that we find this new kind of urban actor strolling the streets and squares. Across the English Channel in Bath during this same time there is a fine illustration of the making of a social company — a 'society' in the original sense — through the management of expressive conduct. In eighteenth-century England, society gathered itself in a number of places, the most important of which were London and Bath. Although quite small, Bath was the eighth largest city in the country at this time and it had risen to a position of high centrality in the doings of the nobility and the well-to-do. Someone like R. S. Neale (1981) tells this rise as a story of speculation and entrepreneurial activity in land acquisition and building; on the other hand, we shall lean more heavily on the poetic imagination of Edith Sitwell (1932) in her account of the city and its society. What fascinates us about Bath was the way in which those who came to gamble, to dance, to see and be seen were united into a single company that in public was ordered not merely in terms of rank, but also equally in terms of their incorporation in the society of Bath.

One could not expect that hereditary rank would disappear as a principle of social order overnight; but it did yield in the face of the growing economic and social importance of the bourgeois classes — merchants, bankers, traders, manufacturers and so on. In many ways, the Bath of Beau Nash was one of the sites in which the transformation of public principles for order was dramatized. Richard Nash was a professional gambler who came to Bath after a somewhat chequered career at university and the Temple. He brought with him little more than a taste for personal dramatization, which he had polished in his years in London studying, or not studying, law, and some experience gained at the Inns of Court in staging public ceremonial. At Bath, as master of ceremonies, a post established by the City Corporation to regulate the public activity of society, he managed to create a social order that allowed both nobility and the rising well-to-do to meet, to dance, to game, to walk, to talk as part of a collectivity ruled only by Nash and *his* sense of public propriety.

An arrival in Bath during these years of the eighteenth century was announced to those resident by a ringing of the Abbey's bells — you were charged for that — and after news of the arrivals had circulated, Beau Nash would pay a visit to offer an official welcome to the city. It was this ceremonial visit which placed all arrivals on the same footing as part of the 'company then resident'; it was Nash's acknowledgement of one's presence which gave standing to the visitor. This is not to say that he would have ignored the arrival of royalty or nobility, not at all, he was something of a snob. However, he could incorporate into the public world of Bath persons who would have found no similar welcome in London society. They would be invited to attend the balls held twice a week, to come to the pump-rooms and assemblies and would be asked to subscribe for the music and entertainments which they would enjoy. At the same time, Nash would suggest what he took to be the general pattern of public life — when and how often one would take the mineral waters, when bathing was done, the time for being in the assembly rooms, for walking in promenades and gardens and so on. Little of this would be necessary for *habitués* of the season, but it did instruct the *arrivistes* in the public manners of Bath society. It was in a display of an acquaintanceship with such forms of conduct that persons exhibited their dramaturgical rights to be treated as members in good and full standing of 'the company'.

This company met in various places and at particular times in Bath. It took mineral waters in the morning; it visited the various subscription libraries during the day; it strolled the gardens and fashionable streets during the afternoon and attended the assemblies for conversation and gambling in the evening. In all these places, Nash was able, in the words of one correspondent from Bath, 'To promote society, good manners, and a coalition of parties and ranks, to suppress scandal and late hours' (Sitwell, 1932). Yet all this was not so easily done. To have the fashionable nobility mix with the country squires and their families and to mix in turn with merchants and their families, all of which was essential for the maintenance of 'the company' as one society, took a firm hand. Oliver Goldsmith reports in his biography of the Beau that one technique he used was to tell the story of an imaginary town in which an assembly, that had succeeded in attracting a good member of upper-class patrons, was disrupted by one noble lady forbidding her friends from dancing with the daughters of tradesmen. When, in retaliation, the traders withdrew credit and called in their accounts, the resultant bad feeling led to the abandonment of the assembly itself (Sitwell, 1932). Nash also would enforce in public his own rules for a dramaturgy of equality among members of Bath society, reproving people for showing any reluctance to mix with someone of lesser rank. Hereditary status had not disappeared from the social world, it reasserted itself outside Bath; but under Nash's rule, the public theatre of society as a composition of all those properly comported had a clear beginning.

Perhaps no better illustration of his control over Bath at this time is available than in his own satiric rules of conduct which were posted in the pump-room where that society assembled to take the waters. Among them we find such as:

1. That a Visit of Ceremony at coming to Bath and another at going away, is all that is expected or desired, by Ladies of Quality and Fashion; — except Impertinents.

. . .

5. That no Gentleman give his ticket for the Balls to any but Gentlemen. N.B. Unless he has none of his acquaintance.

. . .

7. That no Gentleman or Lady takes it ill that another Dances before them; — except such as have no Pretence to dance at all.

At the same time as illustrating the master of ceremonies' authority, however, these rules all too clearly testify to the difficulties which Nash had in managing a socially diverse 'company' and directing its social theatrics to the display of a new ordering of society.

If we shift our views outside the European frame for a time and elevate the level of our analysis above the face-to-face interactions of members of the fashionable world, we can readily pick out Clifford Geertz's (1980) splendid account of Balinese political and social order in the nineteenth century. In this he draws attention to the various meanings of what he terms the 'master noun of modern political discourse, state'. He points out that it has at least three etymological themes condensed within it: 'status, in the sense of station, standing, rank, condition — estate ("The glories of our blood and state"); pomp, in the sense of splendor, display, dignity, presence — stateliness ('In pomp ride forth; for pomp becomes the great/And Majesty derives a grace from state"); and governance, in the sense of regnancy, regime, dominion, mastery — statecraft ("It may pass for a maxim in state that the administration cannot be placed in too few hands, nor the legislature in too many")' (Geertz, 1980).

We do not wich to labour the distinctions, but they do serve a useful purpose; ceremony, ritual, the theatricalization of everyday life may be taken to be not simply the trappings of the state, so much mummery to inflate authority, moralize procedure or conceal exploitation (though, indeed, in some circumstances it may be little else), but as ends in and of themselves. Geertz argues persuasively that nineteenth-century Bali was such a theatre state; a state wherein court 'ceremonialism was the driving force of court politics; and mass ritualism was not a device to shore up the state, but rather the state, even in its final gasp, was a device for the enactment of mass ritual. Power served pomp, not pomp power.' The massive, costly pageants of the Balinese were not mere appendages of the state, aesthetic embellishments subsidized by a reluctant Arts Council, expressions of a domination independently existing, but rather they 'were the thing itself'. The carefully scripted, assiduously enacted ritualism of court culture was, once more, 'not merely the drapery of political order, but its substance'.

Geertz notes that behind this, to us, strangely reversed relationship between the substance of rule and its embellishments lies a conception of the nature and basis of high authority which may be observable in other societies at other times. He considers in some detail the expressive nature of the Balinese state as reflected in royal ceremonials, arguing that, for the most part, these proceedings were aggressive assertions of status. Cremation (ngaben), although practised by priests and commoners, was the quintessential royal ceremony and as such not only was it the most 'dramatic, splendid, sizeable, and expensive; it was the most thoroughly dedicated to the aggressive assertion of status'. Helms provides both Geertz and us with a description at once remote, exotic and replete with the symbology of power:

> While I (Helms) was at Bali, one of these shocking sacrifices took place. The Rajah of the neighbouring State died on the 20th December 1847; his body was burned with great pomp, three of his concubines sacrificing themselves in the flames. . . .

It was a lovely day, and along the soft and slippery paths by the embankments which divide the lawn-like terraces of an endless succession of paddy-fields, groups of Balinese in festive attire could be seen wending their way to the place of burning . . . already the walls which surround the palace of the King of Gianjar are in sight. Straight avenues, up the sides of a terraced hill, lead to the . . . palace; and, higher still, on the centre of an open space, surrounded by a wooden rail, a gaudy structure with a gilded roof, rising on crimson pillars, arrests the attention. It is the spot where the burning of the dead man's body is to take place.

Immediately adjoining this structure is a square surrounded by a wall four feet high, the whole of which space was filled with a fierce, bright fire, the fatal fire which was to consume the victims. At an elevation of twenty feet a light bamboo platform is connected with this place, a covering of green plantain stems protecting it aginst fire. The center of this bridge supports a small pavilion, intended to receive the victims while preparing for the fatal leap.

The spectators, who, possibly, did not number less than 40,000 or 50,000, occupied the space between these structures and the outer wall, inside which a number of small pavilions had been erected for the use of women. This space was not rapidly filling, and all eyes were directed towards the kratona whence the funeral procession was to come. Strange to say, the dead king did not leave his palace for the last time by the ordinary means. A corpse is considered impure, and nothing impure may pass the gateway. Hence a contrivance resembling a bridge had been constructed across the walls, and over it the body was lifted. This bridge led to the uppermost storey of an immense tower of a pagoda shape, upon which the body was placed.

This tower, called the badi (bade), was carried by five hundred men. It consisted of eleven storeys, besides three lower platforms, the whole being gorgeously ornamented. Upon the upper storey rested the body, covered with white linen, and guarded by men carrying fans.

The procession marching before the 'badi' consisted first of strong bodies of lance bearers, with (gamelan orchestra) music at intervals; then a great number of men and women carrying the offerings, which consisted of weapons, clothing, ornaments, gold and silver vessels containing holy water, siri-boxes, fruit, meat-dishes, boiled rice of many colours, and, finally, the horse of the deceased, gaily caparisoned; then more lance bearers and some musicians. These were followed by the young (newly installed) king, the Dewa Pahang, with a large suite of princes and nobles. After them came the pandita or high priest, carried upon an open chair. . . . The procession having arrived near the place of cremation, the badi was thrice turned, always having the priest at its head. Finally it was placed against the bridge which, meeting the eleventh storey, connected it with the place of cremation. The body was now placed in the wooden image of the lion; five small plates of gold, silver, copper, iron, and lead, inscribed with mystic words, were placed in the mouth of the corpse; the high priest read the Vedas, and emptied the jars containing holy water over the body. This done, the faggots, sticks striped in gold, black, and white, were placed under the lion, which was soon enveloped in flames. This part of the strange scene over, the more terrible one began.

The women were carried in procession three times round the place, and then lifted onto the fatal bridge. There, in the pavilion which has already been mentioned, they waited until the flames had consumed the image and its contents. Still they showed no fear, still their chief care seemed to be the adornment of the body, as though making ready for life rather than for death. Meanwhile, the attendant friends prepared for the horrible climax. The rail at the further end of the bridge was opened and a plank pushed over the flames, and the attendants below poured quantities of oil on the fire, causing bright, lurid flames to shoot up to a great height. The supreme moment had arrived. With firm and measured steps the victims trod the fatal plank; three times they brought their hands together over their heads, on each of which a small dove was placed, and then, with body erect, they leaped into the flaming sea below, while the doves flew up, symbolizing the escaping spirits. (Geertz, 1980)

According to Geertz, the ceremonial life of the classical Balinese state was as much a form of dramatic persuasion, of rhetoric, as it was of devotion. For all concerned there was an unbreakable connection between social rank and religious condition. Leaping alive into flames, royal ordinations, royal tooth filings and the like were assertions, made over and over again in the insistent theatricality of ritual performance, that worldly status has a cosmic base, that 'hierarchy is the governing principle of the universe, and that the arrangements of human life are but approximations, more close or less, to those of the divine'.

State ceremonial performance is a feature of almost all societies; but the intense theatricality of the Balinese *negara* is not matched by all contemporary states. To find a parallel concern for the dramatization of the principles of rulership in this century we must look at totalitarian regimes, among which there is no more horribly convincing example than Nazi Germany. Adolf Hitler was no Louis XIV who dramatized kingship before a small audience of courtiers; he was no Richard Nash theatricalizing a new principle of social order in fashionable Bath; he was certainly not a Balinese lord obsessed with status. But he did understand the importance of dramatizing rulership — the principles of state order — and the nature of a capital city as an 'exemplary center', to use Geertz's notion. Further, as with these other cases Hitler too was possessed by his character, captivated by himself as the embodiment of Germany and the German people. He might not completely surrender to the mysticism of Himmler's SS 'religion', but for all that, the anguished, persecuted character of *Mein Kampf*, which was determined to set all to rights, seemed to possess him and motivate his actions as the central figure in the Nazi state.

Of course, no one should think that there was not the massive, coercive power of the state to amplify every dramatic act of ruling the Nazis employed. The willingness of this ruthless totalitarianism to use force in the cruellest possible way is too well documented to require further mention. However, ruling in the Nazi state was not accomplished solely by brutal force; it was also the result of the dramatic communication of the authority of the regime and its central figure, Adolf Hitler. In this we see the great power of theatricalization for controlling the everyday lives of people, expressing in forceful terms the ideals, the policies and the personae of those who rule.

Many, many illustrations come to mind which suggest the great effect of dramatized communication during Nazi rule. We are, of course, very familiar with the gigantic, staged rallies which Leni Riefenstahl's filming has preserved, but not even closely involved participants always recognized the conscious theatricality of the occasion. Thus, Albert Speer who staged many of the Party rallies reports his amazement at the ability of senior members of the Party to reproduce their conduct of the emotional night in Nuremberg, after the event, so that it might be filmed. Part of the 1935 rally was not captured for Riefenstahl's *Triumph of the Will* and had to be reshot after the event in a studio. Here people like Hans Frank, Julius Streicher and Rudolf Hess re-enacted their parts at the rally. Speer (1970) says:

> [They] gave excellent performances in the emptiness of the studio, proving themselves gifted actors. I was rather disturbed; Frau Riefenstahl, on the other hand, thought the acted scenes better than the original presentation. . . . Up to this time I had believed that the feelings of the speakers were genuine. It was therefore an upsetting discovery, that day in the studio, when I saw that all this emotion could be represented 'authentically' even without an audience.

In this Speer is, perhaps, naïve. We are all capable of recreating past events with a good deal of practical and emotional verisimilitude; very few of us, however, do it before cameras as part of the dramatization of rulership.

However, it was not only the grand occasion which dramatized Nazi rule; the fabric of the everyday was permeated with Nazi images, principles and language. The calendar had its important days which commemorated events in the rise to power of the Party or ceremonialized activities which the Party considered important. The Führer's birthday, the anniversary of the 1923 Munich *putsch*, summer solstice, harvest festival and so on gave the calendar a National Socialist order. Uniforms were everywhere; 'Their very ubiquity and variety created an awareness of the vastness of power residing in the Reich' (Grunberger, 1974). The Party had uniforms, the SA and SS had uniforms, the Hitler Youth had uniforms, the German Girls' League had uniforms, the Labour Service Corps had uniforms and so and on. But not only were there many uniforms, there were many variants on even one style of uniform, many decorations which could be worn, many regional colours to notice. Perhaps no one was more involved with uniforms as a communication of power and position than Hermann Goering, and so famous was he for this that one can find jokes about it:

> Sent to Rome for delicate negotiations with the Holy See, Goering wires Hitler, 'Mission accomplished. Pope unfrocked. Tiara and pontifical vestments are perfect fit.' (Grunberger, 1974)

Laughter was possible in the Nazi state; even totalitarian theatricality does not entirely stamp out the comedic; but all too frequently the grandiose, tragic scale on which this regime dramatized itself made laughter a difficult response to produce or sustain.

Fortunately, theatre provides a place for both tragedy and comedy: without the critical distance offered by the comedic, we should be caught in the toils of tragic imagery — condemned to endless stories of fruitless resistance to fate. In dramatizing the authority of a state as beyond examination or critique, there is a deliberate mystification which denies the possibility of distancing oneself from authority in order to laugh at its claims. In the next chapter, we must take the time to establish as firmly as possible our grounds for thinking that one can, and should, elaborate a theatrical metaphor into an adequate social scientific model of organizational conduct.

Chapter 3

All the World's a Stage

I stand in one spot, about two- or three-feet area, all night. The only time a person stops is when the line stops. We do about thirty-two welding jobs per car, per unit. . . . Lots of times I worked from the time I started to the time of the break and I never realized I had even worked. Repetition is such that if you were to think about the job itself, you'd slowly go out of your mind. (Terkel, 1975)

My day starts between four thirty and five in the morning, at home in Winnetka. . . . I talk into a dictaphone. I will probably have as many as 150 letters dictated by seven-thirty in the morning. I have five full-time secretaries. . . . This does not include my secretaries in New York, Los Angeles, Washington, and San Francisco. They get dicta-belts from me every day. . . . I get home around six-thirty, seven at night. . . . I spend a minimum of two and a half hours each night going over the mail and dictating. . . . Ours is a twenty-four-hour-a-day business. (Terkel, 1975)

These two men are describing experiences which are about as far apart as one can get when it comes to working in organizations. One is going through repetitive welding processes on a production line, the other is caught up in the frantic activity of a top executive for a broadcasting company. Yet, despite the obvious differences in their work these people give a sense of endlessly repeating themselves. Indeed, we chose these illustrations to make precisely such a point. From bottom to top of the organizational world, work involves people doing the same kinds of things over and over with hardly a moment's thought.

Moreover, it is not just work which is like this, most of social life has the same quality. We pass much of our days, months, lives in activity with other people that requires only a non-reflective involvement in events made familiar by frequent repetition. It is not difficult to get through major parts of a day without giving thought, without paying specific attention to most of what one is doing alone or with others.

Clearly, to speak about social life, we have to find a concept that comes to grips with its taken-for-granted, repetitive, yet vital quality. A number of possibilities do offer themselves. 'System' and 'regularity' are quite popular choices; but they strike us as too mechanical. They give little feeling for the human life which jostles and animates the social world. 'Rule' and 'order' are rather more attractive options; they are quite widely used among social scientists, ourselves included. Nor should we forget 'norms' — a regular stand-by among sociologists. However, we are here looking for a concept that will convey rather different connotations, one that will lead us more easily into a consideration of the theatricality of conduct. We have chosen, therefore, to consider social life in its taken-for-granted, repetitive aspects as *the performance of a ritual process.*[1]

In selecting 'performance' and 'ritual' as metaphors with which to think about the broad expanses of the social world that require no reflective activity of the persons involved we do *not* wish to imply that the social process is solemn or ceremonial — common notions of what is meant by ritual. Rather we want to point up the fundamental importance of these social practices which occupy our lives so as to serve as the ultimate grounds for society itself. The complex of practices which constitute this process bind us together into a moral and emotional unity that is faithfully captured with the 'religious' overtones suggested in the concept of 'ritual'. By stretching the use of ritual from what we would all commonsensically acknowledge to be ritual conduct — ecclesiastical and civilly religious events — we want to suggest that even the most ordinary of social activities has something of the ultimate about it. The mundane rituals of social life may be taken as the practices through which we make our places and our selves and thus constitute the only reality in which we humans directly participate.

After all, the social life of human communities is the only life which they will have. Eating and drinking, talking and working, all the ordinary human activities are the ensemble of social life. We do not have the option to rerun what we do. When we meet around the committee table on Monday morning, no matter how many meetings and how many Mondays it has been for us, it gets done just once *this time*. We do repeat activities, as should be plain, but each repetition occurs in a unique present of the moment of action. Calling human sociality a performed ritual process, then, allows us to convey metaphorically a sense of its repetitive yet ultimately consequential nature at the same time as it opens up consideration of social life to the complex possibilities afforded by a notion of theatricality.

The enactment of social life is not restricted to Queen's Birthdays, Presidential Inaugurations, the Opening of Parliament or such-like grand events. The ritual process is not something only for special occasions and places; it is all around us. It is mundanely available over breakfast in the way that people are served their bacon and eggs or their tea and coffee. It is displayed in the dress and undress of those present. Anybody who has shared a breakfast table with the same group of people, family or otherwise, has been a first-hand observer of these common rituals which ease our way into the morning world. Watch people going through doors when they arrive at them together; negotiating precedence creates a stir and movement that affirms aspects of the status order of our society. Dignitaries of all kinds will go first, followed through by lesser souls; but among us more common people it is not so simple. Clearly, it has something to do with who 'controls' the doorway and what happens as a result. Women, for example, were ushered through doors; rarely did they control them. Their situation *vis-à-vis* joint passage through doorways was comparable to that of children who are only allowed to play at ushering people through them. Yet, recent years have seen matters of precedence through doors assume minor political importance in relationships between the genders. Women are not now so frequently ushered and in some circles the matter is fraught enough for the resultant status ballet around doors to press home the realization that ordinary ritual is a serious and consequential matter. Of course, life is more than doorways and breakfast tables; ritual performance can be found everywhere; in typing pools, on construction sites, on production lines; it forms the sociality of pubs, restaurants and churches. Rituals are the very stuff of social life, not merely elaborated elements within it.

In these illustrations, we have meant to imply that social life is generally straightforward for those involved. Participation in social rituals is largely non-reflective. People do what they do, they get on with it; they do not think about what they are doing, how to do it or what it means. Rituals are the performance of stable, successful solutions to the problems which repetitive social occasions present. It might be more accurate, then, because few occasions are quite as simple as to have only one solution, if we would consider any performed ritual to be drawn from a *repertoire* of optional solutions.[2]

One of the smaller pleasures of driving in Nova Scotia, for those who favour some uncertainty in their commuting, is the problem presented by vehicle roundabouts. The traffic rotary has long been employed as a technique for facilitating vehicular flow at junctions and the appropriate 'rules of the road' apply when one is passing around. However, different countries solve the problem of getting into such rotary systems in various ways. Priority can be afforded to vehicles already in the system or it can be given to those approaching from one particular direction; in either case, we have a *single*, stable solution to a stable problem situation. Under traffic regulations in Nova Scotia no vehicle has priority in this situation and there is *no* single solution; rather one draws on a *repertoire* of options. Giving or taking priority, however, is no less a ritual performance for all that the accomplishment on any specific occasion might use a solution different from one employed on the previous morning. As you might expect, priority in traffic is something like priority through doorways; the process displays some of the social principles used to bestow and acknowledge status. Generally, little cars give way to big ones, cheap cars to expensive models, women give way to men, slow cars give way to faster ones, older drivers give way to younger ones. All of this is worked out in the fleeting communication of eye and hand signals which drivers use to settle on which solution from the repertoire will solve the particular case that this morning offers of the general problem.

Without the ritual process social life would be not only chaotic but unrecognizable. Indeed, no matter how we conceive the taken-for-granted, repetitive character of the social world, as ritual, system or whatever, it is difficult to think what social life would be without it. Perhaps better, one could think what it would be like, but one could not imagine living in such a way for more than a few hours. It would be like doing everything, always, as if it were the very first time. The difficult moments you and a friend experienced in first inflating your dinghy, in getting it afloat and starting the engine without grounding your propeller on the bottom, in manœvuvring alongside the yacht would always be the same difficult moments. Whenever it came to getting from quayside to yacht, you would have the same painful novelty to contend with and no practised ritual to sustain your efforts. Where would one ever get the strength to up-anchor and motor down the reach if making it from shore aboard left one in a lather of sweat from the concentrated attention?

We do not live in that kind of world, and we do not live there because we can not. We are restricted by the limits of our attention. Human beings, all animals in fact, have restrictions on their attention even when it is most fully engaged. The ritual process husbands attention. At any moment the interplay between ritual and attentive action allows us to move about the social world with practised ease in a performance that is elegantly set off by occasional moments of attentive involvement. After the first twenty or so trips from the quayside to the yacht we have *that* ritual well enough in hand to argue the merits of the outboard we are using with both interest and conviction.[3]

It is in the ritual *process*, therefore, that we constitute most of the social world — beliefs, material objects, people, relationships — as unproblematic, taken for granted, as there for us, as there without attention. We count on them to continue to give us the responses which our involvement expects without further attentive interrogation. We count on this social world as our 'reality'. It serves as a ground against which to figure out solutions to novel problems that emerge from the social process; it is the backcloth for our probing, active attention.

In the ritual process, then, the world is given as it is, or has to be, in order to sustain the performance. Social reality considered most generally is no more than whatever passes unquestioned and unexamined in the conduct of social actors. As we move through the social world, our performances bring realities into existence for us only while we take them for granted. We constitute our surroundings *as an office* by settling down after lunch to routine work on the contents of the 'in' tray. Social reality depends on being unquestioned and unexamined and it can only be so while it is a resource for action, while we attend *from* it and not *to* it. Yet, if people were to stand around in their coats, worn to fend off the noon-time showers, and discuss the routine sexual harassment of female clerks, any office supervisor would recognize a problem that required attention. When any aspect of reality becomes a matter for attention, when it becomes a topic for action, then it is exactly the nature of this reality which is questioned. At such moments, the backcloth of social life becomes the focus of attention and those rituals which had been grounded in its existence can no longer continue.

So, although ritual performance is the general form of social life, particular rituals may collapse with the failure of their solutions to deal with some situation. Any examination of organizational conduct shows the emergence of problematic moments where ritual enactment fails. These incidents can be as varied as emergency discussions over cash flow among executives to union disputes over jurisdiction in some new production process. However, in these and similar moments when rituals fail and an occasion becomes a problem not resolved by a stable successful solution, we discover the emergence of *reflection*. This takes the form of a *conscious distinction between an activity and the person engaged in it*, which is emotionally energized to direct attention at the problem that has emerged with the collapse of ritual process.

This reflective consciousness is a capacity for *actively* seeking out possible solutions to breakdowns in ritual conduct. Rather than the more passive visual imagery in which consciousness and perception are usually presented, we prefer the active, tactile formulation that G. H. Mead uses in his work. For him, consciousness is a kind of manipulative process in which possible solutions to problems are tried out by working with them as if they are, in fact, *the* solution. He wants us to think about hands as the devices for exploring the contours of possibility in a solution because this metaphor captures more of the *activity* which is consciousness than do merely visual images. Taking a simple example of 'handling a problem', we could consider the efforts of a person to find a nut in that box of miscellaneous items we all keep around just in case we need them. Getting a nut to fit the bolt which was holding the portable bed together is not the same as assembling these same beds on a production line. There is no ritual here but rather a conscious direction of attention to finding the right nut among the other nuts, screws, hinges, bolts and so on. However, you can not find the correct nut just by looking at the box; you have to pick your way through them and try likely ones on the bolt to see if they are the right size and the right thread. All this will involve both hands actively exploring the box, picking up nuts in one hand and trying them for a fit on the bolt held in the other, discarding the unsuccessful candidates and trying again until the problem is solved, the nut twirls easily on by hand, and a feeling of satisfaction suffuses one's awareness.

This tactile expression of consciousness is not to be taken literally. We do not actually solve all problems with our hands. Difficulties between spouses often require husband and wife to talk about the problem and change, say, who it is that takes the children to and from school. Again, a consistent failure to get important letters out from an office will require study, some talk and a decision — to change the flow of work through the office, to route all important correspondence to a single person, to discharge one employee and promote another and so on. Thinking about this problem-solving as a 'handling' of the issues, then, is not literal; it is a metaphorical device for getting us to think about consciousness as an *activity*.

But this leaves out of consideration what is for us more important at the moment — the *form* of consciousness. It is an activity directed in search of a problem solution; but it takes the form of an awareness that the activity involved in seeking such a solution is done by an agent. The activity and its agent are not treated as the same. Involvement in rituals presents to the awareness of individuals little sense of distance between agent and action, little awareness of feelings; indeed, there may be no sense of agent at all, just action. Consciousness drives like an emotional wedge into that ritual process, making a space, a pause, in which awareness of the doer can emerge. There, in that moment, affective awareness makes room for reflection, for consideration of both what is or could be done *and* the agent who is or could be the performer. In theatrical terms, through a vital affective involvement, one becomes aware of the distinction between actor and character, between performer and performance.

Consciousness is most fundamentally an awareness of the difference between agents and their activity: it is an agent's consciousness that is directed towards activity. Thus, it is always twofold; a consciousness *of* something — the agent — and *for* something — the action. Reserved into this separation are all the possibilities for knowing that any action is only one among several options and the agent is neither captured by it nor totally revealed in it, that the agent's consciousness is not *necessarily* discernible in any action, that the social world is not a seamless unity of ritual conduct. Consciousness is a protean space, filled with energies of affect, wherein all important speculations — philosophical, scientific, religious, artistic — emerge as efforts to specify the meaning of any action, of action in general. These formulations are attempts to construct a reality — a particular givenness that can be taken for granted from what has become problematic, questionable — an appearance. It is this reflective awareness which we want to claim as a *theatrical consciousness*; we want to have it as a recognition that there is an actor 'behind' a character, a playwright 'behind' a script, a stage 'behind' a performance, a reality 'behind' the appearance.

Our use of terms like actor and character, stage and performance is a metaphoric use of theatrical language, but it is by no means without justification. Theatre as an activity, as a *staging* of reality, depends upon the ability of audiences to frame what they experience *as* theatre. It depends precisely on audiences recognizing, being aware, that they *are* an audience; they are witnesses to, and not participants in, the performance. It depends further on a distinction between actors and the parts they play — characters may die on stage, but the actors will live to take a bow. Finally, theatre depends on a recognition that performances play *with* reality in such a way as to turn the taken for granted into a plausible *appearance*.[4]

What we are saying is essentially this: the recognition of distinctions between mundane reality and theatrical appearance, between actors and their parts, between audiences and performers are the necessary conditions for theatre. Without these distinctions we cannot have theatre. Yet these very distinctions are abilities which are provided for in the reflective consciousness that emerges from the ritual process of everyday life. Theatre is possible, therefore, because human consciousness is fundamentally a theatrical one. Theatrical performance, then, is a paramount achievement of that protean space opened up by reflective consciousness. It is no surprise, therefore, to recognize that the emergence of the human 'theatrical' consciousness out of the ritual process of the social world is paralleled and illuminated by the emergence of theatre from particular kinds of rituals.[5]

However, the transformation of ritual into theatre is important precisely because it displays in concrete, historical cases the parallel which partially justifies our taking the emergence of reflective consciousness from ritual social process as a transformation of ritual action into theatrical awareness. Both theatre and the theatrical consciousness of everyday life are spaces in a ritual world where a form of awareness emerges that provides for reflection on the distinction between actors and their parts, people and their presentations. These are moments which we can summarily consider to be times for reflecting on what must be questioned as an appearance and what accepted as a reality. But theatre and other media of performance like television and the cinema are *unique* in staging action, in playing with reality through staged appearances. It is the conceptual resources which are provided by considering theatre as a metaphor for social life which interest us and which we want to use. But to do that we shall have to say more about what is appearance and what is reality in the theatre.

There is a fascinating tension in theatrical performances which rests between the intentions of the actors and the director and those of the audience. Directors work with actors so as to present a theatrical event which is emotionally involving for the audience. They want to offer performances which are funny or moving or horrifying; they are not interested in having an audience feel it is 'as if' the drama were 'funny', were 'moving', were 'horrifying'. On the other hand, the audience is pulling away from this kind of involvement, trying to hang on to their framing of the events as theatrical. It is somewhere between these two positions — in the tension which is created — that theatre works. The audience must feel involved if the dramatic vitality of a play is to be sustained, but they cannot be taken up into the play as reality lest they cease being audience and become participant.

Knowing this, directors will use a variety of devices and effects to secure a proper involvement; they will try, for example, to horrify their audiences but do so in a way that allows for the distancing which the theatrical frame offers. Mistakes, however, do happen. In the 1981 production of *The Romans in Britain*, Michael Bogdanov staged a scene of simulated buggery which was taken by Sir Peter Hall, director of the National Theatre, as a 'precise and inevitable metaphor about the brutality of colonialism'. Yet, his interpretation and further comment under questioning that all acts in the theatre 'whether murder, poisoning or a heterosexual act were simulated' failed to stay the bringing of a prosecution against Bogdanov for procuring an act of gross indecency (*The Guardian*, 30 June 1981). The simulation of murders on stage apparently maintains that necessary tension, but a simulation of a homosexual rape was so real for some members of an audience that this tension collapsed and they became participant by bringing a legal action.

Yet, the theatrical balance can be destroyed in another way by literally accomplishing on stage what should only be simulated. In some performances of the Roman theatre, for example, criminals replaced actors in a few parts and were actually put to death. But this brutal literalism only led to the audience being uninterested in the play and so involved in the bloody horror of the execution that they neglected the dramatic quality of the performance. 'Death' on stage is both the eradication of a character and a metaphor for something else: it is not literal, not contained in itself, but suggestive of something else. Theatre is a perspective on life, a selection from it, that is presented to an audience and does not work well if that audience's attention is merely literal. The popular Victorian catcall, 'Cut the cackle and get to the 'osses', testified to the focus of that audience on the real live horses to the detriment of anything else going on in the play.

The theatre depends on a dramatic tension that holds the audience in a suspension of mundane consciousness. Within this frame theatrical representations can be inspected — treated as appearances — for what they might suggest about aspects of everyday reality that are taken for granted. Although not always clear, and obviously not altogether shared, directors, actors and audiences draw upon a common understanding that the staged appearances of performance are presented for interrogation. Within accepted conventions — that actors play characters, scenery, lighting, costume and the like present locale, and acting communicates the drama itself— it is the *meaning* of the performance which is at issue. Thus a theatrical frame enables us both to grasp the essential differences between actors and characters, performers and audience, appearance and reality *and* the possible transformation in the nature of some reality which the staged appearance seeks to make plausible.

But, one might ask, how exactly does theatrical performance transform realities? The brief answer is that it does so through metaphor. Whatever goes on in dramatic performance — on stage, television or films — it is always metaphoric of life. The tropes which drama offers might be irony, metonymy, synecdoche, whatever. They are always a theatricalization of life. Performances, therefore, are elaborated metaphors which communicate through rhetorical conventions that allow us to accept sets as locations in place and time, costumes as mundane clothing, actors as characters, dramatic emotion as personal feelings and so on. Of course, the conventions through which life is staged vary widely from the naturalistic to the wholly fantastic or abstract, and they vary equally widely across the performance media — conventions in the theatre are not the same as in films, but they are exactly conventions — well-accepted, shared meanings for the interpretation of dramatic action. This is one significant element in the importance of theatre as a metaphoric resource for understanding social life: it displays *how* life can be accepted *as staged* when that staging is framed by a theatrical consciousness. At the same time, the rhetorical tropes which suggest *how* audiences can transform their understanding of what they take for granted — the metaphoric form of the dramatic action itself— become a second, important element in the conceptual resources which theatre offers to social analysis.

What we are saying is that theatrical performances in any medium transform social realities — be they political, philosophical, scientific, religious or simply mundane — in two ways. First and most obviously, they are transformed by being staged, making their 'appearance' through conventions which persuade audiences to bracket their mundane awareness and frame the dramatic events as emotionally involving symbolic action. Staging that which is not staged — life — is in itself a transformation in what we believe reality to be. The second and less obvious process at work here rests in *the way* in which the particular metaphor of *any* performance — irony, hyperbole, synecdoche, metonymy and so on — interprets social reality. In selecting from life — as does any performance — the complexity of social realities are metaphorically *summarized* in some way such that we can best grasp the process of transformation as achieved through the rhetorical force of specific tropes. The theatre is thus doubly resourceful for students of social action. It shows how life can be treated as staged; how all the elements of theatrical performance can comment on the taken-for-granted events of the everyday world. At the same time, it interprets social realities through the chosen metaphor of a particular drama in such a way as to highlight the relation between, say, people's intentions and their acts, between their acts and the contexts of action, between such contexts and the resources for action that they offer.

However, we forget a crucial point in all this. Theatre is not just *any* staging of life that communicates through the perspective of particular metaphoric forms; it is a staging of life *as action*. 'Acting' — the presentation of plot through characterizations — is the basis of dramatic performances. At the same time, what counts in understanding dramatic action will be such things as the situation of characters, or the means which they can employ, or the purposes which they formulate and so forth. Thus, the crucial *metaphor* of dramatic performance is to treat life *as* action which can be grasped by a focus on what explains it. Theatre is *the* metaphor for studying social *action*, how it can be seen as staged and how it can be explained. In reflecting on realities by staging appearances, theatre is offering us an affective interpretation of the how, what, when, where and why of social action. It is precisely in this we can find the metaphorical resources that we want for the conceptualization of social conduct, and a further licence for taking social theory, whatever its origins, into this same framework.

This does not mean that we believe all social theories to be 'theatrical' or dramatic in some fashion. That would be a silly and exaggerated position to take. Rather, we are persuaded that the interest in understanding social *action* which has brought us to the theatre as *the* place in which to locate our logic of discovery, also makes it important to reflect on the metaphoric nature of social theories as a resource in developing an analytic model of life as theatre. Both dramatic performance and social theory are non-literal representations of some domain; they formally depict situations, persons, events and the like which are elsewhere. Theatre stages life in dramatic performances: theory represents life through interrelated sets of concepts. Both are metaphoric of the domain which they represent, seeking to interpret realities through the scrutiny of appearances. Theory is no less caught up in the rhetoric of tropes — taking part for whole, grasping change as irony, finding analogies between biological organisms and social organizations — than is the theatre. Nor is it less emphatic in locating the explanation for action in acts themselves, or in the purposes of those who are involved in action, or in the recurrent situational constraints which people have to deal with, or in the social instrumentalities which can be used to accomplish our ends and so on. Both theory and theatre are speculations on the meaning of human action that propose conventions through which we can grasp the appearances they feature as representations of realities that we *mistakenly* take for granted.

This notion will not be so difficult to understand with respect to dramatic performance; indeed, we have spent some time discussing it already. However, it is not so obvious how one should think about it in relation to social theory. Let us present a couple of examples here — in a very simpleminded way — and consider what this might mean. Take the work of Karl Marx and his insistence on the paramount importance of economic forms in understanding human life under capitalism. His detailed account of the character and form of human labour as the foundation of capital accumulation is offered as the prime convention for transforming appearances. No matter what institutional appearance is presented, it is always required that one transform it through an effort to grasp how and where labour is present so that one can understand its real nature. Law and religion are appearances which represent the realities of the organization of labour under capitalist conditions of production. Of course, in the lived world, legal and religious action is and has been enormously consequential, and Marx does not make the mistake of thinking otherwise; however, from the point of view of his theory — within the conceptual world that it sustains — both law and religion are symbolic representations of the material conditions of labour. Moving easily between theatre and theory as metaphors for the meaning of action, it is no more strange to talk of theatrical appearances as theorizing about mundane reality than to speak of theoretical appearances as theatricalizations of mundane reality.

If we move down the scale of analysis from societies to individual persons in their relationships, we can consider something like Sigmund Freud's notion of Oedipal fixation. This complex of behaviour represents an earlier, unresolved struggle between sons and their fathers and it offers another instance of a theoretical convention for the interpreting of social appearances. For Freud, individual patterns of behaviour are the staging in the present — symbolic transformations if you will — of past conflicts in the process of individual development. A person's refusal to accept instructions about some aspect of their work, for example, can only be understood (in a Freudian way) by referring to some past unresolved conflicts. These serve as the reality which lurks behind the behavioural appearance of stubbornness.

Of course, not all theatre is a transformation of social reality. Bastard theatre moves only from appearance to appearance: all it has to say is to be found in the performance. The Victorian melodrama, *Sweeney Todd or the String of Pearls*, is a staging that addresses only its own conventions or its sequal. And so it is with social theory which moves only from one appearance to another, from one estimate of the popular support for the government to another and earlier estimate, from one measure of the openness of the occupational structure to another and so on. However, it is *great* drama and *great* social theory which typify the conceptual resources that we want to find in theatre and theory. It is the transformation of appearances into realities which we shall take as *the* norm for both theatre and theory. Yet, it is a self-conscious irony to recognize that this norm is rare enough in both realms for us to talk about classic drama and classic social theory *as typical* in the face of bastard theory and bastard theatre.

Chapter 4

Social Science and the Theatrical Metaphor: Modern Variations

Most social scientific 'data' — surveys and experiments being the major sources of information — are derived from dramaturgical presentations of identity. This is a point which has been noted by a number of scholars (for example: Cicourel, 1964; Benney and Hughes, 1970; Denzin, 1978; Back, 1981). Typically, in experiments we find that subjects are cast inadvertently into their parts according to some experimenter's script: at the same time, respondents for survey interviews find themselves restricted to stereotypical parts — age, gender, occupation, ethnicity and the like — by the interests expressed in a questionnaire format. We create 'puppets', not only in the sense of developing simplified analytic constructs of people (Schutz, 1967), but also in limiting the capacity of our 'respondents' and 'subjects' to perform themselves in their own terms and in their own style.

While these research performances are textually rendered — as Cicourel (1982) remarks — before they are considered to be 'data', it is not difficult to license a dramaturgical approach to the contemporary social sciences when their typical data are obtained either from scripted interactions between interviewer and respondent or from the staged and scripted dramatic episodes which constitute the experimental situation. Yet somehow, we have all been too much concerned for our own research traditions, for the traditional boundaries between disciplines, to notice the organizing power of a theatrical metaphor.

The central theme of this chapter is our effort to respond to the question, self-posed admittedly, 'What use might a theatrical metaphor conceivably be to a reader of the modern social sciences?' In thinking this through we cover much ground in a somewhat superficial manner and occasionally disappear down some fascinating byways: we have tried, however, to offer something more than an explication of hidden and explicit theatrical motifs in social science. We try to link up critiques of 'straight' experimental and survey research, by means of the dramaturgy implicit in these approaches, with the explicit dramaturgy of other research styles. We also manage to say something about what it means to perform, to treat social life as ceremonial, to analyse texts and life as textual. The chapter divides into four sections. First, we look at the relentless application of experimental techniques by social psychologists; then we discuss some work done by anthropologists using images of ritual, performance and text; thirdly, we examine survey research to see how it makes subjective sense to both its authors and its public; finally, we offer an overview of our own tradition — the dramaturgical sociology that has been influenced by Kenneth Burke.

The most *explicit* use of theatrical techniques for staging in social scientific research can be found in the psychodramas of J. L. Moreno and in the exercises of his descendants — the leaders of therapy groups and other members of the Human Potential movement. Moreno wanted to treat the effects of psychodrama as *alienating* an accepted view:

> In the course of a psychodramatic procedure a revision of the reality function within the social context is noticeable. Many of the social values indispensable in the community look unreal. Incidental and fragmentary events grow out of proportion and take their place. The old reality function becomes an *unreality* function. (Moreno, 1943)

In this sense his use of the techniques of the theatre — techniques of improvisation and rehearsal — are Brechtian efforts to estrange persons from their unreflective patterns of living so that they might be able to grasp what they are doing.

This theatrical playing of roles in controlled situations has since become a recognized therapeutic technique and is part of the repertoire of many persons who work in a variety of settings to help individuals and groups develop a fuller range of human responses. An interesting, recent example is Hare's (1985) application of psychodramatic roles as both an analytic and interventionist device in conflict situations. At the same time, such role-playing or the more elaborate staging of the psychodrama is no longer a widely used or even intellectually respectable strategy for *investigating* issues of concern to most psychologically trained academics. Increasingly, they have turned to the experimental situation as the best scientific procedure for gaining accurate knowledge of human conduct. Yet they have done this without much recognition of the theatrical dimensions of their preferred technique.

In its simplest form, an experiment was a practical effort to find out the conditions under which some physical, chemical or biological relationship held. Sometimes a theory would specify the exact conditions and an experiment would examine only their quantitative values: at other times scientists might be interested in exploring the range of conditions under which a relationship would hold. In any of these cases, the researcher has to control some factors which might affect a relationship in order to investigate the effect of still other factors. For example, you would control temperature in order to examine the effect of pressure on gas volume; or you might introduce a new antibiotic to a bacterial culture to see its effect while excluding both other drugs and other bacteria. Extending this style of research into physiological inquiry or into investigations which employ animals as models for humans requires only some slight stretching of a naturalist experimental frame. Even a bright rat will run through its maze without elaborately staged deceptions. The same is not true when using human subjects.

A very early experiment in social psychology reported by Hugo Munsterberg (Penrod, 1983) suggests something of the dramatic staging which researchers employ. In this study, a violent struggle was staged in a lecture hall by two students culminating in one of them drawing a revolver when their professor tried to intervene. The other students, who were not in the 'know', were then asked what they had seen in order to investigate perception under conditions of high emotion. Some later experimental studies have used very elaborate sets in which to pursue the investigative drama. One of the better known (Haney *et al.*, 1973) is the prison set which was built in the basement of Stanford University's psychology building; therein, twenty-four male volunteers played the parts of 'guards' or 'prisoners'. To encourage a realistic portrayal, guards were issued with matching khaki shirts and trousers, with whistles and mirrored sunglasses. The prisoners, on the other hand, wore loose-fitting smocks without underwear, rubber sandals and had their hair covered with caps made from women's stockings. The experimenters set up a prison-like regimen in which meals and toileting occurred at rigidly scheduled times and were supervised by the guards, and so on. These staging details worked only too well. The experimenters abandoned the study after six days because the level of verbal aggression from guards to prisoners (physical aggression was forbidden, fortunately) and the increasingly apathetic responses by the prisoners suggested that the drama of inquiry had become all too much like life. Since the volunteers who became the 'guards' and 'prisoners' in this dramatization of prison life were assigned these parts on a random basis, it was not easy to claim that the differences in conduct resulted from differences in their personalities. The results suggest a much more dramaturgical conclusion; the drama, the parts cast in it, the settings, seemed to catch up the participants into a possession which eliminated their sense of themselves as volunteers 'acting' parts in a simulated prison.

Most experiments, however, are less elaborate in their setting and in the number of parts which have to be cast. Moreover, most involve a different strategy for involving the persons who participate. Unlike the prison simulation, where the situation and the parts to be played were known to the volunteers beforehand, the general pattern of experiments is to conceal both situation and the parts they are to play from volunteer subjects. Thus, in the well-known conformity experiment conducted by Asch (1951), subjects would find themselves members of a group of students engaged in making comparative judgements on the length of lines displayed on a board in front of the group. Everything would seem normal to a subject until the first five persons in the group would make the 'obviously' wrong choice — pick a line that was clearly too short or too long to be an accurate comparison. At that point, a subject could either make the obvious choice or follow the judgement of the previous 'obviously wrong' persons. The subjects did not know that the situation which confronted them was a scenario written by the researcher to evaluate the effect of group pressure on judgement. Save for the subjects, the other persons in the judging sessions were all playing to a script written by Asch which required them occasionally to make the 'wrong' choices with complete conviction in order to frame possible alternative parts for the subjects.

The complexity of experimental 'scripts', as they are called in the trade, varies widely. Some call for a number of players performing parts which are more or less written out by the researcher in order to involve subjects in a seemingly natural flow of conduct. At the opposite extreme, other scripts involve almost no acting on the part of researchers and their 'confederates'. Subjects might be presented with a story of, say, rape during a courtship situation and asked to make judgements about the amount of responsibility or blame which the victim should share (Shotland and Goodstein, 1983). The only variation here would be in the slightly different versions of the story which were offered to selected subjects in order to evaluate what factors might affect attributions of blame or responsibility. An even simpler script is exemplified in one of the earlier studies on the theme 'What is beautiful is good' (Dion et al., 1972). Here subjects were offered one of three different pictures of women, ranging from the physically attractive to its opposite, and asked in the absence of any further information to draw some conclusions about personality traits, marital success and social and occupational happiness. This study indicated not only that some people see physical attractiveness as more likely to lead to preferable life situations than vice versa but, as important, that people will try very hard to have opinions when cast into the part of someone who should have them!

Whether the experimental situation requires elaborate sets, props and many 'actors' or is more like a theatre of the mind in which subjects are presented with hypothetical stories, the classic experiment involves two or more 'scripts' which are identical with the exception of a number of crucial points. It is these elements, present in some scripts and not in others, which are the focus of the experiment for the researcher. The sub-text of the experimental situation, which is hidden from the unknowing subjects, is the effects of these elements on those who participate. Will these mobilize their conduct in the way expected by the scientific dramatist? If they do, then the social psychologist will talk about the causal effect of the independent and manipulated variables. Which is to say, from a dramaturgical point of view, that the parts which the script provided were sufficiently plausible, sufficiently prescriptive, as to cast people willy-nilly into taking them. Yet for all that, only a proportion of the persons involved in an experimental script do take up the proffered parts; typically, many will not. Despite the effort to write a prescriptive drama, in which the participants will fall into the parts which the script offers, many subjects improvise their conduct in a way which defies the researchers' attempts to grasp the meaning of their acting.

The experimental situation which social psychologists stage as a research drama works out predictably when the researcher *already* understands the conditions under which people are likely to do one thing rather than another. Indeed, if there are any doubts about such an understanding, researchers will rehearse — 'pre-test' — their little dramas until the script is smoothly played and the subjects are picking up on the parts for which they are cast. When skilful social psychologists devise experimental scripts, they do so knowing — as both lay persons and social scientists — a great deal about human conduct which is not acknowledged in the claims made about the results of their experiments. Experiments produce predictable results because researchers are skilful dramaturgists: it is not so much the results as the experimental script which is interesting. Admittedly, some experiments fail (although it is hard to know how many in the absence of information on negative findings); hence there will be doubt about any set of predicted results without further information on how a script played out. However, it is only when people in an experiment play the parts for which they are cast, when the expected results are obtained, that researchers believe they have learned something. When people improvise their conduct in an unpredictable way, they believe that nothing useful has been discovered.

From our point of view, then, research which examines human conduct through the staged drama of the experimental situation is a skilful practice that ignores its own skill. Recognizing in its style of research that human life can be viewed as a staged activity, it denies this in reporting what it claims to know. Researchers in the experimental tradition specialize in writing limited performance texts (complete with stage directions), but refuse to acknowledge that what they 'know' is this skill and *not* the findings which they report. In that sense, we are inclined to treat experimental outcomes as only a suggestive resource for dramaturgical analysis. One can look over such results to see if they provide clues to possibly important features of interaction which one would want to examine in detail while doing research. Beyond that, they 'prove' only that experimenters can get their scripts to work in much the same way that theatre directors can get their show on the road.

'Performance' as a metaphor for thinking about ritual action is a notion that has gained currency among anthropologists. Moreover, discussion of ritual conduct usually constitutes it as an explicitly theatrical kind of activity with performers, an audience, costumes, props and a recognizable and repeated text, in contrast to everyday life which seems to be merely lived. The concept 'ritual' is not used by anthropologists as do we, to indicate routine, non-reflective conduct of *all* kinds. Rather it designates specific kinds of activity marked by the dominance of expressive over instrumental conduct, where the focus is on *the way* something is done more than on what is being accomplished. It is not clear whether this use of a performance motif is at least an implicit recognition among anthropologists that ritual and drama were closely linked in the world of classical Greece (an early interest among anthropologists). None the less, the ethnographic diversity which chronicles rituals of many kinds is testimony to how well a notion of performance can serve in understanding these aspects of society.

It would be tedious and to no purpose here if we should try to do more than proffer some illustrations of this diversity. To take a first example from a study of the nomadic I'Kung people of the Kalahari Desert area in Africa, we can see in a description of a dance many of the elements which constitute the performance aspects of such a ritual (Thomas, 1965). The ethnographer presents the dance as an invocation of magical power with which to cure the 'star sickness' — an illness with no symptoms. Although everyone in the band takes part, the major figure is that of the healer — a man whose youth and success in hunting marks him as a holder of the magical power. The dance ritual is usually staged at night with the women's voices providing the music and the men dancing around them in a circular path, stamping their feet in counterpointed rhythm to both the singing and hand-clapping of the women. These patterns of clapping, singing and dancing take much time and practice to perfect and the people begin to learn them when they are children. It is in the midst of this complex of voices and stamped, clapped rhythm that the healer goes into a trance state.

In the ritual which Thomas reports, Gai, the healer, is then described as running off into the veldt and returning out of control to fall through the fire around which the dance had circled. Still in a trance state, Gai then went to each of the members of the band and placing one hand on their back and another on their chest groaned and shook as he extracted the evil from them. This poison was then released as the healer shrieked it into the desert air. When finished this task the healer collapsed and gradually the singing and dancing drew to a halt 'leaving only the children wheeling slowly around the track worn by the dancers' feet, dancing soberly, carefully, without music' (Thomas, 1965).

The implicit theatricality of this account is not hard to follow. With little effort we could find a Greek chorus performing its part as a dancing audience of actors; we have a key actor emerging from the communal chorus to play the part of 'healer' for which he is cast as a result of past success; we see a union between actor and part that allows a trance-like state to be assumed with credibility; we even find the actor who used to play the 'healer' operating as a supporting player and dramatic coach in the healing action itself. And we end with the children rehearsing their future actions as chorus members.

In another ethnography which chronicles the life of the Kapauku people of Papua (Pospisil, 1965), the author separates out ritual from everyday life in such a way as to link it in his narration with discussions of religious belief. However, the metaphor of performance is strong enough to resist this limitation and we find him talking about ritual actions in other contexts. Thus, he notes that if a warrior succeeds in killing one of the enemy in a highly stylized mass combat, he will perform a 'killer's dance' in which he runs around in a small circle with his bow and arrows held low down in his right hand while uttering high-pitched cries. Simple as is this action, it is a part which is available only to those cast into it by their success in slaying an enemy warrior; it does have specific performance characteristics and is set in a particular time and place.

One can see in Pospisil's account of the killer's dance the strength of an anthropological tradition that finds ease in treating ceremonial and ritual as a performance action. It would be simple to go on through ethnographies and show the tradition which narrates ritual in performance terms; but this is not a knowing tradition. There is little explicit awareness that the narration of rituals as performances is a metaphoric frame placed around the conduct; we find little development of performance concepts which might enrich the detailed description of particular rituals. To locate such an enriched performance motif, we have to turn to work which *is* knowing about the use of such a framework. However, in doing that it is necessary to sort out some differences between work which sees 'performance' as some specially signalled activity and that which takes all social life as performance *tout court*.

Richard Bauman (1975) has outlined a performance approach to what he calls 'verbal art' which can be extended to cover all kinds of 'artistry' in social conduct. At the heart of his approach is the notion that in any analysis of social conduct we have to make a distinction between what is framed as 'performance' and what, in opposition, is 'literal'. This distinction is not simply in the orientation of the analyst, but is more properly found in specific 'keying' devices which signal that one should place a frame of *performance* around utterances or actions. Thus, he suggests that such things as figurative language, formal stylistic devices — rhyme, rhythm, harmony in vowel use — conventional openings, closings and announcements that performance is about to begin, patterns of tempo, pitch and stress in speaking and so on are keys in different cultures and situations to a performance orientation on the part of an audience. To extend these to cover other kinds of artistry, we need only add such keyings as movements of the face and body, clothing, make-up, body decoration and hair styling, body posture, choice of background for action and so on and on.

Bauman takes us, therefore, beyond the simple notion of ritual performance, implicit in the narrative descriptions of many ethnographers, to a more general category of actions which are to be viewed as performed because they are signalled as such through some communication that summons audiences to adopt a performance frame. Thus, we would all recognize 'Dearly beloved, we are gathered here . . .' as a 'typical' keying of a wedding ceremony. On the other hand, keyings which are used to begin jokes and stories, 'Do you remember old John and how he would . . .' or 'Have you heard the one about . . .', are equally clear conventions for the framing of performances but are not typically seen as ritual.

To take a longer illustration from the work of Michelle Rosaldo (1980) on the Ilongot of the Philippines, we can show this 'performed' interaction in the oratorical negotiations that constitute the social form employed to heal breaches in civil order. As she describes these oratorical interactions, they are clearly seen as different from the literal activity of everyday action and speaking. They require quite elaborate staging procedures in which both the topics for negotiation and the parties to it are worked out, in which the site and timing for the oratory are agreed, in which the major speakers are decided upon and the supporting, but silent audiences are drawn into the negotiation. At the site of a negotiation the principal speakers for each side seek to gain their ends through elaborate oratorical tactics. While everyone present knows the topic of the negotiation, the rhetorical form avoids mention of that issue save indirectly or euphemistically. Thus, if the object were to secure a bride, then one would find no mention of her, of the interest in a 'woman', rather there might be talk of a desire to 'plant rice'. Clearly, the qualities of a good orator are not found in everyone; one looks for persons who are skilled and witty in speech, who are understanding of human feelings and able to move negotiations along without getting the opposite side upset. Advantages are won and lost in the negotiation with a clever or awkward turn of phrase and these provide moments in which demands for an exchange of material goods can be expressed and honoured. The negotiation, the elaborate speaking in a performance mode, can go on for hours before a conclusion satisfactory to both sides is reached and the encounter falls back into the literal mode of social life.

In this account by Rosaldo (1980) we can detect some of the richness possible when a performance frame is applied; she conveys a sense of casting, of artistic improvisation, of audience, of timing, of sets, of ensemble as these negotiating parties play off one another. However, even though these notions make sense in the context of this description of oratorical bargaining, they are not explicit in the author's account. To find such an explicit development of the performance frame we have to turn to something like Abner Cohen's (1981) effort to understand the élite positions occupied by the Creole people of Sierra Leone in the 1970s. Here, Cohen is particularly concerned with showing how various dramaturgical ceremonials build and sustain the community sense of this small élite.

'Family' among these Creole contains not only those who are genealogically linked, but also those who have become connected through systems of patronage. Funeral ceremonies, then, are opportunities to celebrate the solidarity of the 'family' and through that to dramatize the position of the Creole people. One wake, celebrated at a home of a member of the 'family', involved more than 100 people of both genders in talking, drinking and dancing through the long night. The Western-oriented singing and music of the early evening gave way with the food and drink to an eclectic blend of singing and dancing which mixed hymns, chants and local songs. As if to display the unity of those celebrating the wake, most of whom were Christians, there was even a chant in Arabic in deference to those Muslims present.

Contrast the informality of the wake with the solemn occasion of the funeral service, next day. Despite the principals being the same persons, they were now dressed in formal Western clothes — dark suits for the men and dresses, hats and gloves for the women — and behaving according to a slightly archaic code of decorum that would have seemed proper in genteel Edwardian England. The large congregation was quiet and 'all behaved and acted with the familiarity and certainty of people who were accustomed to such occasions' (Cohen, 1981). The sermon was preached to draw together themes that were religious and secular and the Masonic connections of the deceased were signalled both by the presence of a delegation of Masons in regalia and by the inclusion of Masonic themes in the sermon. Many of this congregation moved on to the cemetery for a brief graveside service in which the immediate family stood closest to the grave, but where the handful of earth flung on the lowered coffin was an act repeated by many of the persons present as an expression of their unity with the 'family'.

We need not pursue Cohen (1981) further to show his grasp of such matters as dress and appearance, the communication of hierarchy in social rites, the use of music and dancing as part of such performances, or the symbolic sharing of food and drink. His volume is rich with such detail that testifies to the utility of a worked-out performance metaphor when applied to ritual action. However, there is still the tacit assumption that performance occurs in some places, i.e. in ceremonial action, and that elsewhere life is merely literal. To be sure, this is the most common employment of a performance frame in the work of anthropologists and it does serve ably as a resource for those interested in dramaturgical analysis. Minimally, it makes a broad array of ethnography available for comparative purposes. This is not so much to facilitate the kind of study which Young (1965) conducted to examine the effects of status dramatization (in the form of initiation ceremonies) on solidarity, as to allow scholars to read ethnographic accounts of ritual conduct for the light which they might shed on dramaturgic practices in our 'deritualized', 'demythologized' organizational societies.

None the less, we cannot leave this brief introduction to the performance motif in anthropological material without drawing readers' attention to a volume by Thomas Gregor (1977) which extends the performance metaphor from ritual conduct to cover *all aspects of daily life* among the Mehinaku Indians in central Brazil. This valuable book takes seriously, in a way that little prior in anthropological studies of simple societies has done, the idea that preliterate people can operate as manipulators of their social masks as do we in our complex, urban society. Gregor does not claim that one can find something like our notion of performed individuality in all simple societies. He does show, however, that making this assumption about the Mehinaku is beautifully insightful about their simple world where people confront each other with no more privacy than that which is won interactionally.

Nowhere does he make a better case for applying a worked-out perform-ance metaphor to the totality of life than when he brings in a film crew to make a pictorial and sound record of daily life. Having told one man that he wanted to show the relationship of husband and wife and their division of labour, he set up the scene:

> Instead of doing the scene straight . . . [Kuyaparei] decided he had better make sure that we really understood what was happening. 'My,' he said as he walked along closely followed by camera and microphone, 'I hope my wife has a fire lit to cook these fish and make manioc bread — they are delicious together.'. . . Villagers watching the filming . . . began to participate: 'Look at all those fish Kuyaparei is bringing home . . . I wish I had those fish to bring home to my wife.' And, of course Kuyaperei's wife couldn't resist getting into the act as well: 'The fire is ready, my husband. You've caught the fish and I'll make the manioc and distribute them.' (Gregor, 1977)

The ability of the Mehinaku to play their everyday roles with conscious theatricality brings them forcefully into our world in this ethnographer's account. The even-handed application of a performance metaphor to both ritual and literal action in Gregor's work allows for an emphasis on the fluidity of life in which we can find out as much about ourselves as about the Mehinaku. Ethnography is at its humane best when we can see our lives in a much simpler world, when *la vie primitive* allows us to understand *la vie humaine*.[1]

Much contemporary work in sociology and social psychology would *not* fall under the rubric of the sciences of action no matter what perspective one would employ. The study of patterns of economic activity, structures of inequality, levels of bureaucracy, occupational differentiation, fertility and mortality in large populations, urban organization and so forth refer only in the most indirect and ironic way to acting persons. Moreover, there is a growing interest in the study of structured processes which deliberately bypasses any consideration of acting persons in favour of a focus on social regularities treated as *sui generis*, as realities in and of themselves. For those interested in studying organizations one can readily think of such work as the social network analysis of intercorporate directorates (for example: Berkowitz, 1982; Carroll *et al.*, 1982; Roy, 1983) or the multivariate analyses largely based on organizational charts with which Blau and Schoenherr (1971) struggled to talk about 'hierarchical levels', 'span of control', 'supervisory ratio' and so on as structural characteristics of bureaucracies. This is certainly not a fruitful place to begin searching for dramaturgical themes.

We are likely to be more successful in looking at material which attends to issues of communication, to socialization in its many forms, to questions about various dimensions of 'identity' and so on. With no attempt to do more than pick and choose among some of these products in a less than systematic fashion, we can locate a thread winding through contemporary sociology and social psychology which is constituted from an unstated concern about the nature of appearance and reality as that is presented through the character of human identities. As the modern world becomes increasingly differentiated, we find ourselves with a diversity of parts to play in the social whirl and no one of them necessarily more really 'us' than any other. In these circumstances, the question of who we really are can become obsessive. Whether or not this is the case, whether or not the majority of people are wandering through their lives unsure as to who they really are is not the point. What is plain is that the question of identity is a live one for the intelligentsia; it forms a theme in contemporary fiction, drama and social criticism. They, at least, are not sure they can actually detect themselves in the many parts which a day might bring them to play. It is not to be supposed, then, that sociologists would be insulated from a similar concern. For them, a puzzlement about the reality of *one* among several identities becomes a scholarly interest in the relative importance of holding such a variety of identities on people's outlook and conduct. In dramaturgical terms this concern is to investigate the effects on an actor of becoming identified with a specific range of parts both for that individual's outlook and ability and for possible future castings.

In this *métier* we can find attempts to evaluate the place of gender, ethnic, racial, religious, political, age, regional and other identities in producing a range of attitudinal and behavioural outcomes. There is a literature on the acquisition and effects of occupational and professional identities. A smaller coterie of sociologists is still interested in understanding the nature of consciousness engendered in persons identified with a particular class. One approach to social deviance rests on understanding the way in which people are cast for the identities of essential deviants. Although these illustrations are only a limited selection, they do suggest something of the varied interest which sociologists show in the nature of identity.

There is a huge body of literature that employs the 'standard sociological variables' — age, gender, occupational status and so on — which might be of interest if dramaturgical analysts could grasp the assumptions through which these variables come alive for researchers as persons' identities. On the face of it, there is little to attract persons concerned for social expression in this kind of 'standard' sociology. Picking a journal off the shelves, almost at random, one can find an article such as Walsh and Warland (1983) which sets out to investigate opposition to nuclear power plants among people in the vicinity of Three Mile Island, Pennsylvania. Addressing this issue with a multivariate examination of a variety of 'standard variables', the study tries to find differences among those who became actively involved after the accident at the power plant and those, the vast majority, who did nothing. Little of promise here for the dramaturgical analyst! And there is not, unless one digs below the surface to ask how those who do it give subjective meaning to the variables which they employ.

It is the old problem, if data do not speak for themselves, how do you get them to make sense? The short answer to that question is that researchers have to be able to invent credible identities of people and their motives on the basis of the limited information which the numerically coded data offer. In this study, 'education' means literally seven categories ranging from 'none' to 'graduate or professional school'. To give subjective meaning to these, researchers turn to their *experiences* of people who can identify the meaning of such categories. Thus, 'education' will mean that university student you met over the weekend, that girl who left school when she was fourteen and can never get a job or the lawyer that you were talking with last week about a divorce and its financial consequences. In other words, variables which appear as operational specifications in a research report have altogether a more personal, a more expressive sense for researchers as they analyse the data. In everyday life we experience each other through our expressions of what we 'are' and what we believe; we live in a world which is dramaturgically accessible. It is this world of common-sense experience which is the fundamental grounding of the interpretations presented by researchers employing the 'standard variables'.

Not every variable has a dramaturgical, an expressive form in the everyday world; but most variables are brought to life in researchers' imaginations as a result of expressive interactions in the quotidian. There they appear as performed characters with motives, contexts, strategies — as identities — which serve as researchers' typifications to vitalize data analyses. What Erving Goffman (1983) in his last publication called the 'interaction order' — the realm of face-to-face contact — is the experiential world for all of us. In that sense, dramaturgical analysts can exploit even those studies which present themselves as stripped of all but the simplicity of quantitative variables; from the dramaturgical perspective such 'standard' sociology can be taken as a simplified and unknowing gloss on the expressiveness of everyday life. Simplified glosses have a place in suggesting the direction of inquiries for the dramaturgical analyst; as a resource they can help to set research agendas.

The task of reinterpreting the broad literature on socialization, both childhood and later, is clearly beyond our aims here. In any case, the mere rewriting of one body of material into the form of a new perspective is a fruitless task — the history of the social sciences is replete with the aridity of efforts to translate old work into new terms without adding anything in the process. We want no part of that. However, we do want to alert those with a proclivity for the theatrical metaphor to the existence of this literature which treats questions of casting and learning parts. It is material form which the dramaturgist can learn, more than work which is in need of assistance from the theatrical perspective. The weakness of the field is that it contains all too few detailed, ethnographic studies of the *process* of socialization: in that way it matches the literature on the theatre which contains as few detailed accounts of the process of acquiring parts.

If we have shied away from reworking the material on socialization and the development of identities, we have equally good reasons for not becoming embroiled with the voluminous investigations into the presence or absence of a particular kind of consciousness among working-class people. It has been a theoretical and political embarrassment for some and a source of malicious delight for others that 'objective' working classes infrequently display an awareness of their position or their exploitation. From a Marxist view, consciousness of class situation results from the conditions under which a class labours to produce the means of its own existence. The experience of working side by side with other men and women in a hot factory, for a pay-packet which is a fraction of the income earned by plant owners, is the form of working-class life that is anticipated to produce an actor's sense of the part in which they have been cast. But castings do not necessarily produce the kind of acting that we think they should. To some extent, it is studies of the *wealthy* and the coherence of the form and content of *their* life (for example, Veblen, 1953; Lundberg, 1969) that make more interesting reading as a drama-turgical resource. Their casting does produce, in most cases, the kinds of acting which is expected: the very rich do know who they are and that, as Gatsby noted, 'they are different'.

Finally, when considering the thread of concern for identity that winds through contemporary sociology, there is the matter of 'labelling theory'.[2] This theory, as has been noted, is mislabelled! It is not much more than the application of some of the main principles of symbolic interaction to the conduct and character of deviant persons; and for those who did the early work, it was precisely that kind of application which they were seeking. To summarize the basic notions of this approach — naturally, one can find it more complexly stated and applied (for example, Becker, 1963; Scheff, 1975) — a deviant is created not by what they do but by how we react to it. In itself no act is either deviant or normal, it takes on that character only in relation to other persons and their responses. To that extent, then, we can do what we choose and if no one responds in a negative way we are without any social 'stain' on our character. On the other hand, if we find something that we do is received with a negative response (even if we think it right) it becomes hard to resist the claim that both the act and the actor are wrong. Of course, some actions, and hence their perpetrators, are widely thought to be wrong; but it is only in bringing that judgement to bear upon the person responsible that the deviant is created.

Now this is a little more complex than the obvious notion that we all learn our morality at, or over, our mothers' and fathers' knees. Certainly, children are amoral, innocent of right and wrong; they have to be morally ruined by the adult world, corrupted into a sense of evil. On the other hand, deviants may or may not be innocent. What moralizes their acts and their persons is the public recognition and enforcement of authoritative social judgements against them. This recognition will often be spread out across a period of time — it might take more than one appearance in court for a person to accept themselves as *really* a drinking driver. Moreover, this labelling casts persons for one *essential* part; it typecasts them in such a way that they can get no other. And this is its appeal for a dramaturgical analyst. Whatever else a person might be — sister, mother, political activist, Protestant — the deviant character is seen as 'essentially' their identity. This identity is fundamentally what they are. Like fate or destiny, the identity of 'deviant' marks them out as set apart from the rest of us. Burdened with this judgement, deviants know the tragic fact that they can only be what they are called, only be what society judges them to be; they can only do what their character can. The essentializing of the deviant label eliminates the separation between character and actor which the theatrical consciousness allows us to sustain, to leave the deviant with only a thread of inner awareness that cannot be socially recognized.

This brief discussion of the casting of deviants as essential characters brings us almost to the end of our journey along a thread of concerns for identity. But we cannot quite get out of the maze without looking for a moment at the issue of 'social roles'. Of course, 'role' and 'identity' are related and often a concept of 'role' is used to talk about what people do in specified social positions — what forms of conduct are identified with them. However, we have left this topic until this point in order to emphasize that even the most dramaturgically based concept among mainstream writing is an unfulfilled promise of escape. Despite the vast popularity of the notion of 'role', the lack of a broader perspective has continued to hinder its conceptual development.

Now all this sounds as if there was one concept of role about which people are agreed when nothing could be further from the state of things. Indeed, the two most recent surveys of this literature do not even agree on what the concept should mean. Heiss (1981) takes the position that since the ultimate dependent variable in social psychology is social behaviour it would make no sense to define roles in terms of behaviour; to do so would leave the concept little to explain. Thus, he treats a role as a set of expectations for how one should behave. On the other hand, Biddle (1979) in the most complete, recent effort to integrate the literature, takes roles as situational behaviours that are to be distinguished from 'expected roles'. Both of these authors recognize in selecting their conceptual specifications that they are struggling against a tidal wash of alternatives. We have no intention either of adding to the alternatives or of swimming against that tide. Nor do we wish to continue the debate over whether some uses of 'role' fail to allow for personal creativity in forming a role. In our view, there is little to be gained in that discussion.

The problems with this approach rest less in its conceptual diffusion than in the failure to take the metaphorical roots of the concept seriously. Certainly, as Biddle (1979) notes, there are few studies of actual roles. We cheerfully talk about the roles of mother, priest, police officer, drunkard and so on with little more than our personal sense of what is meant. But this key omission could well be remedied without thereby providing a broader framework in which to grasp the conceptual links which are possible for a theatrical notion of 'role'. Again, we are agreed with both Heiss and Biddle that there are serious conceptual difficulties with this perspective: we are not agreed as to their proposed solutions. For example, Biddle (1979) argues that the initial heuristic freedom of 'role theory' has served its purpose and the time has come to 'adopt a single, integrated structure of terms and concepts'. Our reservations with such a notion are that it proposes to stabilize the *present* chaotic usage. We see little advantage to static conceptual disorder. If 'role theory' is to develop a 'structure' then it is our view that it would best do so by spinning out the conceptual resources available in the theatrical root metaphor of the term 'role'. The size of that task, if any had the nerve for it, will be more obvious as we look next at dramaturgical work proper. It may well be that, considering the richness of dramaturgical work, 'role theory' will prove to have been a conceptual dead end.

Few dramaturgical writers are found among those using a role-theory approach. Despite the theatrical origins of the term 'role', the development of that area has not been much pursued by those explicit about their interest in a dramaturgical sociology. Nor is much contemporary work influenced by classic figures. Plato, Erasmus, Machiavelli, Carlyle, are little more than footnotes with which we establish a lineage for the use of a theatrical metaphor. Even contemporary classics like Freud and Mead have received little more than cursory attention (for examples: Duncan, 1962; Lyman and Scott, 1975) and have hardly featured in work in a dramaturgical *métier*.[3] With very few exceptions, writers in this approach have gained their understanding of dramaturgy either directly from Kenneth Burke, as did Hugh Duncan, or from Burke as developed in the work of Erving Goffman. Rather than offer, then, a tedious recitation of the many persons and their work in order to survey this literature, we have chosen to talk at more length about Burke and Duncan before moving on to Goffman and some illustrations of the range of dramaturgical work as one can find it today.

In a long life, Kenneth Burke has written a great deal which defies summary in any simple way. Certainly, there is no place in his work that offers much more than a glimpse, a fleeting hint at the fullness of his thought. To that extent, we have to rely upon both secondary analysis and our own reading of his work in order to give a brief account of his accomplishments. One way which sits comfortably with Burke is to divide his work into two periods — early and later — in order to capture something of the difference in emphasis which he has displayed over the sixty years in which he has written.

The early period, which can be treated as restricted to four volumes (1957, 1959, 1965, 1968a), exhibits his concern to grasp human action as dependent upon historically based vocabularies of motives. Burke takes motives as the interpretations we use to make sense of situations which we find problematic; since we all operate from a particular orientation we have developed from our place in the world, he anticipates that such interpretations will be rooted in the interests which we so derive. Motives, then, are interest-based explanations for situations that we cannot accept as taken for granted. In giving such explanations we show not only our rationality — what makes sense to us — we also exhibit the way in which we identify ourselves. If you rattle on about the profits to be drawn from something, or you praise and deplore the planning or the lack of it in some event, or you talk incessantly about fitness and diet, or you rabbit on about last year's, this year's and next year's vacation, Burke understands you to be both making sense of your situation *and* showing who you are. We name ourselves in the explanations we offer for situations that cannot be taken for granted.

However, there is a concern for more than interaction situations in Burke. He also wants to grasp the organization of the social world; specifically he wants to understand the links between the economic order, the vocabularies of motives which are in use at a particular time, and individual explanations for situations. He expresses this analytic imperative in a set of assumptions about the character of social order. Briefly, Kenneth Burke takes the social world to consist of social classes which are hierarchically ordered in terms of an unequal distribution of privilege, property, obligation and authority. As a result of the disparate interests and opportunities produced in such a class organization, people are set apart from each other. If social order is to be preserved in the face both of the glaring social inequalities and isolating effects of class-based experiences, some process has to be available to bring stability. There have to be motives — interpretations, explanations — which give sense to it all.

Here, Burke offers two processes. The first operates through personal allegiances to a variety of authority symbols that are 'fundamentally connected with property relations' (1959). These allegiances are mediated through individual commitments to particular identity claims that both contain and are justified by authority symbols. Of course, there are a variety of such symbols — family, church, state, political party, work — available to persons within a social order of classes: hence, rhetorics of identification — our persuasive efforts to claim to be what we wish — might be rooted in any of the vocabularies of motive that are seen as licensed by authority symbols. The consequences of these processes of identification are twofold, therefore; they justify an individual's place in the social order and sustain, at the same time, the reasonableness of that order.

Plainly, this is too easily said to be done: social orders are not always that easy to maintain. Not everyone finds their claims to identity accepted; not everyone believes the available explanations for social inequalities; not everyone uses the legitimate authority symbols. Thus, Burke proposes 'scapegoating' as a secondary process for stabilizing orders of social inequality. This device marks offences against the legitimated hierarchy and punishes the offenders through a labelling and expulsion of them as deviants from the normal world. Hence, we scapegoat all kinds of eccentricities, life-styles, disabilities, criminalities and the like in order to support the shaky moral authority of the legitimated motives for social order. In this sense, scapegoating serves as a back-up for the everyday rituals in which the allegiances of people to the moral order are formed.

This early period's concern for motives as dramaturgically persuasive, i.e. rhetorical, strategies which are rooted in economically based authority structures is replaced in the later stage (Burke, 1966, 1969a, 1969b, 1970) by a *formal* concern for motives as verbal strategies to be understood through purely linguistic inquiry. This formal concern is the methodological approach to social action which Burke calls 'dramatism'. In any of his stipulations as to the meaning of this method (for example: 1965, 1968b, 1969a) he emphasizes three key notions — 'language', 'motives' and 'action'. Language and the connotations which link words together are the content and form of our mental processes. It is the verbal interpretations of action — what are called motives in this approach — which are the focus of attention. It is the sets of motivational terms, held together by connotational links, which dramatism treats as the explanations for social action. These verbal links, then, become a justification for individuals creating the same relationships with the material and symbolic referents of these terms. Thus, to call a spouse's conduct 'adulterous' is to justify or motivate a hurt sense of betrayal which might easily lead to a serious argument, from there to a lawyer to file a divorce suit, and from there to all the messy divorce proceedings, property settlements and custody disputes. Alternatively, to call that same conduct 'a naïve mistake' is to license discussion, to foster reconciliation and growth in the relationship, to lead to a better understanding of the viewpoints of both partners. A *cuckold* feels, thinks and acts differently than does the *forgiving spouse of an innocent*.

However, we must remember that dramatism is a method of analysis which asserts the *reality* of symbolic action as the defining activity of the human and uses drama, not analogically, but as a formal model with which to explore both action and explanations for action. As a guide to such analysis, Burke offers two basic notions — the Pentad and 'ratios' that are linked together for inquiry into action and its motives. The Pentad is a name which Burke (1969a) gives to the five terms which he claims are basic to any analysis of motivated action:

> In any rounded statement about motives, you must have some word that names the *act* (names what took place, in thought or deed), and another that names the *scene* (the background of the act, the situation in which it occurred); also, you must indicate what person or kind of person (*agent*) performed the act, what means or instruments he used (*agency*), and the *purpose*.

To use these five terms he notes that one only need treat each one as a collapsed question, so that for example *act* is equivalent to 'What was done?' and *scene* as abbreviation for 'In what sort of situation was it done?' (Burke, 1970).

Using these pentadic terms together in an effort to produce something like a complete analysis, he suggests that the most fruitful mode of combining them is pairwise in order to grasp the congruence which makes theatre interpretable and action coherent. Thus, the conventions of drama expect some kind of consistency between, say, the nature of agents and the acts which they perform, or between the acts and the scene against which they take place.

71

We anticipate, therefore, that heroes will be ones who rescue the distressed; or conversely, that those who rescue the distressed will turn out to be the heroes. A rich interior announces a wealthy set of characters, a battlefield signals war and its horrors, a mute telegraph boy with telegram in hand indicates important news and so on. These 'ratios' among the elements of the Pentad are an array of heuristic strategies for grasping the intelligibility of social action, or for recognizing the way in which a violation of dramatistic coherence illuminates the principle which it offends.

Burke's approach to motives and social action has been nowhere more influential than in the work of Hugh Dalziel Duncan (1953, 1962, 1964, 1965, 1968a, 1968b). Most relevant for dramaturgical work is his general perspective on the social order which is available in three volumes (1962, 1968a, 1968b). These books offer a macrosociological view on the social order which contains the emphases of both Burke's early and late period. In particular, *Symbols and Society* is a summary of his work in a quasi-propositional form that can be taken as a sociological reworking of the *method* of dramatism, meant to serve as a *methodological* guide for investigators undertaking a substantive study of the enactment of social orders.

Like so much work in a dramaturgical framework, Duncan makes strong interactionist assumptions; not the least of these is his claim that society is to be taken as the 'communication of significant symbols' (1968b). What is crucial about that communication, however, is the way in which people express the propriety of their actions to themselves and others. This expression is taken as a role-playing activity which enacts ranked differences among people that are based on class, status, age, gender and so forth and displays, at the same time, the legitimations which unite persons across all their differences in rank. As Duncan (1968b) puts it: 'Role-playing is the enactment of a part in . . . a drama of order [that is] . . . the attempt to legitimize authority by persuading those involved that such order is "necessary" to the survival of the community.' The investigation of any particular enactment of social order is to be guided, in Duncan's approach, by the repeated use of the Pentad as a heuristic set of questions addressed to whatever aspect of the process that is under study.

The basic unit of social order in his orientation is the institution — family, religion, the economy, art and so on. In these the social drama of action is expressed through forms like play, games, festivals, parties, ceremonies and the like. In turn, these forms of social drama present their claims to 'inevitable' legitimacy by appeal to 'symbols grounded in nature, man, society, language or God' (Duncan, 1968b) — which the alert will note is one more transformation of the Pentad — that are offered as the result of the influence of one element of the Pentad upon another. To complete a methodological framework, Duncan incorporates notions of both an audience for these rhetorical appeals and criticism of them, as well as a version of Burke's conception of scapegoating.

Duncan's vade-mecum guides us to think about dramas of social order in which such performance is continually emergent from the disorder and counter-order posed by social conflict. Thus, one has to consider all aspects of social order, to think about the dramatization of legitimate order in various institutional forms and also to deal with the endemic threats of disorder. Processes of criticism and mystification stabilize and protect order from this buffeting of disorder. Criticism, for example, forces authorities to adjust to the world as it is experienced by individuals within their institutional domain. On the other hand, mystification places the legitimation of social hierarchy beyond question as long as one is caught in its rhetoric. Just try to develop a pro-Semitic argument within a Nazi order!

Further to this, there are processes of victimage which Duncan takes as horrifyingly pivotal in stabilizing order in the midst of the conflict which is the social condition. If social order is emergent from struggle and conflict, and conceived in moral terms, then one must expect to find offences against this treated as moral affronts and taken as such by the transgressors. In this recognition there rests both guilt, negative feelings about the self and the likelihood of a turn to authorities for some release from these consequences of error. However, unlike one's parents, those who represent institutional authority outside the family are neither easy to find nor particularly approachable.

If this is a problem in small groups, it is exacerbated in more complex social arrangements where the expression of the principles of social order are necessarily remote and less easy to experience. In such situations, it is vital to find some way to personify what have to be the rather abstract grounds for social hierarchy. This is provided, Duncan (1968b) believes, in a 'community drama of social order, with a struggle between a hero and villain who personify good and bad principles of order'. In such dramas — whether in the symbolism of the film or stage, in the actuality of football games, lynchings, armed combat or in that peculiar transformation of actuality that is television news reporting — individuals are provided with the meaning of both order and offences against it, as the consequences of 'sin' are displayed in the figure of the comic or tragic villain of a socio-drama. In this process, we are able to shed our guilt by associating it with the victim and joining in the actual or figurative punishment of this scapegoat to secure our vicarious atonement (see here, also, Klapp, 1962, 1964).

Despite the thorough integration which Duncan makes of Burke, despite his effort to provide a sociological method for the more abstract and literary version of dramatism which Burke has presented, he has been little influential on other writers, either in his own right or as an interpreter of Kenneth Burke. Generally speaking, Burke's influence has been direct or through Erving Goffman. To illustrate some of this work which is directly linked to Burke, one should mention the fine work of Ernest Becker, especially his last volume (1975), that displays his conviction of the importance of Burke *and* Duncan as the key sociological interpreters of the human tendency 'to visit suffering and death on others' (Duncan, 1968b). However, Ernest Becker himself has been little part of the development in dramaturgical writing; perhaps he has been too eclectic, too devoted to psychoanalytic writing or just too successful with a popular audience for most sociologists. More in that main line of Burkean influence, we should exemplify both those who take dramatism as a literal model for social action, and those who treat it as a fruitful analytic metaphor.

R. S. Perinbanayagam (1964, 1977, 1982a, 1982b) has been a consistent advocate of dramatism as a literal model. As he succinctly puts it: '. . . when one talks of the drama of social life one is not engaging in a simple-minded comparison of human relations to what is going on at a theater, but saying something about act, communication and meaning as the fundamental medium of human existence since the evolutionary emergence of symbolicity' (1982a). Thus, in his fine book (1982b) on the use of astrology in the northern part of Sri Lanka, he talks about a 'karmic theater' without meaning that it is *as if* life were a drama of fate. He couples a detailed analysis of the structure of the Hindu belief system with a similar analysis of the system of astrology in order to show their links; this coupled system is then shown to be the rhetoric of self employed by people who live in Jaffna. This book illustrates how Burke's understanding of the terminological basis of self, action and motives comprehends the form of self, action and motives among Hindu users of astrologers; how the logic of astrology forms the motivational logic for persons in Jaffna society.

Within the meanings for life that are drawn from Hindu texts — that speak of life and rebirth, of merit and transgression, of hierarchy as a natural condition of those on their pilgrimage to God, of the patterned character of all events in life — astrological predictions become an organizing device for life. Individuals, from the highest to the lowest segments of society, seek out astrologers to obtain horoscopes for themselves and for those with whom they plan to deal. For example, no marriage can be arranged without an astrological judgement on the suitability of the match constructed from an interpretation of the prospective couple's horoscopes. With the mutual reinforcement of religious and astrological texts, it is not surprising that people are able to grasp the meaning of action by means of the vocabulary of motives that horoscopes use to gloss the *karma* for each person's life.

In Lyman and Scott (1970, 1975) one finds a similar concern to support the 'real' character of life as a dramatic communication. Although less worked out and perhaps less effective than Perinbanayagam's application of a Burkean perspective, in *The Drama of Social Reality* they do take his approach in a somewhat different direction. They turn directly to the texts of a number of Shakespeare's plays and from these and literary criticism of them develop some ideas about the staging of political myths, about human resistance to institutional constraint and about the resort to 'adventure' as an antidote to a modern sense of ennui. In particular, they offer brief accounts of Mead, Freud and Goffman where they contrast the theatre of the mind as it appears in the work of the first two with life as theatre in Goffman. Their own contributions are short attempts to talk about the dramatization of conditions of life. Thus, after discussing the way in which legitimacy is constructed in the myth of ultimate grounds for political rule, they turn to the forms of resistance which occur in response to such dramas of power.

Their discussion of the dramatization of resistance, epitomized in the life, dress and activities of the social bandit of the Old West, helps an understanding of the longevity of that type in both literature and life. And if that social persona seems rather remote in time and place, they offer us the 'adventure' as an emblem of theatrical escape from the routine world in which we live today. Finding ourselves segmented into the many roles which the public sphere requires, the private world can offer a chance for moves towards an integration of the fragmented self. Moreover, it offers chances for the conscious pursuit of activities which require strategy, a suspension of the mundane, and a search for a world of challenge and excitement that can stop the quotidian clock. And if the tourists have taken over the Nile, the Antarctic and New Guinea, there is always the sexual escapade to catch us up into the fantasy of a breathless present where all things are possible. (For a broader array of escapes from the mundane, see Cohen and Taylor, 1976.)

Two major pieces stand out from Joseph Gusfield's work as fine illustrations of the use of dramatism and the theatre *as metaphor* (1963, 1981). In both these works, he makes use of a Burkean perspective without taking it as more than one among a number of viewpoints; dramaturgical realism is for others. The earlier of these two volumes treats the American Temperance movement as an example of status politics conducted through symbolic action. For our money, this treatment is still one of the classic discussions of the difference between instrumental and symbolic politics. It allows us to see political action as both rational *and* non-instrumental and to understand movements like the Temperance as efforts to dramatize the status position and values of collectivities whose place in a community is under threat.

The second of these two — incidentally also concerned with alcohol use — is a volume which adds materially to the fund of dramatistically important works. From a Burkean 'perspective by incongruity' he sets out to understand the public portrait of the drinking-driver as a social problem. He is, in effect, trying to show the way in which that problem is constructed through our scientific knowledge, policy pronouncements, statutory actions and enforcements; but his investigation is not oriented in any conventional way as notions of 'scientific knowledge', or 'policy pronouncements' and so on might suggest. For example, he treats research on drinking-driving as a form of persuasion, as a dramatic rhetoric addressed to the creation of a sense of facticity. As a result, he argues that the authority of science, the facticity on which social policy claims to rely, is itself the product of an artistic rhetoric that overtly denies what is patently the case — that there are alternative interpretations hidden by the glossy presentation.

This concern for authority and its expression in drama-like action is continued when he considers the legal rituals which seek to portray the drinking-driver as a violator of moral order. This theme of moral disorder, however, works against a second one — the drinking-driver as merely 'average, frail and sometimes delinquent' (Gusfield, 1981). It is out of these two themes that legal action directed at drinking-drivers struggles to carve a dramatically consistent world: 'It is an orderly and predictable world, intelligible and legitimate, a world of authority. In creating meaning the dramas of public action shore up a fence against the awesome skepticism of unending alternatives, ambiguous facts, and the confusion of the concrete and particular.'

With some immodesty, as a last example, we draw attention to one of our own joint efforts which employs dramatism as a way of thinking about intervention in organizations by consultants (Mangham and Overington, 1983b). In that essay we have taken up Burke's concern with the processes of mystification which operate by offering only a single explanation for complex, motivationally dense sets of human actions. The claim that Jill is a bad girl because she fell into bad company rejects all blame by laying it at the door of specific bad *agents*; it says nothing about explanations which might draw on *scene*, *purpose* or *act*. Expanding this notion of mystification into a view of theatre as a crucial site of demystification, we go on to discuss interventions in organizations as efforts to display, through a kind of Brechtian strategy of startlement, the motives which are not offered, not considered or not heard.

So much for some brief illustrations of those who are directly in line with Kenneth Burke, both those who take his dramaturgy as a literal model for social action and those, like ourselves, who use it as one among a number of possible metaphors. Yet, we have avoided to this point Erving Goffman, the one person who has been more influential than any single figure on contemporary work in the dramaturgical analysis of social action. One advantage of this, of course, is to have suggested that dramaturgy is not *just* Goffman. His volume *The Presentation of Self in Everyday Life* (1959), the basis for his popular reputation, is both a sociological classic and a best-seller. Too well known, too often written about, the most that we could say of the volume without danger of boring our readers is to remind them of its basic theme.

Goffman is concerned there to show that the ordering of social situations is achieved through the expression of prospective views of self which are received with mutual tolerance. He is not concerned to deal with the conscious creation of these favourable images as much as with the conditions which allow for an acceptable definition of a situation. Thus, he emphasizes the advantages which accrue to those others who serve as audiences to our presentations of self. He notes that there are two streams of information which we provide as we proffer ourselves to others: we say things and we do things. Those things we say, the information we 'give', are regarded as under our control: those things we do or communicate parallel to what we say, the information we 'give off', are thought, on the other hand, to be more involuntary. Our audiences 'may then use what are considered to be the ungovernable aspects of . . . expressive behavior as a check upon the validity of what is conveyed by the governable aspects' (Goffman, 1959). There is, therefore, a fundamental 'asymmetry' in the construction of situational definitions which favours audiences; but since we are all audiences to the other's presentation this becomes a balanced asymmetry upon which we can depend, in most circumstances, for mutual circumspection and charity. We expect a charitable audience for our expressions since we infrequently violate the dramaturgical credibility which they require; so also does our audience. It is from this simple starting-point that Goffman goes on to build up a complex of concepts that treat the co-operative nature of group expressions — 'team performances', the places in which such performances are offered and their backstages, and the various threats to the credibility of performances.

His talent in this volume, as in his other work (1961a, 1961b, 1963a, 1963b, 1967, 1969, 1971, 1974), is the creation of conceptual insights. He develops concepts to talk about some type of person, act, agency or situation (to give this a Burkean gleam) and discards them with the profligacy only the most brilliant can afford. Something of this multiplication of concepts is noted by Peter Manning, when he says of some nineteen pages of *Frame Analysis* (1974) that there are '4 kinds of playful deceit, 6 types of benign fabrications, 3 kinds of exploitative fabrications, [and] 5 sorts of self-deception' (1980). Goffman has left us a mine of ideas. Whether one would feel that his work is 'structuralist' in character (Denzin and Keller, 1981), or 'formalist' following Simmel and Durkheim (Manning, 1980), or prefers to understand him as a Burkean (see also Perinbanayagam, 1982a, b), is not important. We can all find something in him that fits our prejudices. What is not doubtful is the influence that he has had on people interested in a dramaturgical approach to social life: he has inspired both research in his own *métier* and become *de rigueur* in footnotes when the theatrical metaphor is mentioned. Even when a philosopher takes the dramaturgical frame seriously, as does Bruce Wilshire (1982), he uses Goffman as the emblem of this approach in the social sciences in order to explore what he takes as the limits of the theatrical metaphor.

To trace Goffman's influence, however, would be more of a bibliographical than an analytic exercise and it would be of little interest or utility. We prefer to pick a few illustrations of the *kind* of influence which he has exercised as some assistance to an understanding of the resources which are available for those with a dramaturgical orientation to social life. First among these, perhaps, we should mention the work of Rom Harré, who together with a number of colleagues has worked out the 'ethogenic' approach to social conduct. This new name conceals no more remarkable a view of social life than the understanding that the main process of action is 'self direction according to the meaning ascribed to the situation' (Harré and Secord, 1972). In a number of volumes, of which *Social Being* (1979) is the best known and perhaps Harré and Secord (1972) the clearest, he has outlined cogent philosophical criticisms of neopositivism and the application of a single-minded experimental technique to social psychology. As one might anticipate from a philosopher at Oxford, there is much concern with the conceptual weakness of social psychology which has resulted in particular experimental 'paradigms' becoming the actual specification of the object of research efforts (Harré and Secord, 1972). Not only does this leave the actual object of interest unclear for Harré, it also assumes an unwarranted passivity in human beings which will inevitably defeat scientific attempts at understanding.

To remedy this, Harré and his colleagues propose a different model of the human — as active, self-conscious and rule-following in conduct — and proceed to ask how that kind of organism can best be studied. They treat the 'episode' — a meaningfully bounded social interaction — as a basic unit of analysis. Within this they are concerned to understand the organization of conduct in terms of nested hierarchies of rules which are followed by persons with conscious plans. While various models for the formal structure of episodes can be found — ceremonial, game — they have some preference for a dramaturgical one. This allows not only for the theatre as a set of model conventions with which to examine the episode, it also allows for the participants and observers to adopt a theatrical distance — 'role distance' in Goffman's usage — from which to monitor and analyse the conduct. In both Harré and Secord (1972) and Harré (1979), Goffman and Burke play important parts in providing conceptual resources that are woven into the proposed analysis of episodes. However, it must be said finally that Harré, as with Wilshire (1982), is unable as a philosopher to consider the human as merely an actor playing a character without inquiring into the nature of personal identity for those acting social roles. The radical dramaturgical position is hard to follow.

A second illustration, this time of a body of literature which has been influenced by both Goffman and Burke, can be taken from work which treats of the verbal explanations for conduct.[4] The issue here is the way in which language is used to bridge the gap between what has happened and what was anticipated, the relation between deeds and the words which define what they are to mean. Stokes and Hewitt (1976) call these attributions 'aligning actions' and consider them 'verbal efforts to restore or assure meaningful interaction in the face of problematic situations of one kind or another'. 'Aligning actions' serve two purposes in their treatment which enables the concept to pull together much of this literature. First, such actions serve to assist individuals align themselves to joint conduct which has become problematic; second, they restore fractures in the link between action and expectations, conduct and culture. Aligning action, thus, smooths the path of social relations in all its idiosyncratic particularity so that the 'shoulds' and 'oughts' of our anticipations are guarded intact, no matter that they are violated in practice. However, as Perinbanayagam (1977) notes, most of the material on verbal motives relates to the provision of meaning to an event which has happened; it is present talk addressed to past deeds. Therefore, he bypasses much of the more recent work to return to Mills (1940) and Kenneth Burke, in order to suggest the importance of prospective as well as retrospective motives. In this essay and more extensively in Perinbanayagam (1982b), as we have discussed earlier, he shows the importance of motives for people's organization of their action.

For a third illustration, pointing to an area which has been neglected till now, we would suggest Arlie Hochschild's *The Managed Heart* (1983) as an attempt to deal with emotions and emotion work through a dramaturgical understanding that is partly Goffman's and partly Stanislavski's. In this volume she is concerned to understand how emotions are managed by a flight attendant so that they can be situationally staged to correspond not to the attendant's feelings, but to the airline's policy. This staging process she calls 'emotional labour' and she tries to show the way in which attendants are trained in both 'surface' and 'deep acting' in order to allow them to present themselves in line with corporation policy while dealing with passengers. She is marvellously persuasive in describing how attendants learn to feel, and to say they feel, that the aircraft cabin is 'their living room full of personal guests'. We are reminded with this volume of how much the theatre is about feeling and how little attention has been given to that by dramaturgical sociology.

Finally, we have taken Heilman's (1976) delightful monograph where he displays a native ability to participate in the activities of a modern Orthodox synagogue and gain, at the same time, sufficient dramaturgical distance to analyse the theatricality of those same activities. In many ways this is an exemplary work; Heilman is able dramaturgically to frame his conduct as an observant Jew and, at the same time, be a true member of his community. The dramaturgical perspective does offer that capacity; very few succeed as well as Heilman in putting a theatrical frame around such deeply cherished practices and beliefs. As he notes in the preface: 'If the book succeeds in its purpose, the reader will finally know little if anything about the meaning that the Orthodox synagogue has for the faithful; he will only see how Orthodox Jews, *as social beings*, act in their congregation.'

Indeed, what we do learn is the way in which the synagogue as a building serves as the setting for a broad cast of characters to act out their parts in daily prayer, on *Shabbos* and on holy days. We discover the semiotic properties of clothing, hats and wigs; we learn of changes in scenic quality which marks areas within the various sections of the synagogue. We observe, with Heilman, the staging procedures which construct the particular cast for a service from among the actors present; we are caught up in his description of prayer services as varying between the ensemble of unison prayer and the jazz-like improvisation of many individual voices; we are amused, as is he, by a father's half-serious complaint about the rapid swaying movements made by his son as an accompaniment to prayer, that it is 'one of the hazards of a yeshiva education'. Yet, as we focus briefly on that activity, known by Jews as *shokeling*, it is also serves Heilman as a sign that indicates — in conjunction with other behavioural features — whether or not a person is a modern or traditional Orthodox Jew, whether this is an important part of the service to which all are obliged to give public attention, whether this person is pious, whether a younger man and his father share the same orientation to Judaism and so on. And so this volume proceeds, opening up a world that is alien to a non-Jew, for an understanding which treats the members of this congregation as engaged in the expressive formation of their world, like any other social actors.

Perhaps with this last illustration, we have been able to fill out what use we think a theatrical metaphor might be to those reading the modern social sciences; what a dramaturgical approach does that 'mainstream sociology' does not and cannot accomplish. Using a dramaturgical approach makes it impossible to employ 'stock' types of persons and characters (the familiar variables of gender, ethnicity, age, occupational status and the like) without accounting for their creation in some social process — whether that he conscious or non-conscious. Thus, for example, Jews can never be simply Jews, to be compared with Protestants and Catholics in terms of their proneness to suicide, mental illness, divorce and so on. Nor can air stewardesses simply be one instance of the uses and misuses of women's labour power.

Jews are more than Jews: air stewardesses are more than women. Neither can be reduced to a 'mere' character or stock type without an assumption that people are no more than *one* of their characters. Taking dramaturgy as *the* metaphor means that one has to recognize such analyses are no more than 'type casting', that it is an exigency of situations and not a requirement of persons. People are all the many parts that they can play and should not be confused with the requirements of their religious or occupational identities. Our concerns spill out from the use and application of this theatrical metaphor, rather than from a preoccupation with categorizing, typing and organizing the kinds of social life that one believes exists. Our task in the next chapter will be to elaborate this metaphor into a model suitable for social scientific inquiry.

Chapter 5

The Theatrical Model

The theatre is in darkness. In the centre of the room, surrounded on three sides by the audience, the stage is barely discernible under the safety lights. Gradually it emerges as the lights are brought up; cold, steel blue reflecting upon a scaffold of a set; brutal, metallic, functional. A throne and a banner emblematically declare that we are in the royal palace.

Enter the Younger Mortimer. We know, since we have sat through the previous scenes, that Mortimer has rebelled against Edward II and is now acting as Protector. We have seen him change from a rebel with a cause to one who displays considerably more personal ambition than desire for the common weal. We have witnessed his transformation from raw sensitivity to cunning and guile, from relative poverty to relative wealth, from influence to considerable power. He now appears before us arrayed in splendour and yet far more uneasy than when we first met him as a hot-blooded, justice-seeking young nobleman. His movements are nervous, we can see anxiety in his face, almost feel the sweat upon his hands. He talks as if to himself and yet addresses us directly:

> The king must die, or Mortimer go down.
> The commons now begin to pity him:
> Yet he that is the cause of Edward's death
> Is sure to pay for it when his son's of age;
> And therefore will I do it cunningly.
> This letter, written by a friend of ours,
> Contains his death, yet bids them save his life:
> (*Reads*) *Edwardum occidere nolite tenere bonum est,*
> *Fear not to kill the king, 'tis good he die*
> But read it thus, and that's another sense:
> *Edwardum occidere nolite tenere bonum est,*
> *Kill not the king, 'tis good to fear the worst.*
> Unpointed as it is, thus shall it go.
> That, being dead, if it chance to be found,
> Matravis and the rest may bear the blame,

And we be quit that caus'd it to be done.
Within this room is lock'd the messenger
That shall convey it and perform the rest;
And, by a secret token that he bears,
Shall he be murder'd when the deed is done.
Lightborn, come forth!

Lightborn, a hired assassin, appears — spotlit at the back of the stage. He does not enter. He is suddenly present. Mortimer moves downstage as if to be as far away from the person he summons as possible. Lightborn is dressed in black from head to toe but wears a strong white make-up which emphasizes his cold stare. He speaks evenly throughout, and is clearly proud of his calling; he has all the chill inhumanity of the professional. Mortimer speaks to him:

MORTIMER: Art thou as resolute as thou wert?
LIGHTBORN: What else, my Lord? And far more resolute.
MORTIMER: And hast thou cast how to accomplish it?
LIGHTBORN: Ay, ay; and none shall know which way he died.
             Mortimer moves towards Lightborn, anxious and concerned:
MORTIMER: But at his locks, Lightborn, thou wilt relent.
LIGHTBORN: Relent! Ha, ha! I use much to relent. (*Contemptuous, dismissive, scornful*) ·
             Mortimer retreats downstage, distancing himself even more.
MORTIMER: Well, do it bravely, and be secret.
             Both men are now isolated within pools of cold light. Lightborn lists his techniques with delight. Mortimer is both fascinated and repelled.
LIGHTBORN: You shall not need to give instructions;
             'Tis not the first time I have kill'd a man.
             I learn'd in Naples how to poison flowers,
             To strangle with a lawn thrust down the throat,
             To pierce the wind pipe with a needle's point.
             Or, whilst one is asleep, to take a quill,
             And blow a little powder in his ears,
             Or open his mouth, and pour quick-silver down,
             And yet I have a braver way than these.
             Mortimer crosses to Lightborn almost against his own better judgement, but drawn by the authority of the man.
MORTIMER: What's that?
             Pause. Lightborn looks at Mortimer, the latter is unable to hold his gaze.
LIGHTBORN: Nay, you shall pardon me; none shall know my tricks.
             Mortimer retreats downstage once more.
MORTIMER: I care not how it is, so it be not spied.
             Deliver this to Gurney and Matravis.
             He holds out a letter. Lightborn does not move. Mortimer gestures with

> *the letter. Lightborn does not move, but slowly stretches out his arm.*
> *Mortimer hesitates, crosses to him, thrusts the letter at him.*

MORTIMER: And every ten miles and thou hast a horse.
Take this (*gives money*): away, and never see me more!
Retreats once more downstage.

LIGHTBORN: No?

MORTIMER: No, unless thou bring me news of Edward's death.

LIGHTBORN: That will I quickly do. Farewell, my Lord.
> *The light snaps out and Lightborn disappears, leaving Mortimer alone*
> *on stage. The theatre appears to be very cold and still.*[1]

We have a couple of difficulties immediately. Our purpose is to offer an account of the resources which are available in the theatre when that is considered as a realm of metaphor for describing and analysing social conduct. We wish, therefore, to talk about theatre in sufficient detail that it stimulates our conceptual imagination in moving backwards and forwards between theatre and social life in order to know more about both, yet we do not wish to lose our focus on conduct in organizations in a welter of detail about theatre — fascinating as that detail may be. After all, there are many volumes that have been written about theatre in all its aspects and we neither can nor wish to add another.[2] Rather we wish to add to our understanding of social relationships through an emphasis upon social life in all its repetitive aspects as ritual performance. Thus, like a number of other commentators, we take the notion of performance as a necessary point of departure for our excursion into the theatre; a necessary but not sufficient point, since we shall have occasion to move from it to a discussion of the conditions that allow for performance.

Starting with performance is not merely a way of getting directly at social action; it is also a way of beginning that is recognizable to anyone not actively involved in the theatre, for most of us participate there as members of audiences. It is a way of beginning, furthermore, that allows us to employ a mode of analysis of social life that is compatible with our efforts to develop the theatre as a framework for metaphorical invention. It does not require much thought to see that we can avoid another, and perhaps fatal difficulty if we adopt such an approach. We can avoid the problems created by an infinite regress. The difficulty is something like this. We want to use a theatrical metaphor as a device for analysing social life; to do that we have to present an account of the theatre so that we have a sufficiently rich understanding of theatre in which to develop our concepts; what kind of metaphoric framework do we use to develop an analysis of the theatre? We can not use a theatrical framework to analyse theatre; that would be self-referential and impossible. We have yet to develop a theatrical framework; how can we use what is to be developed? On the other hand, if we use some other metaphoric framing in order to develop this account of theatre, are we not simply laying ourselves wide open to the charge that it is this analytic framework and not the theatrical metaphor which is the root of our conceptual invention about the character of social life?

What we are suggesting here — starting with performance — is a way out of the problem. This way is available in our adopting an interactionist position towards the analysis of theatre without further reflection on how such analyses are done. Obviously, we cannot present an account of anything, theatre or any other social world, without presumptions about that world and how it is to be grasped. We must start somewhere with some basic assumptions and we cannot (at the same time as we analyse) subject these assumptions to close scrutiny. Thus, we have chosen to start with interactionists' assumptions, to situate our account of theatre in the tradition taken for granted. We do this since it is the tradition in which we work and feel most at ease as social scientists: we also recognize that we could have started in many other ways, with other assumptions, out of other traditions of inquiry. Yet, one must accept some tradition of inquiry, must take some matters for granted. As interactionists, then, we start with the event of theatre as it is given us in performance. This is the event which we have to understand in terms of what it is and how it is possible.

Without overly anticipating the analysis, it can be said that we shall try to show how performances in the theatre are presented as *givens* that successfully hide the conditions which make them possible. Any performance is offered as the only one possible; no hint of an alternative is suggested. *Edward II* is just that. Yet this givenness of a performance is no more than a persuasive communication made to an audience. The performance is for them and without them there would only be a rehearsal. No audience, no performance. What is hidden in any performance is how the naturalness of the staged reality is accomplished. How our attention is engaged, what in the acting, setting, lights, sound effects and so on allows us to suspend disbelief and assume a theatrical consciousness, these are matters for investigation. Yet such an interest in the mechanics of the performance, the techniques of acting, the text of the play, would take one out of the sense of givenness which is available to the properly attentive member of an audience. It would take one on to speculation about the nature of the creative process, to an investigation of the conditions which allow the performance to be accomplished. It would take one to consider rehearsals, casting, directors and designers. Further afield, it would take one to examining the entertainment industry, the financing of it, the environment in which it takes place, the workforce that produces it, the sites in which performances are given, the general characteristics of audiences; and finally it would lead one to inquire about playwrights, their plays and the story-telling traditions out of which dramatic art is constructed. But we begin with performance.

In the theatre we find that it is useful to break down the activity in terms of where things take place. The performance takes place on stage defining an arena in which the dramatic action is presented as a given that refuses to acknowledge (save under special conditions) either those who are backstage or those who constitute the audience and front-of-house workers. Yet coming off the street as prospective members of an audience, the first theatrical workers that we would meet are those whose task it is to get us into position and prepare us for the performance. They take our money, our coats; they sell us programmes and drinks; they help us find our seats in the auditorium. But none of these front-of-house workers is readily welcomed on the stage or even backstage. It is almost as if their contact with members of the audience makes them unfit to be part of the mystery which constitutes performances as givens. In our time, the gap between the stage and the front of house, between performance and audience, is a crucial one. It is a separation that constitutes for audiences a preliminary set of cues as to what is to be framed as theatre and what not.

From the point of view of performance, what counts is that any audience be able to enter into the appropriate theatrical consciousness that will allow for that givenness which successful playing requires. Of course, what is entailed here will be quite variable; different times and places will exhibit diverse conventions for audience involvement. Today, audiences at theatrical performances expect to be silent, save for applause or laughter. We may be appreciative and amused and express that: we rarely exhibit disapproval or other emotions. In the eighteenth century, audiences were noisy and expressed a range of emotions: poor actors knew that disapproval could be clearly signalled with a volley of rotten fruit. But quiet or noisy, approving or critical, audiences have to be minimally attentive and minimally aware of the way in which the communication of theatrical reality through costumes, scenery, lighting, acting is to be framed as drama. The assumption of a theatrical consciousness by members of an audience allows them to distinguish the actors from the characters that they play and suspend their disbelief in the appearance of the stage so as to construct them as a theatrical reality.

Not everyone, however, adopts a theatrical consciousness towards a performance. Audiences may contain not only those properly involved in the givenness of some playing, they may also have those bored by it all, those who came along to be seen in the right place, those interested in a particular actor, singer or dancer — 'fans' and so forth. From the viewpoint of the performers, these particular 'side involvements' among members of an audience are not a problem; they are much more concerned about the presence of claques and critics. Both are vociferously responsive to the performance, yet neither is properly involved. Members of a claque are paid to give noisy support to a particular artist and thus are within the critical distance required of an audience. The balance between belief and disbelief that enables a drama to engage an audience in the theatrical reality implies that its members neither be part of the performance nor detached from it. Yet, if claques are too close, becoming part of the performance (knowing collaborators), then critics are too distant, taking no responsibility for the dramatic communication save for its appraisal.

It is only with some kind of 'paying audience' that is properly involved with a performance that we have the conditions for the dramatic moment which suspends quotidian disbelief and treats theatre as reality. The other element in this dramatic moment is, of course, the playing that is taking place on the front stage. Theatrical reality is jointly constructed by performers and audience across that space which separates them. Whatever reality it is that is communicated by the playing that takes place on-stage, the perspective on this which counts is not one from backstage, it is the viewpoint from out there, from the position of their audience. It is to such a perspective that scenery, lighting, make-up and acting are directed in the creation of a dramatic reality which involves members of the audience. Paramountly, it is the acting which takes on the burden.

Acting is the craft practised by actors. It is the routine communication of a character through speech and action by persons who are not themselves the same as the characters they play. Paradoxically, in a performance there should be no communication of acting; the portrayal of a character should be 'natural'. Notwithstanding the experiments of Craig, Artaud, Brecht, Grotowski, Brook and others, nothing is more likely to destroy the vitality of a dramatic communication than a sense that it is acting which is going on, that some artifice is being used to make the characterization credible.[3] A further paradox of dramatic performance is that this concentration on natural portrayals, which is accomplished for the audience, cannot acknowledge that audience save under special conditions.[4]

One can sum up the accomplishment of a natural performance, from the viewpoint of acting, with the notion of ensemble playing. Although this may only be possible in the best theatrical companies, or only for some moments in others, it is a commitment and ability to play off each other (and not strive for individual brilliance) in the interests of presenting a dramatic unity that conveys with it no sense of acting. It requires loyalty to the play, to the collective presentation; it needs discipline from all the actors; finally, it mandates control over the common problems of acting such as upstaging, stage fright, corpsing, drying and prompting, going over the top and so on. In the extract from a performance which serves as a preface to this chapter, the actor playing Mortimer can literally upstage the one playing Lightborn by abandoning his rehearsed movements and seeking to dominate the scene. To do so would draw attention to himself, to be sure, both as character and performer, but it would wreck the overall sequence of moves and moods, activities and emotions, that have been so carefully elaborated through hours of rehearsal. Equally, should the actor playing Mortimer forget to pick up his 'prop' letter or his 'prop' money at the beginning of the scene, the consequences could be dire for the performance as a whole: 'Deliver this to Gurney and Matravis' (*Holds out nothing*) Collapse of all concerned.

Yet, attention to ensemble is only one element in the service of a convincing performance and that, in turn, is framed before an audience with concerns for pacing and timing that are sensitive to that audience and its responses. Again we have the paradox of playing to an audience that we do not acknowledge in the playing. Timing deals with working a performance around an audience's responses, seeking to elicit particular responses, without communicating any awareness directly that there is an audience. In comedy, one waits for the laugh before going on to the next lines. Building up the audience's expectations for the climax is a more complex business, as it involves both a shaping of the performance from beginning to the end and an interplay with the actual audience so that it is prepared for the climactic moment. None the less, even on those occasions that allow for the audience to be directly addressed — the soliloquy or aside are common examples of this — the rapid return to playing that does not recognize the audience is a display of the delicate balance which enables actors to play to an audience without a demonstration of this intent. The actor playing Mortimer in *Edward II* has to tread a careful line between addressing us as Mortimer and yet not creating in us as audience any desire to respond to him. In effect, he signals that he is talking *at* us rather than to us; he must take us into his confidence without drawing attention to the very device by which he achieves that relationship.

To assist actors in persuading the audience to accept the dramatic reality which they are staging, we find a number of 'props' being used. It is more common today to find that a play is presented with little in the way of a set than in the last century; but the amount and kind of scenery, make-up, lighting, music and special effects has been highly variable in a variety of theatrical *milieux*. Make-up, for example, can be highly differentiated in terms of various performance contexts. Clowns in the circus wear individualized faces that are copyrighted and reproduced exactly for every performance. In this way, they fall in with other traditions that conventionalize all or parts of the made-up face, such as Japan and China where the characters are communicated in part by unchanging facial appearances. The actor playing Lightborn signals the long tradition of the presentation of non-human creatures by his demeanour and his make-up; the white, featureless expression he adopts giving rise to associations of death. On the other hand, we have theatrical forms of make-up which seek to give the effect of naturalness from the distance at which the audience will view them. Cruelly distorting when seen in close-up — hence, the notion of 'theatrical' applied to heavily made-up faces in everyday life — they are realistic at a distance.

Costume as well is intended to be seen at a distance. The richness of a king's robe and the jewels of his crown are reduced to more prosaic material if one gets too close. With costumes — and we do not say 'clothes' of theatrical wardrobes — we are still dealing with props which support characterization, that give depth and veracity to the way in which actors present themselves in particular characters. The change from the rough, honest clothes of the provincial feudal vassal effected by Mortimer in the early scenes of the play to the richly embroidered gown in which he appears before us in the scene we have been discussing signals something about the change in the character. Something that we as audience are meant to apprehend. Equally obvious, the sharp contrast which obtains between Mortimer and Lightborn, dressed in black, emphasizes that which is transacted between them; Mortimer, the corrupted soul, is now dealing with the embodiment of Satan (Lightborn = Lucifer); how are the mighty fallen.

When we look at the sets against which the play goes on, they serve as a general communication of context for the dramatic action. Rather than giving density to characterization, the scenery offers a more general context of place and time. The more definite is the scenery, the more specific the context it imposes on the dramatic actors. In Britain, the earliest scenery was quite simple, little more than painted slides that were pulled out from the sides of the stage. Over the centuries, however, sets became more and more complex and reached some kind of a peak in the nineteenth century in the great spectacles, the horse-races, train wrecks and so on, which so dominated attention that situations counted for much more than any character. The extravagant scale of such settings that seem to fit in so well with the Victorian era is no longer dominant in contemporary theatre, although one still finds vestiges of it in such areas as grand opera — think of the triumphal march in *Aida* with the animals, captives and ubiquitous spear carriers parading across the stage. Modern sets can be very simple indeed, and some are constructed, as in *Edward II*, in order to convey little sense of place or time so that attention is willy-nilly on characterization.

The issue of naturalistic production is not merely the expense of getting a level of accuracy that will convince anyone looking closely. It is also the difficulty of signalling this accuracy. Clearly, this is raised in having, say, nothing but rich silk for the dresses; but how does one signal this to an audience that might not recognize the fabric? Yes, extravagance cannot be easily overlooked. A train crash, hundreds of extras cannot easily be ignored; but what about the accurate rendering of a worker's home of the late seventeenth century? If that set actually contains pieces of authentic or reproduced furniture of that period, to modern eyes they are antiques, and what are antiques doing in a weaver's cottage? We have to remember that staging is just that, it is the persuasive communication of time and place, of character and action; it is not authenticity that one offers but a representation which offers an audience all the information that it requires to draw conclusions that make sense of the dramatic action. Naturalistic staging is just one style of presenting that information and it no more solves the problem than does any other.

However, in all this talk about sets, costumes, acting and audiences we have to remember that we are talking about what goes into making a performance. We have been trying to understand what it is that assists in constructing the givenness of performances; but we have said very little about the character of performances themselves, what they are like, what they are about. Most importantly we have to remember that any performance presents all that is necessary to make sense of it *in its own terms*: at the same time it conceals the conditions and techniques through which it is offered as a given (unless there is some collapse of the theatrical reality). Yet it presents itself not through a plot or a text, but through the acting of characterizations. Certainly, plays do have plots and usually there will be a script or text that was used in rehearsal; but those are not available in the performance itself. It is only at the end of some drama that we can reconstruct what was the plot, what the story of the play was about. In performance, therefore, we experience only characterizations; through these we gradually understand what the play deals with and how we are to make sense of it all.

The text of a play, therefore, is only available in a performance as an attribution to it; it is not communicated in the playing. On the other hand, it is possible that some people will bring a sense of text to a performance. A critic might come to *Edward II* with the text in hand to see what has been cut or rearranged; young candidates for examinations that have some set play or another for study will be likely to be following the action with the text which they have brought. If one is attending the performance of some classic drama for the twentieth time, it is difficult not to have a textual sense of the action and to be more interested, then, in such things as the quality of the acting, the sets and costumes and so on. In the late 1970s, a cult audience built up for the film *The Rocky Horror Picture Show*, and people would attend screenings of it dressed as their favourite character. These audiences would chant the lines in unison with the characters on the screen. Yet, all these situations are unusual and point up what is crucial to the experience of theatre in the characteristic situation. We are much more likely to be at a performance for the first time and will not and cannot know what it will be about apart from what is communicated during the performing. Thus, the dramatic vitality of our experience is kept intact and our involvement with the characters and their activities is made possible. A sense of text, then, is antithetical to this dramatic experience and its possession indicative of something unusual.

Yet, if we as members of an audience are usually present for the first time, this is not the case for actors. This might be the 'first night', of course, and everything will be a little more tense; more likely is it that we shall be one audience among the many that have given some show a long run and what is novel for us in the audience is routine for the actors. Routine performance of characters presents a number of difficulties for actors unless they are able to slip into their characters easily and carry off their performance without great effort. Failing that capacity, which is like allowing oneself to be possessed by some other personality, actors have to look around for techniques that enliven their characterization. It is then that one can find the exercises for getting into character, the little tricks which are played to break the monotony and so on.

It is also here that one finds the occasional lapses of theatrical reality as people forget their lines or cues, or some element of the staging which has been taken for granted for weeks is out of place, breaking up routine and forcing actors into unpractised improvisations. Simon Callow, in his splendid book *Being an Actor*, to which we shall have recourse on a number of occasions, writes about the problem and the solution:

The third crisis, four months or so in, is the loss of character. The thought patterns are no longer clear, the character's attributes have become mannerisms, a voice and a walk empty of any impulse. A glance in a mirror has no transforming power. This is a very troubling sensation. A feeling of complete falseness overcomes you from the moment you reach the stage. Something nags away at you all the while you are talking. Your face hangs heavy on your skull as if it were a mask. The remedy for this is to write out your entire part in the first person in character. It compels you to rethink every scene you are in, and restores the eyes and ears of the character to you. (Callow, 1984)

Such is the experience of the theatre for audiences and actors. But it says nothing about the content.

What is theatre, in its broadest sense, about? What do performers mean, refer to, communicate? Over and above the *form* of theatrical performances which we have talked about as a *staging of reality*, is there something to be said about content, about the kind of realities that are staged? The short answer is yes, but the longer version would require more than a little attention to literary theory and histories of performance. To be only somewhat more lengthy than a one-word answer, we would say that theatrical performance always refers both to itself and beyond. It is always at least self-referential in making sense in its own terms. At the same time, dramatic performances make internal sense only because they employ a framework of motives that are humanly sensible. Thus, they refer in general terms to what people do, do not do, what people feel and do not feel, and why. The sense which audiences make of these motivational frameworks will clearly vary; at different times and in varying contexts the same play will convey quite dissimilar notions. Thus, theatre can be both supportive of some established order and subversive; it can challenge received notions or reflect them approvingly back; it can celebrate the virtues of establishment heroes or propose new heroes from among the ordinary people. We will argue later, however, that the theatre is primarily concerned with feelings, that its very form is antithetical to discursive thought. In essence, we will claim that the success of a performance may be measured as a function of the extent that it causes us, the audience, to apprehend relationships and emotion. It fails if it becomes only a talking shop, an instrument for propaganda, a lecture theatre or a political forum. What we see when we go to the theatre is an abstraction from actuality, a selected and edited version of that which most of us can recognize as human encounter unfolding before us and resonating with some element of our own experience, real or imagined. It has the semblance of happening around us, unrehearsed and edited, as in life, by the performers; if we are caused to think that it *is* rehearsed, that each move *is* practised and choreographed, our attention is drawn away from the import to the mechanisms and that peculiar relationship between performers and audience is put in jeopardy. Discursive thought is the enemy. Notwithstanding the current vogue for breaking up that which is transacted between the actor and the audience and inviting the latter to become active, that which is presented is emblematic, an objectification of feeling and thought which requires a degree of passivity on our part if we are to receive it. The art of the performer is to cast us into that peculiarly receptive frame of mind so that what we apprehend appears natural and real. It is the crafting of this 'givenness' that will concern us for the rest of this chapter. The central defining characteristic of theatre is, of course, live performance before an audience. The final product, the interactions we witness occurring before our eyes, are revealed only in performance and, ideally, appear to be spontaneous and yet matters of consequence with a rhythm, flow and 'naturalness' not unlike social life as we experience it in 'real time'. Theatre consists of moments of performance which, like everyday social interaction, once performed and experienced are forever lost.

The fact that theatre in essence consists of the finality of performance means that preparation prior to performance is all important. A great deal of effort goes into constructing the appearance of spontaneity and preparing for the immediacy of performance. Mistakes before an audience are not easily corrected without a breaking of the all-important frame, so very careful pre-planning and rehearsal become mandatory. The process of arriving at a performance is a creative one and it is to the nature of this that we now turn, to enrich our understanding of the theatrical metaphor.

> I usually produce a blueprint which is there to be destroyed . . . the anarchic process is very important. . . . (Peter Wood, 1981)

What unfolds before us on the stage as we sit through *Edward II* is the result of a process of group creativity. Just as individuals produce paintings, literature and music, so groups produce films, operas, dances and plays. The process is a fascinating one and one which we believe — and will demonstrate later — has much to say about the nature of ordinary social intercourse. To arrive at a creative product one works long hours. The process consists of running things up provisionally — working from some set of ideas, some blueprint — taking a look at what results in the light of standards deriving from experience and knowledge, modifying, rejecting or accepting the whole or aspects of it, before moving on to develop other ideas out of that which has so far been achieved.[5] A process which is fundamentally that of discovering the problematic and rendering it less so through provisional, cobbled-together attempts to come to terms with it.

The director of *Edward II* had some initial ideas of how he thought the play ought to be performed; his preliminary blueprints (more accurately, his preliminary 'working drawings') were based upon a critical evaluation of other productions and other performances out of which emerged a group of problems to be addressed and resolved by actually doing something — the suck-it-and-see approach to creativity (the tactile approach) — acting in order 'to see what we are doing and where we are going'. For example, the scene which prefaces this chapter presents a problem for the director and the cast; the relationship between the characters is problematic: what is the relative power and status of the two characters, and having 'discovered' that, how is it to be emblematized in performance? In order to determine the answers to these questions, the actors and the director 'try it out'. Directors, therefore, are likely to study plays carefully so as to become aware of the conditions the texts present for interpretation. In so doing, directors try not only to understand the actual lines and to appreciate the development of the plot, but also to come to terms with what Stanislavski has termed the 'sub-text', the feeling that is to be objectified.

In his work, the concept of 'sub-text' is employed to refer to what 'lies behind and beneath the actual words of a part'. He describes this as that 'which makes us say the words we do in a play. . . . It is the manifest, the inwardly felt expression of a human being in a part, which flows uninterruptedly beneath the words of the text, giving them life and a basis for existing.' In more familiar words, the sub-text is the director's (and actors') 'naïve' theories of action and motives which enable them to formulate characters whose conduct will 'make sense'. What follows is part of the conversation which followed a number of such 'runs' (try-outs). Much talk of getting the 'right feel' and of 'holding the stage':

First phase, when Mortimer is being urged to hold his ground and dominate the set.

DIRECTOR: I felt that quite unnecessary, absolutely unnecessary, when you walk up and down. I think that we'll lose that. . . . I think that you, Mortimer, you have your conviction and confidence. Just stand there and do nothing at all. No gesture, no illustrative thing . . . just you . . . in a way here, as in a lot of the play, you are saying to the audience . . . OK, I'm here . . . but I think particularly here we see the emanation of your power, the emanation and weight of your power should fill whatever space you are in, Westminster Hall, this small rehearsal room. . . .

MORTIMER: From the beginning of Part II of the play onwards, that should be there, growing all the time?

DIRECTOR: Absolutely. In fact, you get stiller and stiller, more and more powerful, as the play progresses. Absolutely.

Second phase, director talking to both actors about a sequence in which Lightborn catalogues various forms of murder with which he is familiar:

DIRECTOR: Then we come to murder at close range and I think the words to go for are 'lawn' and 'throat' — 'to strangle with a lawn thrust down the throat, To pierce the windpipe with a needle's point'. . . . You did something, Lightborn, the first time which you haven't done today which I thought was very, very good. When you are talking about the 'windpipe with a needle point', your hand came into physical proximity to Mortimer which was actually very threatening. It caused Mortimer to move away very fast, 'I care not how it be done' — not necessarily a physical move, but a kind of quick verbal escape perhaps. . . .

In the final stages of rehearsal, the problems are being discussed and further resolutions arrived at in the light of what has gone before. The actors are now experimenting with Lightborn still and Mortimer moving:

DIRECTOR: I just wonder, Lightborn, if you are actually coming on too far — following through what we have just been discussing. If we kept the distance greater . . . the pressure that is put upon Mortimer may be quite considerable. . . . Let's give it a try. Just come to the top of the steps, no further, and let's see what happens. (*They run the scene as suggested.*)

MORTIMER: What was interesting about that was that I feel that I have to move. I have to break in order to get rid of him. . . . The only thing to be wary of is that . . . being disturbed by somebody's presence is one thing, but being overrun is quite another. . . . Do you see? I don't know. What do you feel?

DIRECTOR: I thought the distance made by Lightborn — actually Lightborn not moving at all — made him extremely strong in the scene. Whilst you don't exactly dance attendance on him . . . you know the sort of thing I mean.

MORTIMER: Yes. I mean, it's all about power, isn't it? And this cold, calculating sod has it in this scene, doesn't he? I start off on top and end up just wanting him out.

The director's initial blueprint indicated that in this scene Mortimer, the proud, upwardly mobile baron was to be the dominant character, but playing it in that manner did not 'feel right'. The 'runs' which followed modified and virtually upended this perspective.

Creativity in the form with which we are concerned (that which occurs in the theatre) rests upon the notion of blind variation and selective retention. A widely held view is that creative products such as *Edward II* (and, as we will subsequently argue, some elements of social and institutional life) occur through a process in which those concerned: (a) critically interact with prior products, are in touch with the 'tradition' within which they are working and from which they derive their professional standards (standards, however, which do not totally constrain them); (b) proceed by a process of trial and error in a 'necessarily indeterminate' manner to discover and render it less so, with each resolution suggesting a partially new set of possibilities; completing the process (c) when a stage is reached which in the opinion of those involved represents an appropriate breaking-off point (Briskman, 1981). This final stage is the most difficult to define and to account for — perhaps the words of a composer best sum up the sort of notion we are trying to encapsulate: 'I recently spent three months collaborating with Peter Porter on an opera on the subject of Orpheus. I then literally had to tear the whole lot up and start again (the second time round I finished it in five weeks). It wasn't right. Often it can be very nearly right, but it's when it's most nearly right that it's most difficult because what you've done, although it's wrong, is all you've got. . . . And of course you may find at the end that you've pretty well written what you did the first time, but with a few tiny, crucial changes' (Burgon, 1982). The process of creativity can be rationally accounted for (even though stages in it may appear to be non-rational) and may be retrospectively described, but it is, at the same time, unpredictable and relatively free from rules and routines; the kind of foolishness March and Simon (1958) talk about: 'Treating action as a way of creating interesting goals.' The envisaged end is likely to change as the work already done reveals an unexpected character and suggests unforeseen possibilities.

The end point of the creative endeavour is a performance which is in fact adjudged 'creative' if it is thought so by those who are considered to be the best judges. Part of this judgement is concerned with the novelty of the performance, part with its value. The finer points of this need not concern us at the moment, for our interest is in the nature of the theatre and the resources the employment of a theatrical metaphor places at our disposal. At the minimum it affords us the opportunity to think of conduct as performance; an abstraction and editing of reality which imposes itself upon us. Going backstage, as it were, it also allows us to consider the broad notion of group creativity. Actors, technicians, set designers, musicians, property masters, lighting artists, costume designers, directors and producers interact to 'discover' ideas and emotions from within a particular text and seek to render these 'discoveries' meaningful to an audience. We will argue in the final part of this book that as on the stage, so in social and organizational life: actors interact so as to discover what it is they are about and perform so as to emblematize or objectify that meaning. The process by which they do so has, we will argue, many features of the process which occurs backstage in the theatre.

Rehearsals, in part, are about getting characterizations to work, having actors work on getting the right 'feel' to their portrayals, making them intelligible and consistent from situations to situation, and making them fit in with the other characters in the play. In effect, this means that a characterization is shaped over the whole of its presence in the play so as to render it coherent to the overall interpretation. In many situations, this requires a summing-up of the character into some kind of a notion about what it is *essentially*. Exactly what such an essence might be is not in any way fixed in the theatre. Certainly, different eras will have their own ideas about the essence of human character and those are sometimes recorded in 'stock' characters. Yet, depending on interpretations, this essential character might be expressed in terms of a relationship to another character, to the situations presented by the play, to some action taken, to some internal 'personality' feature of the character and so on. None the less, getting the right 'feel' is conducted jointly with the other actors, who are also working on their characterizations. The object is to get it right *together* so that the ensemble playing will communicate the essential characters of all and through them the plot will be intelligible for an audience.

Theatrical consciousness involves an awareness of the differences between actors and the parts that they play, and this is no less so for actors than members of audiences. However, this is an awareness that is generally unhelpful for actors during performances. Becoming self-conscious during a performance creates difficulties in creating a convincing portrayal of one's character. As in everyday life, so on the stage, the more we are aware of ourselves in the course of action, the more likely are we to stumble, trip, forget what we are doing and generally communicate an inappropriate absorption that destroys the naturalness of characterization. Thus, the typical bracketing of self-awareness of actors during performance, whether they be more classical than 'method' in their styles, communicates nothing but their characters. This acceptance of the character's domination over one's self has been likened to a kind of shamanistic possession (Cole, 1975; Travers, 1981). Shamans, in order to achieve the ability to heal or prophesy, believe that they must give up control over themselves to a spirit which then possesses them and uses their bodies. When actors talk about the characters that they play they convey a sense of there being another personality which they present.[6]

Such an involvement with the parts that are played, for good or ill, makes them consequential for actors. It is not simply the case that actors impress their personalities, their personal style on the parts that they play. The characters that they play also affect actors' personalities; although rarely to an extent that a person becomes nothing other than their past and present characters. No more than the rest of us are actors only the parts they play; they too are selves in making and claiming identities. Like anyone else they are sons and daughters, husbands and wives, lovers and friends, believers and agnostics, supporters of this team or that; but their work is different. As actors, their selves are involved in assuming and acting the persons of dramatic characters. This process consists of a number of different aspects. There is first of all a grasp of what it is to be an actor, as a life, a vocation, as a job. Within that identification of what it is to be an actor, individuals must deal with three elements of assuming parts that affect how they experience themselves. They have to accept or reject a casting offer; they have to work out their characterization of a part using more or less of their personal experience; they have to accept or try to reject the experience of playing a part as being a personal experience.

Getting into a part is no easy business, not simply because of the technical demands of a part but also, and perhaps as importantly, because of the effects that the part could have on how actors conceive of themselves. It is no light matter to discover that one has the resources, either in personal or imaginative experience, to give a convincing portrayal of a mass murderer. Actors have to live with that realization. Yet if getting into a part is more than mere

95

technique, so also is getting 'down' again. Becoming dispossessed of one's character can take time, and during that interval between stage and everyday reality actors are between social worlds — in a liminal moment that has the individual insecurely attached to either social world. Getting back down is not merely shedding the character and reasserting one's own personal style; that would be comparatively easy. Getting back down involves two questions: what of the part do you take with you and second, to 'whom' do you get back? Experienced actors will have biographically available an array of parts which they have played, many of these will have affected their own personal style and sense of identity; there is no getting back to basics! It is not surprising, perhaps, that most performances are followed by social gatherings where conversation is superficial and drinking often deep, where there is much gossip and little 'shop'. Having played parts on-stage or in rehearsal, actors play with them afterwards as they get back down.

Our focus here is upon the theatre as a resource and consists of trying to describe and understand the processes which occur in developing a performance. The discussion of actors and acting may have taken us some distance from the idea of rehearsal. It would be difficult if not impossible to grasp the slow process of developing characterizations, learning lines, blocking out movement if one had no sense of what it was that actors were getting into. Thus, actors acquire their lines as they rehearse; they become fixed as a characterization is worked out. Often it is only in particular positions on the stage in relation to other characters and after specific cues that actors will know their lines. Actors read through their parts, through the whole play, and they will begin to have some recall of the part before the rehearsals are far advanced, but that complete, natural ability to play a part without seeming to say the lines results from knowing the character in relation to the other characters and not simply from knowing the lines. On the stage, as in everyday life, remembering is specific to one's role.

So, rehearsals proceed and actors acquire an increasingly solid feel for their characters as they learn their lines and movements about the stage; but none of this is done mechanically or routinely (routine is the form of performance, not rehearsal). Rather, roles are characterized out of the improvisation of joint actions. Naturally, this is a time-consuming process and one that will depend on the kinds of acting techniques employed. Those more inclined to use 'method' approaches will be eager to play improvisationally off others in building up the characters; they will alter their playing in rehearsal to take account of changes in others' work. On the other hand, actors more committed to the 'classical' style will wait for direction as to how they might change and play off the others' characters.[7] To help in this process, directors often employ dramatic exercises that limber up acting techniques, assisting actors to gain access to relevant memories, to experience unusual capacities of their voices or bodies and so on.

So the director appears after all our talk about the rehearsal process which has seemed to give actors the key place. They do have the key place in performance, the stage there is dominated by acting and the director is present only emblematically in the style of the production. However, rehearsals are the directors' place to make a mark, to construct an interpretation of the text that will communicate through the actors to what their vision is. To work at all, directors have to select a cast of actors who may take a variety of attitudes to their presence in the theatre. If being an actor is a master status, then being in work allows one to be 'really' oneself; yet, others might be there for the money or unable to engage in such an undemanding part unless it be merely for money. There is a large range of attitudes that individuals can bring, but from them a director has to build an ensemble to communicate the interpretation of the work that displays how he understands it. This often leads to some ambivalence in the relation between directors and actors, and respect for actors is far from universal among those whose trade is directing.

We can see something of that relationship in the style of directing which is employed; these vary from autocratic to the participatory with every intermediate combination that one could conceive. It is through that style directors shape characterizations in order to communicate the plot and the meaning which they believe it presents. They coach actors in rehearsals, comment on the improvisations, work with those who are having difficulty, remind persons of the importance of ensemble and generally take responsibility for getting the work ready for performance. They also work, in parallel with the rehearsals, on matters of costume, lighting, sets and effects so that the emerging form of the production is complemented by these. Indeed, there will sometimes be effects and lighting rehearsals without actors. All this effort is finalized in the dress rehearsal, when for the first time all the elements of a production are assembled for the actors' and director's judgement on its verity.

We have said enough to demonstrate the range of possibilities recourse to the theatrical metaphor allows. Working both from the notion of performance from Mortimer, splendidly arrayed, talking to Lightborn, cold and still, centre stage, we can explore the processes which go into the making of this performance and, should we so wish, can go on to explore the conditions — artistic, cultural, economic and political — which support and constrain the event.

Obviously an exhaustive work upon the utility of the model for our understanding of conduct in organizations would require a detailed comment upon each and every aspect of it. That, as we have indicated earlier, is not our present intent. Rather we will seek in the following chapters to speculate about elements of the model; we will, for example, be concerned in the next chapter with the nature of performance and rehearsal, with the idea of expressive behaviour and the nature of creativity. We will also make some more general comments upon the utility of the analogy. In subsequent chapters, we will reflect upon settings, properties and costumes and their deployment in and around organizations; we will examine the notion of characterization, acting and self in a little more detail and, finally, we will consider at length the notions of interpretation and of leadership as evidenced by the activities of the director.

Chapter 6

Organizational Appearances and Theatrical Realities

Six men are sitting in a large room. It is a converted tithe barn with timbered beams and white stucco walls. The conversion has evidently been undertaken with taste and considerable sums of money have been expended. The barn now serves as a boardroom with a splendid, highly polished, craftsman-built, rectangular teak table dominating the scene. Around it are arranged some thirty chairs; those to one end unoccupied and drawn up to the table in disciplined lines, whereas at the other end of the room, the chairs are in disarray as their occupants sprawl around the focal position at the head of the table, that of the managing director. The room has five large windows providing glimpses of the courtyard beyond, which is backlit with a cold wash of winter sunshine. Heavy velvet curtains, floor to ceiling, are complemented by expensive carpeting. Portraits of the Heseltines, founding members of the company, evidently dour and no-nonsense men, cover the wall opposite the windows, each a silent witness of the proceedings undertaken in their joint family names.

Philip, who is the managing director of one of the subsidiary divisions, is talking. He is a tall, somewhat spare individual with the severe expression one might associate with those whose purpose in life in former times would have been to smell out witchcraft. He has a lean and hungry look, an almost cadaverous appearance exacerbated by his severe, charcoal grey suit, his white shirt and dark-blue tie, his cold, rimless spectacles and his sparse grey hair, which he wears cut almost brutally short. He is outlining his intention to undercut his colleagues in a sector of the market hitherto not exploited by his division. His tone throughout is peremptory:

PHILIP: . . . So, as I see it, that's it. We are going all out for that end of the market. We recognize that in so doing we may be treading on a few toes, but that's the price that will have to be paid.

He places his pen carefully on the table and sits back. The atmosphere is tense although, at this stage, no one seems prepared to respond. Eventually Derek, the managing director of the parent company, speaks. A small, somewhat diffident man, he derives his authority from being a member of the founding family. His face is destined to join those of his ancestors on the wall. He is dressed somewhat casually, even unconventionally, in a worn sports jacket with leather patches at the elbows and cuffs, and tan corduroy trousers. His ill-fitting shirt is of a loud check and he sports a bright-red tie. He is a good ten years younger than most of his colleagues — in his early thirties — and is conscious of both his age and the source of his authority.

DEREK: OK. Fine. Thank you, Philip. Very . . . er . . . clear. (*Waits. Looks at each person in turn. No one, other than Barry, head of the service division, meets his eye.*) Well? What do you think? (*No response.*) Philip has laid it on the line. . . . Proposed a course of action . . . which will throw us into direct competition with each other. . . . What do we think? . . . Tony? . . . Michael? . . . Barry?

Barry needs no second invitation. A large, florid and excitable man whose every gesture exudes energy barely under control. He wears a dark-grey suit complete with waistcoat and sports a bright handkerchief thrust into his top pocket; although clearly designed for a man of his height and girth, his clothes give the impression of being about to burst. His hair is unruly, as are his tie and the papers scattered on the table in front of him. He peers at his colleagues over the top of his reading glasses which from time to time he thrusts back upon his nose with clumsy irritation.

BARRY: I'm willing to jump in if no one else is. As I see it, what Philip is proposing is a direct challenge to the way we have operated up till now . . . to be precise and pedantic, a direct challenge to both Tony and Michael — as service division, we follow rather than lead (*derisive laughter around the table*) . . . which won't stop me jumping in. Not to put too fine a point on it, what is being proposed will wreck the company . . . let's not kid ourselves about that. . . . It's a complete bollox for us to set out to screw each other in this fashion. . . .

PHILIP: Bollox or not, it's what my division intends to do.

BARRY: Not if we don't agree it you're not! That's why we are here — to sort out this kind of thing. You can't just declare you are going to do something like this and expect us to cheer you on, you know.

PHILIP: I have profit responsibility for my division and am free to determine my markets and my prices.

BARRY: Your freedom stops, old son, where my nose begins — to paraphrase somebody or other. It's not up to you — or any one of us — to decide on a shift like that. . . .

TONY: He's right, Philip. It's not a runner. It's never been the policy to clash head on in the field.

Neat, precise, the mind of an accountant, the appearance of a business graduate. Thirty-two years old and a rising star in the organization, well organized, smooth, ambitious and cold. Tall, well shaven, neat well-trimmed hair, tailored-fit, monogrammed shirt, jacket carefully arranged on an adjacent chair. Calculator and a small portable computer sit on the table before him. Managing director of one of the other divisions.

PHILIP: Look, I'm responsible . . . I'm held accountable . . . for the profit, you are as well . . . in pursuit of targets. . . .
BARRY   (*interrupting*): Agreed here.
PHILIP: Put up by me and rubber stamped here . . . in pursuit of them it is up to me how I go about it. . . .
MICHAEL   (*incredulous*): Rubber stamped. . . .
PHILIP: Don't play the innocent, Michael. You know as well as I do . . . you'd be the first to complain if we chucked your figures out.
BARRY   (*cutting across the exchange, ignoring it*): What happens if I decide not to provide the support? Advertising, for example, that's a central service. What if I decide that there is no sense in running campaigns to fight each other.
PHILIP: It's your job to provide the service, and in any case, we wouldn't be so stupid as to knock each other. . . .
BARRY: It's my job as a director of the company to maximize overall profit. That's your job as well.
PHILIP: What I propose will do just that!
TONY: What you propose will lead to anarchy. Simply sticking a load of figures before us and saying 'Take it or leave it' is not the way to go about things. . . .
PHILIP: That's good, coming from you, Tony! What about the decision to go into own brands? As I recall that, you did that without any consultation with us — I knew nothing of it until the goods were on the lorries.
TONY: That was months ago, and in any event, you didn't need to know about it. It didn't affect your division.
PHILIP: It had implications for the company as a whole — profit implications, policy switches. . . .
TONY: Barry knew about it, Derek knew about it. . . .
PHILIP: Derek is behind this proposal of mine. We've discussed it and he's for it. (*This revelation is greeted with surprise by Tony, Michael and Barry.*)
DEREK: Yes. I said that I would support it. (*Shuffling and muttering around the table. Philip is clearly pleased with the turn of events. Tony and*

Michael appear nonplussed. Silence. Barry appears to be weighing up the pros and cons of a course of action. He decides.)

BARRY: So what? So Philip nobbled Derek before the meeting. How does that change anything? He didn't nobble me, or Tony or Michael. As I understand it, in this brave new world we now inhabit, it's not up to Philip and Derek, or Tony and Derek, or, for that matter, *me* and Derek to fix on a one-to-one basis. . . . It's up to us. Us as a group.

(*There is a long pause. All seem at a loss as to how to proceed.*)[1]

This chapter will be concerned primarily with the notion of *performance*. We will seek to understand that which distinguishes performance from *rehearsal* and that which constitutes a good rather than a bad performance. Given the nature of the theatre and of life, both of which will prompt our speculations, much of the first part of the chapter will address issues such as *appearance* and *reality*, and the nature of *expressive* activities. Lest our imaginations prove too unruly, we have disciplined ourselves to return at frequent intervals to examples drawn from conduct observed in a range of organizations. In that which follows we will draw heavily upon the text which opens this chapter. We would advise, therefore, that it should be read through once more before proceeding.

A theatrical event is a communication between actors and audience in the context of a meta-communication about the framing of this event as a theatrical *staging* of action. Theatre is an opportunity for mundane opportunities to be inspected as appearances in order to consider their meanings. As such, theatre creates space for awareness. This space and this experience, moreover, are available only in the performance itself and only then while the theatrical frame, the awareness of the frame on the part of audience and actors, is unquestioned. Meta-communication of this theatrical frame varies from place to place and from time to time; it will be different across performance media (although for convenience we are discussing the stage rather than television or the film); however, today a number of devices are commonly used which induce the audience, in particular, to give a theatrical attention to what takes place before them. Thus, the stage is lit, the auditorium is not; the seats are arranged to face the action on stage and sightlines are carefully respected; there is usually a physical separation of the stage from the auditorium and so on.[2]

The power of what occurs within the theatre to command attention is strong. This is largely because its images are intended to be both seen and heard. Furthermore, it unfolds in time and those who would know the outcome must persist until the end. The opening words of the exchanges which form the preface to this chapter set up an expectation such that — as in the theatre — one wishes to discover the resolution. Not only the resolution in terms of form, such events are expected to have a shape, but also in terms of plot. In the theatre questions are raised, clues are scattered around (why all this talk of guns, what is the importance of the statue, or whatever) and we, the audience, want an answer. As in the theatre, so in social life, this talk of 'wrecking the company', a strong air of antagonism, argument, conflict, where will it all lead? Conflict on- and off-stage serves to provide a strong commanding focus; events which focus attention are often referred to as 'dramatic'.

The theatrical frame, however, is a delicate one and can be readily shattered unless elements of the performance provide support for it. When attention focuses not upon the work in its entirety but upon the materials or techniques which have been used to create it, the frame is likely to break. Someone dropping a prop off-stage (or on, if it is not assimilated into the action), a glimpse of a stage-hand behind a curtain, overemphatic music, exceptionally ingenious effects (such that attention is drawn to *how* something is done rather than *what* is realized) serve to undermine theatrical reality. In particular, it is the way in which actors appear to be possessed by their roles that is the major contribution. Thus, the way in which actors present themselves on-stage, not as themselves but as their characters, nothing but their characters, is the key to maintain the audience's attention to the staging of theatrical reality. Any hint in the playing of their parts, any suggestion that there is an actor present in a character (unless that is provided for in the theatrical framing of particular dramatic genre) will erode the taken-for-granted nature of this special form of consciousness. If an actor forgets a line, audibly breaks wind, has problems with his costume or his props or loses his wig in the middle of the action, the reality so delicately maintained until that point is rendered more precarious. Not that the consummate or even the average performer cannot recover; he can, since it rarely takes long for an audience to be drawn back into the action.[3]

The parallels with normal everyday intercourse are obvious. Should Barry, one of the social actors presented in our opening scene, knock the water jug over in his exuberance and impatience, the frame will be temporarily broken; attention will move from what he has to say to what he has done. All concerned will be temporarily distracted. Similarly, should anyone present signal that he is not invested in the part that he is proffering then, again, the appearance will be shattered. In such circumstances, as in the theatre, others present are made aware of the actor *as such*, the person behind the role; the appearance of Joe, or whoever, *as* planner, personnel manager or whatever fails to be an imposing one and we glimpse the actor behind the part.

Some will find this talk of appearance disturbing; it will be maintained that what we see on the stage are appearances, but what is done in the office, on the factory floor, in the boardroom, is 'real', that there is nothing of the illusory about it. Our position is not in accord with such views. We take it that what occurs in organizations when it ceases to be mere behaviour (the unreflecting scratching of an ear, a crotch or a nose) is a matter of performance. Performance, as a concept drawn out of theatre, implies what is happening is a matter of creating realities, of transforming appearances into the taken for granted. Clearly we are not going to get away with such a claim without a deal of elaboration. To sustain our point, we turn first to the theatre and then to conduct in organizations.

Although a successful staging of reality is such that it commands our attention, it is clear to most of us that it is a staging, a realization that does not require consequential action on our part. The sight of Macbeth with a dagger should not be such as to cause any one of us to call the police, any more than Iago's actions concerning Othello should result in us referring him to the Race Relations Board. In the theatre, we are expected to — and for the most part do — retain an aesthetic distance from that which is enacted in front of us. It is not just that we suspend disbelief; to be sure we do that but we do it knowing that what we are about to be involved with is theatrical transformation of the world we take for granted, an abstraction from that which we take to be reality. A matter of a very different order of consequence from matters of the more mundane variety with which we have to grapple at other times and in other locations. Dramatic art, as other forms of art, is an abstraction from actuality, one that we recognize as such. As Langer puts it:

> the surest way to abstract the element of sensory appearance from the fabric of actual life and its complex interests, is to create a sheer vision, a datum that is nothing but appearance and is, indeed, clearly and avowedly an object only for sight (or for whatever sense or senses the art is intended). . . .

So, a theatrical performance is an abstraction from the 'blooming, buzzing confusion' of actuality which we recognize as a staged reality, an appearance, from which we maintain an appropriate aesthetic distance. Discursive thought is the enemy of such illusion, as is distraction, error and inconsistency. Dramatic art seeks to impress motives upon us but does not invite action nor, *at the time of its realization*, reflection on the transforming of mundaneity by dramatic appearances.[4]

As in the theatre, so in social life. That which Barry and Philip are engaged upon is a performance. They display to each other and to those temporarily rendered speechless by their energies an abstraction from the totality of events and perceptions that involve them. They struggle to sustain a consequential reality, to have taken for granted that which they are offering in expressive form. They seek to impress upon each other their definitions and their feelings; their performances are successful to the extent that they prevent each other thinking about what is occurring. A performance as a whole is worth while to any one of them to the extent that it becomes the commanding if not the sole focus of attention of all of those in the boardroom. What Barry is attempting to impose upon his colleagues is an emotive view of what it is like to be him and to experience life as he experiences it. He is not inviting anyone to *think* about it any more than Philip is in his response. The language they use, the expressions they assume, the physical gestures they employ, are attempts to impose ways of being, experiencing and seeing upon others. Neither succeeds if the other(s) focus upon the portraits, their papers, the clothing of either Philip or Barry, the accent of one or the other or the quality of the light filtering through the windows. If, as we have taken it to be, a theatrical performance is an abstraction from the actual, then what Philip and Barry are about is as much to do with performing as what the actors playing Macbeth and Iago are about.

A successful performance from the point of view of the actors is one in which 'you hear everything as if for the first time. The performance is not so much new as newly revealed, the varnish stripped off, the paint bright again, detail discernible. . . .' For the actor in such circumstances, the text 'is sunk into your bones, so that it comes unbidden; it is the inevitable, the only, response to what is said to you' (Callow, 1984). It is not a matter of technique but of immersion. There is a story about Olivier that is apposite. One night, he gave a performance of Othello that was so outstanding that not only did it bring the audience cheering to its feet, it also elicited spontaneous applause from his fellow actors. After the curtain calls, Olivier, apparently in a towering rage, locked himself in his dressing room. Eventually one of his colleagues approached the great man and asked: 'What's the problem? Don't you know you were brilliant tonight?' Olivier replied, 'Of course I fuckin' know — but I don't know *why*.'

Immersed in his performance, no doubt, but not totally possessed by it. Again to quote Callow: 'Your relationship to the play is that of rider to horse. *It* is the energy: you are the direction. You must be above it and on top of it' (1984). A bad performance for Olivier and Callow, as much as for Barry and Philip, is one in which they lose control, do not exercise direction over the energy, are ridden rather than ride. A bad performance is also marked by the other extreme — too little possession. As a performer (on- or off-stage) one can be either overwhelmed or underwhelmed by creative energy. When the latter, one is no longer the agent, *it* is not working; one is behind the beat all the time, out of focus and out of key, uncoordinated and slow to pick up and develop cues. One is acutely self-conscious and excessively aware of one's impact upon others. In extreme circumstances, one suffers *stage fright*, an inability to find words, a flatness and a stumbling, awkward incompetence.

A good performance, therefore, consists of a staged appearance which we as performers are controlling and directing with no consciousness of our control and direction; a bad performance, one where both we and our audience are conscious of the contrived nature of what is being offered. In social life as in the theatre, interaction is a mixture of good and bad performance. We occasionally bring the house down but we do not know why. More often than not, we stumble through our lines seeking — at best — to avoid embarrassment. And by and large we are successful, since life itself is 'a dramatically enacted thing'. As Goffman (1959) notes: 'It does take deep skill, long training, and a psychological capacity to become a good stage actor, but this fact should not blind us to another one: that almost anyone can quickly learn a script well enough to give a charitable audience some sense of realness in what is being contrived before them.'

What is the nature of the staged reality we experience in the theatre and what does it tell us about the interactions we witness and participate in within organizations? Eschewing for the moment other kinds of performance, such as that practised by stand-up comedians, high-wire acts and magicians, we can follow Langer in asserting that 'all art is the creation of "expressive forms" or apparent forms expressive of human feeling'. A work of art, in dramatic form or not, is

> . . . an expressive form created for our perception through sense or imagination, and what it expresses is human feeling. The word 'feeling' must be taken here in its broadest sense, meaning everything that can be felt, from physical sensation, pain and comfort, excitement and repose, to the most complex emotions, intellectual tensions, or the steady feeling-tones of a conscious human life. (Langer, 1957)

Feelings require a different form to embody them than do our ideas; as Langer points out, our experience of being human, of subjective reality, is not something that can be addressed in lectures, essays or books like this. To express and impart something of that which we feel, we need a different form. Be that form music, opera, painting, sculpture, poetry, literature, dance or theatre, it is art. If this is true, and we are taking it to be so, it follows that whatever it is that is embodied in a particular work of art — say a play — even though it may use words to achieve its effect, is not itself reducible to words. By definition, the artist is dealing with non-discursive notions; no amount of analysis can dispense with or explain fully the experience of seeing *Othello*, listening to Mozart, standing in front of a Turner.

We have to face up to a difficulty here, because in seeking to come to terms with our purpose, it is likely that you, as a reader, will have concentrated upon the words, the script, the verbal interplay between Barry, Philip, Derek and Tony. The study of scripts and transcripts (such as these are) does not provide the experience that we wish to address. Much can be gained by careful reading of such material (we would not offer it were this not to be the case), but it must always be remembered that the script is not the perform-ance; it is but one aspect of it. Nor is it necessarily of greater importance than the more ephemeral aspects of performance in seeking to understand what goes on in the theatre or in social life. Just as plays are something to be acted, so social life can be judged with what we take to be accuracy only when seen (Baker, 1925).

Let us pursue the theatrical parallel for a moment in an attempt to focus some of the difficulties we are likely to encounter throughout this chapter. The ability to preserve scripts rather than performances has been a feature of literary and dramatic criticism for generations. Even allowing for the fact that plays have been regarded as a kind of poetry written to be staged since the time of Aristotle, thus throwing considerable emphasis upon the script, the inability to record performances (until the twentieth century) has meant more attention has been paid to words said than to any other aspect of performance. The result has been that many believe they can understand a play by studying the script and ignoring other aspects of dramatic art. Others believe that performance is a matter of technique and tend to devalue the script. So on the one hand we have literary souls who assume that the script on the printed page is the complete work of art, and on the other hand those who in their comments ignore the script and concentrate upon the production.

The situation in the social sciences is not dissimilar. There are those, usually of a cognitive bias, who believe that all that is needed for an understanding of what is occurring in a particular circumstance is a transcript. There are others who believe, for example, that attention to non-verbal behaviour is of considerable importance, or that the setting is a most significant factor or the personality of the performers is the key to understanding what is going on. There are some, of course, who see no need to enter the theatre at all; for their understanding is derived from a knowledge of the social and economic conditions rather than from performances.[5]

This tendency to reduce performances (on-stage or off) to elements, however necessary, is fundamentally misguided since it detracts from the fact that what occurs before us (on-stage and off) is an audible and visible presence. The words, the settings, the non-verbal gestures, the costumes, the lighting, are in and of themselves nothing more nor less than signs or indications. The sentences that Barry speaks or that Tony enunciates, Philip's gestures, Derek's crumpled jacket are part of a whole that is apprehended as a whole. Just as no playwright worthy of the title creates a play that can be realized only in a reading, so no record of an interaction can be fully complete nor can any element of that interaction stand separate from it. Each element contributes, none can stand alone. Although for purposes of outlining what it is we are about in this section of the book, we shall have occasion to speak of scripts, settings, dialogue, characterization, acting and the like, we are not construing them as separate functions. Our context throughout will be performance: visible and audible action taking place in space and time.

Works of art consist of successful attempts to convey that which is not accessible by any other means — subjective experience — and they do so in an integrated fashion. Reading the script of *Othello* is not the same as being present at a performance of *Othello* when actors, movement, setting, light are articulated in a satisfying whole (see Langer, 1957). What we are saying, therefore, and in so doing we are not saying something that has not been said a number of times before, is that what we see when we watch a play is an artistic expression contained within a form constructed by several hands and embodying what those involved know about emotions, ideas and feelings. The whole causes that which is internal and subjective to each one of us to be rendered less opaque. Those involved in mounting the performance, seek to present an objectification of feelings — an externalization or display of emotion — not a discursive *debate* about the nature of subjective experience.

Othello is not a set of ideas concerning jealousy, nor is it an indication of what Shakespeare felt about jealousy, it is — as a fully realized performance — an image, an externalization of feeling.

Back to the boardroom. We would maintain that a great deal of interaction which occurs in organizations is expressive, constituting objectification of feelings rather than anything else. It is possible to see the exchanges between Barry and Philip, for example, as monologues in which they reveal their subjective states to themselves, to each other and to the other actors. It is possible, and social commentators/critics such as ourselves do it every day, to regard the patterns we perceive, the feelings that we apprehend passing from them to us as representations, images of their relations. To consider the exchanges as expressive abstractions, art in the sense of that which is selected and edited from actuality realized in performance.

The scene which opens the chapter illustrates the issue of performance as expressive of feelings. The nature of the performance enacted is one with which each of the principals is familiar; it has the character of *ritual*. Indeed, this is the term we favour for thinking about repetitive sequences such as these. Not that we are talking about ritual in a religious sense, but rather as a sequence of actions that give shape and substance to the interactions, actions and exchanges. For example, Philip and Barry know full well what the pattern is. However novel it may appear to us seated in the stalls, to the principals and to their immediate audience, their colleagues, it has all the flavour of a long run. Philip is seen to assert his independence, Barry to challenge it. On other occasions, it could well be Tony or Michael who will declare their intentions; it is always Barry that challenges. Often he is supported in his attempts to curb what he takes to be the excessive independence of individual divisions by those he is not directly confronting. Nearly always, the resultant disagreement is resolved by appeal to Derek; on many occasions — as in this example — he has previously sanctioned the course of action which precipitates the squabble.

What we have in this scene is a sequence of action 'in which (1) the situation is specified; (2) the several players have interlocking roles to follow, and (3) the players share an understanding of what is supposed to happen'.[6] The scene with which we are currently concerned has been elaborated over a long time; all concerned are thoroughly versed in the combats they enact. Whatever the apparent force of the confrontations, each knows the outcome: the issue will be actually determined, as it always is determined, by Derek. He who sets the whole scene in motion and, on becoming tired of it, calls the curtain down. An element of creativity breaks into this scene, however; the ritual is threatened by Barry:

BARRY: So what? So Philip nobbled Derek before the meeting. How does that change anything? He didn't nobble me, or Tony or Michael. As I understand it, in this brave new world we now inhabit, it's not up to Philip and Derek, or Tony and Derek, or, for that matter, me and Derek to fix on a one-to-one basis. . . . It's up to us. Us as a group. . . .

This radical departure from established ritual occasions a long and embarrassed silence; no one knows how to proceed. Barry's cue line prompts no response. Eventually, Tony chooses to ignore the comment entirely and to return to the ritual within which he can operate more comfortably.

TONY: So, it's been agreed, has it? Between you and Derek? I'm not sure I'm going to be happy with that, but at the very least, I'd want a clear direction from you, Derek. . . .

In this illustration the alternation between performance, the routine and the ritual, and what we may term rehearsal, the less routine, more creative elaboration of ideas and feelings, is momentary and barely acknowledged: the capacity of the actors to rehearse is severely constrained by the setting and by the overall established pattern of behaviour which appears to rule out such meetings as occasions in which breakdowns in performance can be identified and considered. There is an overarching pattern which holds that the 'play must go on', one which allows little or no room for improvisation other than that which brings the performance back into line.

In contrast, the following scene highlights the expressive nature of the interaction by challenging its substance:

DEREK: Hang on a minute, we are getting a bit heated about this, aren't we?

PHILIP: Look, Tony, ever since we were divisionalized in the days of Frank Tobias, it has been accepted that matters which cross divisional boundaries have to be sorted out at this level.

TONY: Agreed. But this is not a cross-divisional matter. It concerns me and my people — nothing to do with you and your set-up.

PHILIP: Look (appeals to Derek), we've gone through the set-piece. We all know the pattern by now, someone raises an issue in here, we toss it backwards and forwards and end up submitting to your ruling, so don't let's waste any more time on this. I say it's cross-divisional, Tony says it's not. It's up to you to rule, Derek.

DEREK: Well, I'm not.
(Philip and Tony appear to be somewhat disconcerted by this comment, as do others.)

PHILIP: I didn't quite catch that, Derek. . . . You are not what?

DEREK: I am not prepared to arbitrate.
(Embarrassed silence.)

TONY: Someone has to decide, we can't do it for ourselves. . . .

DEREK: Why not?

PHILIP: Why not? Why not . . . because we can't — if we disagree, only you can resolve it — that's the name of the game.

DEREK: Well, I'm not playing it any longer. I've been put in this position too many times lately. You each bide your time, then open up on each other in these meetings and expect me to sort out the consequent mess. I've decided not to, that's all — it's pointless, since next week we will go through the same performance and the week after that, and the week after that. . . .

TONY: There is no other way.

DEREK: Well, we are going to have to find one.

PHILIP   (*after a pause during which exasperation, resignation, abstraction and the like are severally expressed non-verbally around the table*): What do you suggest?

DEREK: *I* have no suggestion.

TONY: Great! I mean, how are we to proceed? *You* are refusing to play this game, as you put it — *you* have got to suggest another.

DEREK: To do so, even if I had one in mind, would only serve to perpetuate the problem. The appeal is always to me. I am suggesting that the problem is *ours*, not mine, and that *we*, not me, should sort it out.

TONY   (*less aggressively*): Sounds like an invitation to hang ourselves to me.

PHILIP: I've spent so long disagreeing with him (*indicates Tony*), I would not know where to begin.

The contrast between the two forms of interaction is, we believe, sharp.

The second scene has a different character. To be sure, part of this performance has been elaborated over the years and persists in this series of exchanges. None the less, Derek's refusal to enact his traditional role is something that everyone else present has to take account of and needs time to accommodate within their normal repertoire. Initially the actors simply switch their aggression from each other and direct it somewhat less forcefully at Derek. He refuses the casting implied by this conduct; he neither retaliates nor retreats. Instead, he responds quietly and cogently to the points made rather than to the manner in which they are made, persevering in outlining a possible new role for himself. In doing this, he is withdrawing a necessary condition for the continuation of their performance, refusing to be its audience. At this moment, the encounter begins to assume the character of rehearsal rather than that of performance although, of course, since the participants must serve as audience to each other as they construct and interpret a revised situational script, elements of performance persist. In fact, neither Barry's challenge nor Derek's shift in role is completely unrehearsed. Some weeks prior to the playing out of the scenes reproduced above, the same group had met to discuss its performance. Off-site, in a draughty hotel room ('Available for Masonics and wedding receptions'), under the guidance of a consultant, they had attempted to take a meta-theatrical perspective on their activities as a team. As can be seen in what follows, although performance characteristics persist, there is a clear attempt to objectify different emotions, to elaborate new routines, different rituals:

BARRY: . . . In our management meetings, many of the papers are slung around at the meetings. We just don't make ourselves prepared for serious discussion.

TONY: There are two aspects to that, aren't there? The mechanics — getting the papers out, reading them — and expectations of Derek. . . . What you think he wants to hear from you.

BARRY: OK, so Derek is one of the problems — we've aired that already and I'm quite prepared to come back to it but, for me, the key question is: 'Are we one company or three companies?' What I hear Philip saying is that, what he is really saying is that we are three companies. I don't agree. We are in the same group and should behave as one rather than trying to behave as three.

PHILIP: As usual, a gross misrepresentation of my views.

DEREK: But, for example, on the German business, you circulated no papers on that. Not even I knew anything about that until a couple of hours before the meeting. . . .

PHILIP: I think you have put it unfortunately. I certainly was not intending to surprise anyone . . . it was not by some Machiavellian reasoning that I delayed the presentation.

BARRY: Coming back to the point. . . . Fundamentally, I believe that everybody should have the right to challenge anything that is happening within the total business around the table, because no one of us can really operate in the absence of any other part. . . . If our support is not forthcoming, you just castrate yourself before you've started, so you have to bring it out into the open, you've got to get the influence and the opinion of the people around you that you are going to depend upon. . . .

MICHAEL: I'd like to agree with Barry, and here I go smoothing again! But at the end of the day, somebody's carrying the can for something, and it isn't that group of people sitting around the table on Monday afternoons. It's an individual; not us, *one* of us.

TONY: OK, but if you raise something you must expect some criticism. Even though it's your baby and you are totally defensive and everybody takes a hard position, but whether you like it or not, you are influenced by that fight.

BARRY: You still tend to move . . . tend to try to reconcile views. You are a peculiar beast if you just go straight on down headlong down the course that you set when it's in opposition to the majority of people.

PHILIP: The situation where influence is available does not necessarily mean to say that it is taken.

BARRY: OK, but I would like the opportunity to listen to what you want
           to do, and to raise some issues so that at least I understand what
           you are doing and we've had a frank discussion.
DEREK: How do we do that? Have a frank discussion. Some of us —
           Philip, probably Tony — think it's illegitimate. Where does that
           leave us. . . ?

Clearly, this particular rehearsal did not succeed in resolving the issues; as
we have seen, some of them surfaced again in other scenes. None the less,
the example illustrates the point that in order to develop a revised performance, Derek and his colleagues must improvise and test out a number of
relationships. If they take themselves to be one company, their performances
with and to each other ought to be expressive of such a relationship. The
expressed nature of their relationship will be different if they take themselves
to be distinct and each contesting with each other. In the first extract we
presented, the relationship as one of division and conflict, a routine with
which each is familiar and one in which, for the most part, they can each
give a convincing performance. The other extracts from their exchanges show
them at work questioning the bases of their performance, seeking to define
what it is they ought to be about in order to convey that essence in their
future performances. In these extracts, we are witness to the actors in rehearsal
rather than in full fig.
   It is clear that the discussion of creativity in Chapter 5 relates to the process
that occurs almost daily in organizations. The social actors we have been
concerned with in this chapter stage performances which, on a number of
occasions, are subject to revision almost as soon as they appear. Managers,
in particular, spend a great deal of their time seeking to reduce equivocality
by imposing a frame upon and attempting to constrain themselves and others
to perform within it, and then abandoning it. Using the language of the
earlier chapter, we can see that some interaction in organizations is marked
by the suck-it-and-see activity which characterizes creative rehearsal in any
setting. As we have attempted to illustrate, what unfolds before us as we
witness the interaction of Philip, Barry and the others is the process of and
the results of a degree of group creativity. The last illustration shows them
in the activity of running things up provisionally — working from a set of
inchoate ideas, taking a look at what results in the light of standards deriving
from experience and knowledge and then modifying, rejecting or accepting
aspects of it, moving on to develop further ideas out of what has been
achieved.
   Barry suggests the problematic — the nature of our management
meetings — and Tony elaborates upon it, only to have his elaboration rejected.
The process of seeking to find the nub of their poor performance and felt
dissatisfaction continues throughout this passage but, as we can see by their
later behaviour, a degree of agreement as to its nature — the arbitration role
of Derek — results in some attempt to do something about it. In a sense,

Barry's blueprint, which identified preparation as the key weakness of particular performances, has been torn up in favour of the one that focuses upon interaction with Derek as being at the heart of the problem. Resolve this and we have the makings of better performance. We would argue that interaction in organizations proceeds very much in this 'necessarily indeterminate' manner to discover that which is problematic and render it less so. The process, if it is a creative one, is unpredictable and relatively free from rules and routines. Social actors, no less than stage actors, interact so as to discover what it is they are about; they are simultaneously *doing* and understanding and modifying that doing. Again we can but reiterate the point made earlier about regarding action as a way of creating interesting goals. In the mode which we have referred to as rehearsal, Barry, Philip and the others are discovering and shaping their performances; to a lesser extent (like good stage actors), they do the same as they actually perform. At one end of the continuum, perhaps, are staged performances or presentations such as to a group of potential investors or to each other when seeking funding; at the other end are rehearsals such as those we outline, where improvisation is much more obvious and appropriate.

We have illustrated the difference in form between performance and that which is relatively less finished, less routine, which we have termed rehearsal. We will have occasion to return to this distinction later when we discuss text; for the moment we wish to re-emphasize the notion of performance as expressive. To many brought up to believe that all that occurs in organizations is or ought to be rational and that relations between members are largely if not wholly instrumental, our assertions will come as a shock. It is, of course, a matter of focus; we are attempting to understand conduct in organizations through recourse to the metaphor of theatrical performance, not attempting to explicate or understand, say, decision-taking or the institution of accounting systems. We are thus interested in what any interaction signals about the nature of relations within the organization; all interactions are expressive, all symbolize the state of play between the actors.

To us, audience to their interactions, they are not simply instrumental, they express in every line, every gesture, the nature of the relation which obtains between them. What is true for us as audience is also true for the actors; Barry knows the nature of his relationship with Philip and is aware that it is as much a matter of feelings as it is of reason. Relations in organizations produce and sustain emotions and are of consequence.

To understand why this should be so, we need to take a moderately lengthy detour. If that which we have advanced as being the nature of art is correct, that it is substantially a matter of the externalization and display of non-discursive feeling, the objectification of emotion, and if art persists (as it has in most societies) it follows that it illustrates or puts us in touch with something fundamental to the human condition. Far from being a frill, an expensive pastime of little consequence, art may be taken to signal something of great import about the nature of our existence *qua* humans. That something, we believe, is concerned with relationships and emotions, power and passion. Ordinary, everyday intercourse within a theatrical frame is also a matter of relationships and emotions. Barry's relations with Philip are a matter of consequence to them both; it is not simply that Barry wishes Philip to conduct his affairs differently. Were Philip to comply, it may indeed make for a more efficient company, but it would also imply a shift in the power balance which obtains between the two actors; Barry would experience a gain and Philip a loss. What is more, the movement would be obvious to all, and both would be likely to react emotionally.

Although, for many other writers, some distinction must be drawn between 'technical acts' and 'expressive acts', from within our tradition no such distinction is valid. Organizations are enacted hierarchies and may be conceived of as scenes and settings within which order is enacted consequentially or symbolically. Our focus, as commentators of a dramaturgical persuasion, is upon the meaning of action. It is of no value to us to seek to distinguish between what others may well term technical/instrumental on the one hand and expressive/relational on the other. We are interested in the action — what occurs — and our concern (the same concern us that of an audience in a theatre) is to ask what it means.

Thus, for example, Derek's refusal to arbitrate in the boardroom may be understood as an expression of his power to interrupt the particular ritual which has — to date — marked such occasions. His refusal produces astonishment but it also produces no small degree of anxiety, since that single act symbolizes a challenge to the status quo and potentially throws all previous relationships into disarray.

To understand why this should be so, we need to provide a sketch of the relationships which may obtain between Derek and his colleagues and that which may obtain between them as peers. For the sake of simplicity, we will concentrate upon the scene concerning Derek, Philip and Tony. Our starting-point, which is worth hanging on to, is the assertion (derived from Kemper)[7] that a large class of emotions 'result from real, imagined or anticipated outcomes in social relationships' (Kemper, 1978). Given this, let us consider the Tony/Philip relationship. In this interaction, there are a limited number of possible outcomes: Tony may gain power or status, he may lose power and status, he may continue as before on both dimensions, he may lose power and gain status, lose status and gain power. Similarly, Philip may lose, gain or maintain his level of power and status. Our scene is complicated by Derek's presence but the principle remains the same.

What we have at the onset of this scene is a situation with which all three of them are familiar. Philip challenges and Tony denies the ground . . . 'this is not a cross-divisional matter', which may be read as 'my territory, within my jurisdiction, nothing to do with you — piss off!' Tiring of the scene, Philip gives up the attempt to change the balance of power (which was half-hearted in any event) and looks to Derek: 'I say it's cross-divisional. They say it's not. It's up to you to rule, Derek.' This ploy, of course, has the advantage of not *directly* affecting the relations between Tony and Philip, neither wins nor loses *vis-à-vis* the other. Once Derek has ruled (as he has done so often in the past), either Philip or Tony wins or loses, to be true, but Derek is the agency and it is Derek to whom regard or hostility will be directed by the other two. It is, nevertheless, still a matter of power and status and the ruling — whatever it is, even if it were to be that of a Solomon — would be the occasion for emotion. What Tony, Derek and Philip take themselves to be is intensely bound up with their relations with others and these relations are essentially ones of power and status. Derek's refusal to arbitrate — 'I'm not playing it [the game] any longer' — throws the usual struggles into disarray; it threatens the nature of the relationships which have been built up over the years:

There is no other way.
Well, we're going to have to find one.

It generates anxiety and anger:

Great! I mean, how are we to proceed? *You* are refusing to play this game, as you put it — *you* have got to suggest another. . . .

We could go on but it would become tiresome so to do. It is clear that what is being improvised here and in many of the sequences with which we have been concerned is a matter of power and status and these improvisations are matters of consequence. What they enact is not simply technical or instrumental, it is expressive. Normal interaction for these actors celebrates their relationships, abnormal circumstances where the established patterns are broken simply serve to highlight this aspect of their activity. A great deal of ordinary, everyday intercourse in organizations is marked by expressive activity; just as on the stage people *do* things and in so doing effect and affect patterns of relationships, so in social and organizational life, people do and in so doing emblematize their relationships.

Despite this apparent digression upon the nature of relationships, we are not suggesting here or elsewhere that our perception of such emblematizations, be they in a work of art or elsewhere, occur in a non-reflective fashion. To be sure, Derek, Barry, Philip *et al. know* they have a problem; they do not need to spell it out. Severally they appear to grasp the meaning of what is occurring — a shift in their relations — without much need for self-conscious reflection. The realization appears as natural as recognizing that the portraits of the Heseltines on the wall are portraits and not human heads, that the object around which they are sitting is a table. None the less, we do not wish to fall into the folly of assuming that there is something direct and unmediated either in what they do or what we do when apprehending a work of art. The theatrical metaphor, at least in so far as we have elaborated, offers an opportunity to separate actor from action, consciousness from mere behaviour. We do not have to take it; we can go to the theatre without attending in this manner and we can interact with others in a relatively mindless fashion. Such, we would maintain, is not always nor, perhaps, often the case.

To understand the point we are groping towards, we need to return to the theatre and to the words of Simon Callow:

> Self conscious as the audience is, so are you, thinking all the time — and this is death to a performance — what did they make of that? or, hell, I fucked that up. It's almost impossible to be in the present with this performance, unless you've reached a high state of Zen and are able to say: The play alone matters. A semi-Zen state, and almost equally useful, is to say, Fuck the lot of you, I don't give a shit what you think, this is GOOD and I'm going to enjoy myself. I'm doing it for (whoever you like: Laurence Olivier, the Queen, the author, God) and the rest of you can go and jump in the Thames. . . .
>
> If you don't attain it, or something like it, you're condemned to the somewhat nauseous condition of looking in on yourself, observing and commenting. Paradoxically this is also the condition of really extraordinary performances, with the difference that the alter ego who's looking in on you on the first night is terribly slow and stupid, and can't understand what's going on at all, whereas the guy who sees you when you're being brilliant has winged feet and an IQ of 150. He's there *before* you, solving, suggesting, steering. (Callow, 1984, emphasis added)

Callow, the consummate stage actor, here provides us with some clues as to the nature of performance. A poor performance — a first night for him — is often characterized by a degree of reflection either before or after action. Reflection normally does not sit easily with action; too much thought paralyses us. What we are suggesting is that in some circumstances (perhaps many, we do not know), our performance is steered by reflection that occurs almost simultaneously with the action. The good actor giving a fine performance is part action, part thought, the latter 'solving, suggesting, steering'. The gap between thought and action is, in these circumstances, infinitesimal. Likewise for the good manager; one part of him solves, suggests and steers as another part of him acts: the sum is the performance.

The ability to experience intuitively and indirectly in this manner is not evenly spread throughout the population, nor is it maintained at the same level within any one of us. Those of us who have little experience of the kind of frustration that Barry exudes are less likely to be attuned to the expression of such feelings than those of us who have had similar emotional experiences. Those of us who attend a performance with strong emotions may find it difficult to apprehend anything that is occurring on the stage; we import our feelings rather than respond to those objectified before us. Theatre history is full of events where the audience import emotions into the auditorium and cause uproar. It is also full of circumstances where antipathy towards a particular actor is the reason for trouble. In everyday social interaction each of us is able to recognize occasions where the emotions we import colour the encounters and occasions where we so dislike or like the principal social actors that we are quite unable to grasp what is being said.

Just as there are people for whom art is of little or no consequence, so there are persons who do not consider relationships to be important and ignore the expressive character of interaction. Such people are few since, in our view, power and status are pervasive concerns of humans, but, few though they may be, they parallel the kind of person who goes reluctantly to the theatre and fails completely to grasp its meaning. The kind of person who takes *Oh What a Lovely War* to be simply a musical and *King Lear* to be a tract about the problems of housing the old and infirm.

The appreciation of particular performances, of course, is also a matter of language. A play in Greek may be incomprehensible to many of us, as would one in Erse. A play in Elizabethan English may also cause us some labour, the more so when we are both unfamiliar with the terms used and the conventions of the time. As audience to the interaction of a group of scientists, a group of space engineers, television moguls or whatever, we may experience similar problems of language and convention which may make it difficult for us to grasp readily and intuitively what is happening between them.

Finally, familiarity, while making it easier to grasp import, may also dull our response. It is hard work to become involved in *King Lear* for the fifth or sixth time, *The Wild Duck* for the third or fourth, *Peter Pan* for the thirtieth or fortieth. It is hard work to listen to Barry and Philip going through what appear to be the same routines time and time again; there may be some new material, but, given our familiarity with their act, we are likely to miss it. In order for us to refocus upon the interaction, there has to be an extra dimension, not simply the same old plot, there has to be a quality to the performance which grabs and holds our attention.

That quality, often, is a matter of possession. In everyday life, although we are all totally possessed at times, few of us are completely possessed by one role all the time. Remember Ward Quaal, the workaholic we introduced in Chapter 3.

> I talk into a dictaphone. I will probably have as many as 150 letters dictated by seven-thirty in the morning. I have five full-time secretaries. . . . I have seven swing girls who work for me part-time. This does not include my secretaries in New York, Los Angeles, Washington and San Francisco. They get dicta-belts from me every day. . . . My personal secretary doesn't do any of that. She handles appointments and my trips. . . . I dictate on Saturday and Sunday. When I do this on holidays, like Christmas, New Year's and Thanksgiving, I have to sneak a little bit, so the family doesn't know what I am doing. (Terkel, 1975)

Quaal is an awesome figure. He is so utterly possessed by the role that he plays to do his work that he cannot shed it even for those holidays that *he* knows (there is still an actor possessed by a role — they are not completely one) to be 'sacred' to the family. Quaal's possession by an occupational role turns every situation into an occupational setting and leaves us with the same uneasy confusion which actors in character present when they invade the auditorium. Possession by roles is expected, but it is tolerable only when restricted within particular situations.

Indeed, just as actors can only be on-stage in performance if they are possessed by a character, people can sustain their presence in most situations only if they are possessed by their role. A wonderful illustration of this may be found in the article on the management of fear among structural iron-workers by Haas and Shaffir (1978). In this article, they show us how much more likely it is that these fearless performers on the high steel are in fact men possessed by fearless roles than men without fear. After gaining the confidence of workers they find that the workers are just as frightened as they are on the 'iron', but have to adopt a role of fearless competence if they are to be trusted by other workers (if they are to sustain their capacity for the joint action — the ensemble playing — necessary to being an ironworker).

From our viewpoint, ironworkers have learned to be routinely possessed at work by a role that has a fearless quality, although they can strip it off in after-work drinking and confidence sharing with this outsider. Nothing displays the nature of this possession better than events which surrounded the fatal fall of one worker off the 'iron'. As one of Haas's friends recalls the accident (which is incidentally complete with a 'naïve' theory of action — a sub-textual account of the power of fear over the older workers):

> Maybe, I was too new then, but anyway the older guys up there just froze. They wouldn't move, and they wouldn't come off the iron. I had to go up there and bring them down one by one, and some of the guys were so scared I had to bring them down almost by carrying them. (Haas and Shaffir, 1978)

Confronted by the collapse of the ritual performance, those who depended most strongly on the quality of possession by the fearless role (something which younger workers were still making part of the routine) were like any actor in the grip of stage fright. They found themselves literally dispossessed of their roles and unable to operate on the stage high above the ground.[8]

The initial scene we presented from the boardroom is convincing, conveys something to us because Barry, Philip, Tony, Michael and Derek play their parts with total conviction; they are possessed by the characters they enact. Should we for a moment descry behind Barry's occupational character a warm, pipe-smoking, self-effacing, non-combative being, his performance as a challenging, aggressive iconoclast would cease to have credibility. Contrast his approach with that of Derek in the later scene when he reveals that he is no longer willing to play arbitrator; his colleagues *as* audience and co-partici-pants in the action do not believe in this new characterization. They do not consider that he is possessed by the role. We, as audience, grasp the ambivalent nature of his commitment and both we and they are witness to his struggle to create and sustain the characterization. More of this and many other matters relating to characterization later.

What we have been striving to do in this chapter is to indicate the nature of performance and the utility of the general metaphor when applied to conduct in organizations. Theatrical performances can be considered as events which occur in the presence of audiences who are led into assuming a theatrical consciousness — a willingness to concentrate upon an appearance of reality — and then assisted to sustain this level of attention by the actors' possessed portrayal of characters.

Chapter 7

Julie Harris's Legs

The dramaturgical perspective such as the one we are propounding has, of course, no problems accommodating the notions of staging, settings, costumes, properties and cues. In this chapter, we will be concerned in particular with some aspects of signification and communication in the theatre and in social/organizational life; specifically with the communication of ideas and effect that arise from the organization of space, the wearing of costumes and the assumption of properties. Our stance throughout will be that not only do these elements of performance inhibit, facilitate or function as a catalyst for actions, they also serve to predict and prescribe it. They guide responses by signalling the kind of behaviour that is expected; settings, costumes and properties communicate the situation and the rules that elicit performances. Orwell drew attention to the impact of setting upon waiters in *Down and Out in Paris and London*, and his comments will serve us well as an introduction to this chapter:

It is an instructive sight to see a waiter going into a hotel dining-room. As he passes the door, a sudden change comes over him. The set of his shoulders alters; all the dirt and hurry and irritation have dropped off in a instant. He glides over the carpet, with a solemn, priest-like air. I remember our assistant maître-d'hôtel, a fiery Italian, pausing at the dining-room door to address an apprentice who had broken a bottle of wine. Shaking his fist above his head, he yelled (luckily the door was more or less soundproof):

'Tu me fais — Do you call yourself a waiter, you young bastard? You a waiter! You're not fit to scrub floors in the brothel your mother came from. Maquereau!'

Words failing him, he turned to the door; and as he opened it, he farted loudly, a favourite Italian insult.

Then he entered the dining-room and sailed across it, dish in hand, graceful as a swan. Ten seconds later, he was bowing reverently to a customer. And you could not help thinking, as you saw him bow and smile, with that benign smile of the trained waiter, that the customer was put to shame by having such an aristocrat to serve him. (Orwell, 1933)

Of course, the stage radically transforms all objects and bodies defined within it, giving the mundane an overriding significance which is less evident

119

in the normal social function: 'On stage things that play the part of theatrical signs . . . acquire special features, qualities and attributes that they do not have in real life' (Bogatyrev, 1971). The very fact of the appearance on a stage of, say, a spinning-wheel or a set of cooking-pots depresses the practical function of them in favour of the symbolic or expressive role, 'while in real life the utilitarian function of an object is usually more important than its signification, on a theatrical set the signification is all important' (Brusak, 1938).[1] In the theatre, settings, objects, costumes, performers and movements become signals. As spectator we 'frame' that which we observe in such a manner as to make ourselves hyper-attentive. We are aware of the set (so much so that we occasionally applaud it), we understand that the dress signifies, that the actor signals someone other than himself. The performer's speech — its tone, pitch, accent — all signify. Everything is potentially significant; even those non-intended aspects of the performance are observed. Groucho Marx illustrates this point well in his amazement at the scratches on Julie Harris's legs in a performance of *I am a Camera*: 'At first we thought this had something to do with the part and we waited for these scratches to come to life. But . . . it was never mentioned in the play and we finally came to the conclusion that either she had been shaving too close or she'd been kicked around in the dressing room by her boyfriend' (quoted by Burns, 1972).

It is clear that no one can pay simultaneous attention to the various levels of communication that are involved in a given performance. It is rare, however, that anyone should need so to do since it is probably rare for all channels to be transmitting simultaneously. 'Information' as Michael Kirby (1976) notes, 'is usually presented in a discontinuous fashion. It comes in sudden bursts or "bits" scattered irregularly through the performance like stars in the night sky.' The curtain rises and we take in the setting, for the moment it is the foreground, the point of attention. An actor appears and we take in his physical size, his posture, his movement, his position (upstage, downstage, centre, left, right), his relation to the set, his costume, his make-up and so on. He speaks, he moves, he gestures in time and space and is joined by others who introduce further signals. The lights change, music plays, technicians either are or are not seen (Brecht or not-Brecht) — all signify and the meaning of the performance unfolds through time. At any given point in a performance, what is happening is characterized by a 'density of signs' (Barthes, 1964); all channels may be operative or just one or two of them. The problem of selecting information from the many channels open to us is modified by the principle of relevance: we select out for attention those aspects of performance which appear to confirm or negate that which is of importance to us. Thus in *Edward II*, we pay attention to the *character* of the king (or Mortimer or whoever) since we know from experience that characterization communicates plot. We pay attention to who the characters are and thus to any information that helps us realize this understanding, in order to participate fully in the story. As in the theatre, so in social life: we are interested in what the use of space, the setting, the décor, the costumes and the make-up (beard or not, blonde or brunette) tell us about the people with whom we have to interact. On a recent visit to the office of a very senior civil servant, correct in every aspect, one of us was startled to find the incumbent dressed in a Fair Isle slip-over, casual trousers and a brilliant red tie. His characterization of the part of civil servant as supported by this element of his presentation was such as to indicate change in the attitude of the particular department (plot). The shock of finding a person dressed in this manner in such a setting highlights the rule. In many circumstances the setting, the built environment, be that a room or an entire building, provides us with a clue as to the behaviour appropriate to it. Experience and cultural expectation has taught us to expect little grey men in little grey offices dispensing little grey platitudes. Fair Isle slip-overs in such a setting are in a very real sense shocking, somewhat akin to seeing Lear on a unicycle. Without the help a setting normally provides, interaction becomes somewhat more difficult and demanding.

We do not have the time or inclination to go into detail with regard to all of the potential signifiers — language, tone, hairstyles, make-up, noises off and so on — fascinating though such a pursuit may well be. For present purposes, we will confine ourselves to a discussion of the use of space and to some comments upon stage décor and properties.

To borrow a title from Peter Brook (1969), we can claim that the stage is in essence an 'empty space'. The designer and director begin with a playing space (often a raised platform) and seek to 'fill' it visually and acoustically. In Chapter 5, we devoted some time and space to a sequence in which the director of *Edward II* experimented with his actors in order to discover and emblematize the nature of their relationship as characters, Mortimer and Lightborn. Who stood where in relation to the other was taken to be a matter of consequence and who moved to and/or away from whom was also reckoned to be a matter of importance. Directors and producers have known about interpersonal space for years; since the earliest of stagings, conventions have arisen which accord centrality (literally) to some characters and peripherality to others. A production in *King Lear* which creates scenes in which the fool dominates the stage, as did a recent famous one in Stratford and London, presents a focus which radically transforms our view of what is happening. Fools normally inhabit the edges of staged and 'real' life; playing them centre stage is an *inversion*, perhaps even a *perversion*, of hierarchy. Given that a director wishes to say something about his performers in terms of his own culture, he can and will adopt divisions of the performing space that reflect those in everyday discourse. He will, that is, signal the nature of the dramatic relationships between performers by the appropriate use of space. Those he wishes to depict as 'intimate' he will have close together, more formal relationships will be distanced. He will organize the space and will block the movements of the actors so as to reflect the relationships; most directors will be very concerned to choreograph the performance so as to create visually interesting patterns and, at the same time, to emblematize relationships. Interestingly enough, so clear are some of these spatial signals that one director, Scott Burton, has been able to present eighty interpersonal situations in minimal sets, simple costumes, virtually no make-up and very little speech — that is, almost exclusively in 'proxemic' or spatial terms — and have the audience succeed in distinguishing unambiguously the relationships obtaining among the five actors (Argelander, 1973). Apparently we are able to read intimacy, friendship, leader–follower patterns and the like with little more than spatial clues. Social scientists such as Hall (1966), and others[2] have come late to a field well understood by those working in the theatre.

In the scene with which we began Chapter 6, we may note that Derek sits at the head of the table and that Philip sits next to him and opposite Tony. Michael sits next to Philip and some way down the table, almost distant from his colleagues, sits Eric, the secretary, surrounded — even barricaded — by his files. Antagonistic relations such as those sustained by Philip and Barry or Philip and Tony are difficult to maintain if the protagonists do not face each other. Eric's diffidence and essential functional relationship with the others is evident in his position, his paraphernalia and his posture; Derek's ascribed authority symbolized by his position at the top of the table, his role of adjudicator dramatically underlined by his literal position between Philip and Tony. Barry's ambivalence is signalled, for those of us who care to read it so, by the degree of distance he maintains between himself and his putative colleagues. He sits back from the table, not wholly withdrawn but not wholly of the company either. Moving his chair up to the table and leaning into the circle, as he does when animated, serves only to emphasize the nature of his relations with the others.

It is probably not necessary to labour the issue of space much more, it being so manifest to any one of us giving more than a moment's thought to it. It is used to communicate hierarchy, as in the notion of the 'top of the table', or even the 'top table' and, of course, in the very idea of the 'top of the organization'. The headquarters of organizations are rarely found in the basement (except in times of war), although few corporations go as far as Allgemeine Rechtsschutz:

> At Allgemeine Rechtsschutz AG, a West German insurance firm, employees will have unmistakable evidence of their standing on the corporate ladder when a new $2.8 million headquarters opens in Düsseldorf at the end of the year. Each storey will be occupied by a progressively higher echelon of workers, from 360 typists and clerks on the ground floor to president Heinz G. Kramberg alone at the top of the twelfth floor. Kramberg says he ordered the staircase design to 'encourage ambition and provide a visual image of our organization structure'. (*Stairway in Success*, Newsweek Inc., 24 Oct. 1966, cited in Steele, 1973)

Similarly, the presidents of corporations are rarely found inhabiting small cubby-holes of offices, any more than professors have to live in tiny rooms behind the library boiler house, as may some of their research students. The Civil Service in the United Kingdom has norms for the allocation of space which reflect much more than need; the more senior you are, the greater your entitlement to space and privacy. Such an allocation of territory and properties is not merely a joke.[3] The size of the office is a code which members of the organization learn to decode very quickly; behaviour in a three-window office is thus expected to differ from that demanded in a single-window one. Although, of course, factors other than the setting influence performance, it is possible to assert that location, distance from the most powerful, size and decoration of offices communicate not only information about the resident but also about how he or she would like others to behave when in his or her room. Such are the apparent 'rules' governing such settings that it is occasionally quite difficult to violate them. One of us, faced upon his assumption of office with a large 'standard issue' professorial desk, attempted for some weeks to dispense with it in favour of a smaller one such as used by typists, and was met at every turn with objections by administrators who appeared to see his action as at best foolish, at worst revolutionary. Notwithstanding the fact that status and dominance are much less important in academic offices than in those of business executives, there is no doubt that they are often structured and furnished so as to reflect hierarchy as well as character. It may well be that it is the social situation that influences actual performance, but it is the physical setting that provides the cues for it.

Look around any 'modern office'. Landscape and modular office design presents a splendid illustration of the emphasis modern management places upon flexibility and frequent change. Such offices, with their rapidly movable partitions, their potted plants and system desks signal that life in this kind of setting is likely to be in a constant state of flux; space can be expanded and contracted, new work patterns can be introduced. Communication and interdependence is the order of the day. Individuality, on the other hand, is discouraged. It is rare that such offices promote individual privacy; standard spaces, standard desks, standard chairs, standard potted plants are favoured. Any acknowledgement of idiosyncratic behaviour signals chaos and renders the environment ambiguous since it cannot be designed to reflect that which is of major importance to organizations — status and hierarchy.

Weick (1969) argues that:

> . . . organizing is directed toward resolving the equivocality that exists in informational inputs judged to be relevant. . . . Any item of information contains several possibilities or implications. It is more or less ambiguous and is subject to a variety of interpretations. If action is to be taken, the possibilities must be narrowed and the equivocal properties of the message made more unequivocal. Organizing is concerned with removing equivocality from information and structuring processes so that this removal is possible.

From this perspective, a major function of the physical setting, of any physical setting within any organization, may be seen as an attempt to reduce the ambiguity of social position and power by making distinctions between social actors. These distinctions may be gross — amount of floor space, degree of protection by the presence of outer offices, floor level, depth of carpeting, quality of the furniture or more subtle — access to windows, pictures (reproduction or original), provision of executive toys and so on. It is clear in most organizations from the settings who are the powerful and, equally important, who are to be lumped together. Standard equipment implies, at the very least, standard hierarchical levels within which distinctions, if any, are to be finely drawn. Such settings, and there are many of them, are concerned with and designed to express order and control as well as flexibility and change. In fact, as a number of studies have shown (Sloan, 1972; Sommer, 1979), offices designed for privacy and reflecting 'an unplanned quality' may promote greater satisfaction and higher productivity, but they have the grave problem of signalling a 'lack of discipline and control' (Sommer, 1979). A clear characteristic of open-office landscaping is that it transforms settings that may have been relatively private into relatively public ones. Behaviours such as failing to maintain a tidy desk which may have been tolerated (or not even known about) in a less public space now become subject to control. Such untidiness is taken to reflect upon the corporate image and must be discouraged, as must eating at one's desk, reading the newspaper or simply sleeping. New forms of office environment are not only adopted to improve communication and facilitate interaction, they are also adopted to create the impression of increased efficiency. The users may not like them, but that is not the point. Protest, however, may be successful. Rapaport (1982) reports that people in Columbia Records Division, who were forbidden to personalize their open-plan offices, fought the attempts at control and won. Their argument was that they were creative people, artists, and that they wished the setting to reflect this. They wanted and got a cluttered, chaotic and highly personalized environment.[4]

One further example, this time concentrating upon the meanings we the audience construct around settings and properties. Recently in England, a television franchise was reassigned to a group where dominant members were not 'television men', that is to say, for the most part they had not come up from the studio floor. They were, and are, primarily business men. One of the first actions of the new regime was to strengthen the perception that they were not of the industry by re-establishing the main offices on the top floor of the building, well away from the studios and the production areas. They provided themselves with rich and splendidly furbished offices clustered around that of the new managing director, signalling to everyone else that the power lay here and not in the programme department. This reorganization was effected to enable 'the managing director to be able to call in his people' quickly and reflected, above all else, his particular style of management ('Drop everything and do this') as well as — it was thought — his attitude towards 'those who create the wealth — the programme makers'. Thus an initial concern — these people do not know about television — was turned into an attitude — they do not *wish* to know about it — by the creation of a particular setting which, in turn, catalysed a series of actions. Senior executives no longer had any contact with the operating level and became more and more isolated despite resolutions to 'walk the floor'. Lower-level employees regarded their behaviour and continue to regard it as deliberate and the physical separation as an expression of a desire not to be involved with the product on the part of the executives.

Consciously or unconsciously, we interpret the settings within which we find ourselves in a variety of ways. In part and on occasion, we are prone to ascribe motivation and intention to those who promote certain physical arrangements. We acknowledge that what we perceive to be their intentions affects our feelings and our emotions, that settings have some meaning. Communication occurs through multiple channels. We often pay more attention to what is implicit or literally unsaid than to the more obvious signals that surround our everyday encounters.

As we have indicated in Chapter 5, space is not only used to signal hierarchy. It can also convey something about character, although the distinction to be drawn is often a fine one. Lightborn's relative lack of movement, his holding of his position throughout the scene with Mortimer, conveys the impression of a strong, resolute, chilling character. One with no doubts, no hesitations and no waverings. By contrast, Mortimer's agitated demeanour, his movements towards and away from Lightborn tell us a little more about who he is in this scene. A person made uneasy, not only by Lightborn, but also by what he is commissioning him to do; think what difference it would have made had the director and actors concluded that Mortimer stand firm, centre stage, and have Lightborn move towards him. Not only does the relationship change but so does the expression of character.

As in the theatre, so in social life. In Chapter 6, Derek, for example, occupies his position at the head of the table with a degree of diffidence. Given that he wishes not to exert authority nor to arbitrate, a move from this central space would, of course, be highly symbolic. Such, however, is his ambivalence that he does not make it and his continued occupation of this spot while advocating a move to joint decision-making serves to highlight the struggle within him. A manager of our acquaintance, recently appointed to a post in the National Health Service, has declared that he will have no office since the job as he defines it is 'getting around and getting things sorted out'. What a splendid image it conjures up, a peripatetic problem-solver. His forfeiture of personal space appropriate to his rank is a dramatic gesture which proclaims to all who he wishes to be taken for in the brave new world he hopes to be able to create. Similarly, Robert Townsend's (1978) denial of desks to himself and his managers, recorded in *Up the Organization*, is meant to signal something about himself as a dynamic, iconoclastic person, as well as dramatizing notions such as efficiency. In depriving others of personal space, Townsend signals what kind of characters he wants around him — doers, get-out-and-about people, not sitters and thinkers.

Before we are aware of movement through space in the theatre, we are aware of settings. When the curtain goes up, we are confronted with the organization of space. Given that the stage is of limited dimensions, what we see is organized for us by the director and his set designer. Even an empty stage is the result of a choice. Settings, as every theatrical designer and every architect worth his salt knows, are important. Kenneth Burke has defined what he calls 'ratios' by which he means the relation between different aspects of a play (and different aspects of social life). Any script (theatrical or social) will imply a 'scene–act ratio' in which the scene or setting in the terms we have been using above 'both *realistically reflects* the course of action and *symbolizes* it'. Clearly, from such a perspective the setting in a theatre is not a frill, not simply a piece of decoration to amuse the audience and enrage the accountants, but it is part of a unified, aesthetic process. The setting is not separate from but essentially part of the action. Burke illustrates his point in a discussion of the setting in the final act of Ibsen's *An Enemy of the People*:

> In Act V, the stage directions tell us that the hero's clothes are torn, and the room is in disorder, with broken windows. You may consider these details either as properties of the scene or as a reflection of the hero's condition after his recent struggle with the forces of reaction. The scene is laid in Dr Stockmann's *study*, a setting so symbolic of the direction taken by the plot that the play ends with Dr Stockmann announcing his plans to enrol twelve young *disciples* and with them to found a *school* in which he will work for the *education* of society. (Burke, 1969a)

This is an excellent example from the theatre of the vital connection between setting and action, as well as setting and character. The final scenes of *Edward II* provide another such example, when the deposed king is crushed with a table and disembowelled with a red-hot poker; a symbolic and ritual act which signals in a horrifying manner the end of his homosexual activities. Occurring, as it does, within the dark and narrow confines of a foetid dungeon, the image clearly reinforces the act. The scene played in full light in a large white space would have been much more difficult to render effective.

Those who are responsible for the ratios in social and organizational life are often well aware of the need to reconcile them. Most of us would have difficulty in suspending disbelief in a doctor who operated out of a garden shed or, for that matter, a landscape gardener who operated out of a surgery. At a level often beyond the threshold of attention, we know that settings tell us something about action, about character and about purpose. The confidence trickster arranges to meet us in the Ritz, not the local Holiday Inn. Settings in social and organizational life, no less than upon the stage, need to communicate their intended nature and must be congruent if they are to elicit appropriate performances.

An important caveat to this whole discussion needs to be introduced at this stage. We have argued that, while in any circumstance there is always the possibility of an idiosyncratic definition — the Fair Isle slip-over in Whitehall — it is usually the culturally encoded setting which cues the behaviour. We know what is expected of us in Westminster Abbey just as much as we know how to conduct ourselves when confronted with the McDonalds fast food setting. Both settings produce 'astonishing degrees of behavioural uniformity' (Kottack, 1979), since both cue customers into ritual practices. Meanings in the Abbey and in McDonalds are not constructed *de novo*, they are learned and thereafter cued by the setting.

As we noted in the early chapters, much of what we do consists of habitual, routinized behaviour which we termed ritual performance; our responses in a number of situations tend to be unreflective, consistent and uniform. We operate in settings with which we are familiar and, providing the ratios are not violated, we identify a setting almost subliminally and perform in line with it. None the less, however automatic our response, at one level it occurs because we can decode the setting, we are familiar, that is, with the culture it encapsulates. To illustrate, let us return to the stage. In *Edward II*, the whole notion of kingship is symbolized by the crown. To those of us brought up within a particular culture, there is no problem in taking this object as representing something more than gold and precious stones. To those not educated to the tradition, the crown *is* nothing more than metal and jewels. Encoding and decoding is a matter of consequence. In simple societies, the codes may be simple and widely shared; in a complex, multi-cultural modern society such as the one most of use inhabit, the codes proliferate and the decoding becomes much more difficult. Thus settings become less legible and behaviour within them much less predictable. Football grounds are no longer places where people simply go to watch football; for some, they have become arenas wherein they can perpetrate violence upon their adversaries; for others, places to advertise whisky, cigarettes, television or whatever; for still others, places which can be utilized to realize finance and exercise power. A football stadium no longer simply elicits a limited range of behaviours.

Somewhat of a digression, but one with some point. Settings, even in the theatre, have ceased to have the impact they once had (and may still have in somewhat less complex societies). In *Edward II*, the setting, consisting largely of scaffolding, is not specific enough to be a guide to behaviour. It signals images of imprisonment and brutality rather than those of opulence and freedom, but we need more than it to make sense of that which unfolds before us; we need coherence between it, the costumes, the properties, the appearances and the manners of those who inhabit it. The set is not as specific as Westminster Abbey nor, for that matter, as McDonalds. It is certainly not as instantly legible but nor, for that matter, are a great many of the settings within which we find ourselves. Westminster Abbey, it must be remembered, may nowadays be the setting for a tour (or several), for a recital, for poetry reading, for state occasions and for protest meetings; nowadays we need more than the setting to cue our behaviour. Signs inform us that 'This is a House of God. Please act accordingly'; the problem is knowing what is appropriate; kneeling reverentially is likely to be physically difficult and almost certain to set off a thousand tourist cameras.

Clothes, or costumes, as we refer to them in the theatre, play an important role in placing people and, having placed them, inducing appropriate behaviour.[5] Mortimer is splendidly apparelled on set and we read his change of dress to be significant, just as we read Lightborn's black clothing to be selected and not randomly thrown on from that which is available backstage. Our man in Whitehall selected his Fair Isle slip-over in order to signal something about himself and his attitude, choosing to be deliberately incongruent with his setting. Most of his colleagues still dress in clerical grey and are even classified after an element of their clothing, forming a recognizable class — that of 'the old school tie'.

That costume communicates and is used to express explicit messages about not only status but also identity is clear to all who work in the theatre. It is the commonplace also with the many who work for such magazines as *Vogue* and *The Face*. Rank and status is not only communicated by badges and insignia, it is also more subtly conveyed in the cut and quality of the material used. It does so even — perhaps particularly — in times of rapid change; élite groups — 'leaders of the pack' — may be recognized by their clothing. The April (1985) edition of *The Face* captures well the impact of clothing in contemporary culture:

It is eight o'clock on a Saturday evening and beneath the scaffolding that skirts the Town Hall, the Corn Exchange public house is filling up. Inside, the video juke-box flashes the pop hits while outside, three well-built men in dinner suits have just started their shift on the entrance. They belong to an organization called Unit Control, and they have been hired because they can handle the violence that flares up in Leicester every weekend.

. . . Around the corner, two pubs — Asquith's and Winston's — stand opposite each other, their respective doormen exchanging wisecracks across the street as their potential enemy journey from bar to bar. Dressed in designer-name sportswear, Yves St Laurent tops and Fiorucci jeans — a look meant to spell 'smart prole' — the enemy are only boys: boys who are tattooed before they can shave, boys who have fallen into the habit of carrying Stanley knives in their pockets. . . .

. . . At the end of this year, Moore has decided, he will retire from working on the doors. In a neat dark-blue suit, with a white shirt and a quietly snazzy tie, he looks like a patriarchal movie-villain with a heart of steel — which may well be the desired effect. . . .

The two groups, roaming youths and bouncers, signal their presence to each other and, more importantly, know that they are so doing by their dress.

Tonight this branch of the Baby Squad has forsaken its customary casual style in favour of a consignment of T-shirts, freshly stolen that very afternoon. Their tribute to 'Wham' turns out to be ironic, but practical. 'We wear "Wham" T-shirts to take the piss. We're barred from every boozer in the town and every nightclub because the bouncers don't like us. So we get into the boozer by going a bit incognito. We're not soft-heads, we wear "Wham" shirts. This season, when you go to football, everyone will have "Wham" T-shirts . . . anything so long as you look the same. You're less likely to get nicked if everyone is wearing the same T-shirt — it's camouflage.' (*The Face*, April 1985)

Once upon a time it was all much simpler, sumptuary laws proscribed items of clothing as a way of preventing certain groups of people from expressing or claiming high status. Dress, then as now but then by law, was taken to give important clues to identity, role and status. In his splendid discussion of clothes in the eighteenth-century city, Sennett (1974) argues that clothing signalled role and thus facilitated social interaction. Elements of this still obtain. The Queen of England has recently declared that scarlet robes may not be worn by characters and functionaries within the Established Church other than by her express permission. This declaration means that a large number of cassocks must now be replaced (so important is the symbol to the Queen that she has volunteered some money for the replacement); it also means that those entitled to wear scarlet — those precious few — will not only be seen to be distinct and important but are likely to experience themselves as such. I am a scarlet cassock person and must live up to that characterization. Others, not permitted to wear scarlet, now have a clear signal of hierarchy to which they can attach the appropriate sentiment. Thus, for the social actor, properties and costumes may well signal the character one is expected to assume; for the other social actors, these same accoutrements may signal not so much who you are but where you are in the hierarchy.

For an actor to appear without make-up, costume, props and setting is very difficult. Actors need to know who they are and what they represent; the accoutrements and symbols are of as much help to them as they are to the audience and to their fellow actors. A crown symbolizes kingship and, within limits, cues the actor into the assumption of a particular set of gestures, a specific demeanour, a certain tone of voice and so on. A suit of chain mail not only limits one's possible movements but its assumption may well bring about (rather than simply add to) a military posture. What one wears signals something to oneself as much if not more than it signals to someone else. Thomas à Becket, for example, when he became chancellor to Henry II of England, continued to wear a hairshirt beneath his no doubt splendid chancellorian gowns to remind himself that — in essence — he was a man of God, devoted to poverty rather than that which he outwardly signalled to the world. The writer of this passage is surrounded by symbols of his own status and position in life as he sits writing this; word processor signalling a degree of technological control over his surroundings, books signalling his image of himself as an academic, confirmed by the gown hanging behind the door (in gorgeous green, red and gold), flute on the music stand representing his aspirations to musical glory, half-built bicycle is a sign indicating his sporting and mechanical pretensions. All are expressions of and support for a particular identity. The assumption of a particular set of clothes signals in some cases a move from rehearsal to performance. The Italian Wind Quintet take themselves and what they are about much more seriously when they are wearing ties and tails than when rehearsing in sweat shirts and jeans.[6] Managers going off-site for a strategy meeting (as with the Heseltines discussed earlier) often dress informally to signal to themselves the more playful and creative nature of that which they are about. Similarly, the white coat confers an identity, the briefcase, the stethoscope, the slide rule, the phone in the car, the executive toys, the heavy carpet, the large (or small) desk, the venetian blinds, the receptionists and secretaries, the deference of the chauffeurs and the lift attendants serve to suggest and confirm a particular characterization. I am an important person because I number among my props a Jaguar motor car, a personal computer, a leather briefcase with EIIR embossed upon it or whatever.

Dress is an important cue to behaviour but, as with setting, one which is less imperative in modern societies than in traditional ones. None the less, as books like that of Thourlby (1978) indicate (following on from ideas generated by Goffman), a good living may be had in advising others how to 'dress for success'. First impressions still count and judgements are made quickly, often upon clothing alone. For those who wish to make it, particular suits, colours, arrangements and styles are important; this year, as *The Face* has it, 'Derrières are simple' and one is invited to 'Raise a look to a peacock's crest, treat a torso with jackettes and blousettes, smooth to a fine line below the belt. . .'. It will not get you to the boardroom of ICI, but it will get you noticed as a leader of fashion.

Properties, or accessories as they are termed in the fashion industry, are important to the manipulation of personal fronts. No self-respecting member of the Baby Squad would be seen in public without his Stanley knife, just as few executives dispense with their briefcases (which, apparently, are filled with items such as sandwiches and clothing rather than documents) when visiting the City. These items, as much as space, costume and setting, have meanings that serve to organize social relations (Douglas and Isherwood, 1979). An item as innocuous as a wristwatch, for example, has a meaning which may have little or nothing to do with its role in showing the time (Wagner, 1975). Not only is the possession of a Rolex or a Cartier watch an indication of wealth, but the very style of the watch says something about you as a person. An acquaintance of one of us takes great pride in showing people his ancient Longines watch — 'Forty-five years old and still going strong' — and signals his delight in it as a personal symbol of his resistance to change. He appears to regard himself as a quality product, a wind-up version of modern man and all the better for it. Watches, of course, communicate sexual stereotypes; the male type strong and function related (often with a welter of gizmos that the owner is at a loss to operate), and the female type, delicate and aesthetic. Those who doubt this kind of analysis should try dressing against type in this detail alone and see what it does for them. Even Rocky Marciano would create some identity confusion appearing in public with a delicate piece of machinery strapped to his weighty forearm. Women, of course, wishing to stress their competitiveness in a man's world, have long affected suits, trousers, shirts, ties, short haircuts and, inevitably, male accessories such as briefcases, sports cars and heavy black wristwatches. The trade the other way has been less in evidence but, recently, has accelerated with a number of men now using not only deodorants, but perfumes, and some investing heavily in personal jewellery, such as ear-rings.

It seems reasonable to assert that settings, clothing, accessories, hairstyles and make-up elicit conduct in a similar manner. All such cultural material (and any of the items is encoded with cultural meaning) can act as a mnemonic device that communicates behaviour. Generally speaking, a city suit in a setting which is recognized as an office reminds those of us confronting it of the kind of relationship to be acted out. Should a visit to the head office of our bank result in us being ushered into a setting of pastel shades and tinsel and confronted with a man dressed as a clown, the best of us will have difficulty in pressing on with our request for a loan.

We are all accustomed to reading signals in the theatre and in social life. We are, for the most part, accomplished in the art of synecdochism — the taking of the part for the whole. We do not *see* an entire castle on the stage but simply a part — a series of turrets, for example. We do not see, even in the most naturalistic of sets, an entire room (there is no ceiling, no fourth wall) but we take the part for the whole. Similarly in social and organizational life, we take one element to be representative of a whole:

> The outer door, in bronze and glass, is placed centrally in a symmetric façade. Polished shoes glide quietly over shining rubber to the glittering and silent elevator. . . . A minute later, and you are ankle deep in the director's carpet, plodding sturdily towards his distant, tidy desk. Hypnotized by the chief's unwavering stare, cowed by the Matisse hung upon his wall, you will feel that you have found efficiency at last. (Parkinson, 1957)

Any aspect of social and organizational life can, like any aspect of a theatrical scene, be 'foregrounded' or 'framed'. Such notions are essentially spatial metaphors (but not exclusively so); the placing of the desk, for example, highlights it. It may, of course, be highlighted by its being not placed where one could anticipate it: a small desk pushed back against the wall in an otherwise plush executive office frames it in such a manner as to signal 'informality'. Normally in the theatre, as elsewhere, the performer is foregrounded; in particular it is the lead actor who attracts the most attention. All other aspects of the production are 'transparent' in the sense that they support the star. It is possible, of course, for the star to be 'upstaged' by another performer (accidentally or otherwise) or by an element of the set or of 'effects'. The 'storm' in a recent production of *King Lear* at Stratford-upon-Avon succeeded in drowning out the actors. Similarly the Pope's transportation (his Popemobile) has been known to attract nearly as much attention as himself. Occasionally in the theatre, however, attention is deliberately focused upon the support system such that it is granted unusual prominence and significance. The spotlight upon the crown, for example, a favourite device of directors of Shakespeare's history plays, or the image of an empty throne. Brecht deliberately foregrounds costuming in *Galileo* when he has the newly elected pope enrobe in full view of the audience — the clothes stand for the assumption of and trappings of high office. In similar fashion, Parkinson's executive foregrounds certain aspects of his office, trusting that we, the customers or clients, will take the part for the whole — the tidy desk as representative of order and efficiency, the carpet and the Matisse of wealth and success, the 'unwavering stare' of reliability and steadiness.

There is, of course, nothing perverse or odd about this. In all cultures, we find elements of settings, costumes, occasions or whatever which are, as it were, paradigms for the whole: symbols that may be regarded as microcosmic. The elaboration of doors and entrances in a case in point — signalling to the world the rank and importance of the inhabitant. The acquisition and display of a particular drink is another apparently trivial but significant one; a whole life-style is encapsulated in Pimms No. 1, as indeed it is in the consumption of caviare or the wearing of the kilt.

Front lawns are interesting examples of synecdoche. In a recent and very popular television series *The Good Life*, the nation was both shocked and amused when the inhabitants of a detached house in an affluent suburb ploughed up their front lawn in order to grow vegetables. Their fictional neighbours showed as much rage as would any neighbour in such a setting should anyone suggest, let alone execute, such an outrage. Rapaport (1982) documents such a case in Wisconsin where court action was instituted by the municipality of Wauwatosa to prevent the occupant from growing vegetables on this sacred front region. He notes that the lawn has a central role in communicating meaning, often being put in and maintained while the house which backs it lacks furniture and fittings. Lawns, like doors and entrances, communicate adherence to a particular notion of status and respectability. A lady in the city of Bath has frequently and resolutely insisted upon painting the door to her house in a famous Georgian Crescent in a bright yellow, as a sign of individuality. The council and the other residents consider her action an affront and have successfully prosecuted her for her temerity. Informally, it has been remarked that her kind of behaviour disqualifies her from living in such a district.

All, however, may not be what it seems. The quote from Parkinson (1957) concludes:

> In point of fact you will have discovered nothing of the kind. It is known that a perfection of planned layout is achieved only by institutions on the point of collapse.

None the less, until we have information which causes us to pause, we continue to take the part for the whole. As confidence tricksters have shown time and time again, careful manipulation of settings and properties can fool a great many of the people for a great part of the time. Just as in the theatre we accept the conventions that help us to 'suspend disbelief', so in social and organizational life we are more than prepared to take at face value the settings, costumes and properties which we encounter. Indeed, if anything, we are much more attentive in the theatre, much more open to communication at multiple levels than we are, for the most part, in everyday life. We are likely to notice the scratches on Julie Harris's legs and ponder their significance, their relationship to anything else which is occurring on the stage. In social and organizational life, we either do not notice that, say, the phones in the plush office do not appear to be connected or we accommodate our observation within the generally reassuring setting. We appear to have a deep-seated desire to be bamboozled by social fabrications. We are, that is, only too ready to take the part for the whole; the 'expensive' advertising signals massive resources, the large cars achievement, the modern office block solidity. As in the theatre, we are 'taken in', led gently to believe in what transpires within these settings. How many of us insist upon inspecting the certificates our doctors hang upon the walls of their surgeries? How many would refuse a request to pull over made by someone dressed as a police officer? Social 'props' may well be deceptive but, for the most part, they not only support performances, they catalyse them. A formal setting promotes formal behaviour, an informal one the opposite.

Meanings, of course, are a matter of context. Even front lawns may be ploughed up in times of war when the overriding purpose becomes one of self-sufficiency. It is not that lawns provide much space for vegetables, but their utilization signals that 'Digging for victory' is important, an activity highly valued by all classes of society. Similarly the adoption of particular clothes must be seen in context; a student appearing at one of our lectures in a suit and tie is unusual, but not so if we discover that he is *en route* for a job interview. Derek's sports jacket does say something about him and his attitude to his subordinates and the company he runs. Those unaware of his role as owner, however, could misread the relationships, could take the coat to signal an informality that is not operative.

Which brings us back, in concluding, to the issue of the transmission of signals and their receipt. In certain circumstances, our attention is as sharp as when in the theatre; we notice the scratches on the legs and speculate about their intent. This happens in social and organizational life when we are confronted with the novel. An initial encounter with people working in a computer room is likely to be very confusing to those of us unfamiliar with the way relations are culturally encoded in such settings. After a relatively short period of socialization, however, we will be able to read the signs and not long afterwards we will be taking them for granted. Some settings, however, are quite difficult to read, however familiar we are with them, because others define them in a manner which we find disturbing. There is, for example, a seventeenth-century church in Shaftesbury which, having been declared redundant, is now used as a sports centre. It is difficult to exercise violently or with boundless joy and mirth in such a setting. It is equally difficult to shop in settings where the goods are displayed in profusion but the check-outs are few and well camouflaged. Such settings signal all too clearly 'choose', but less distinctly, 'pay'. As we indicated earlier, the very multiplicity of settings available to us and the plurality of interpretations render our world less certain than that of the member of a traditional society. The result is that our reactions have to be multiply cued, we can no longer tell what behaviour is expected in a particular building, explicit signs are necessary to tell us to 'HAVE FUN' in churches or indicate the directions of the cash desk. Bank tellers have their name and function displayed on desks. In effect, by increasing redundancy, the likelihood of the appropriate behaviour being elicited is much increased.

All of which, of course, has been well known to generations of theatre directors:

> In our production generally, we were very careful to construct a continuous, naturalistic façade. We researched the period in order to make historically accurate props and costumes. There were a real Christmas tree, real lamps, a stove that glowed when real coal was put into it, real children and a real baby (often cut from productions for expediency), real embroidery, real knitting, real cigar smoking. . . . We improvized important scenes from the past, before the play begins: Krogstad courting Mrs Linde, Helmer in his illness being examined by Dr Rank, Nora borrowing the money from Krogstad. One long improvization was simply a day taken at random out of the Helmer's lives — the maids cleaning and working in the kitchen, Helmer working in his study, Nora playing with the children and doing her embroidery. . . . The purpose of all these exercises was to develop 'relating' in the Stanislavski sense, establishing connections between the actors and each other, as well as between the actors and their surroundings. It was important that the actors behave as if they know one another, were used to each other's presence, were in some cases intimate with one another, and were in surroundings that were very familiar, filled with memories of the past. (Hornby, 1977)

The director worked hard to give the impression that the characters were 'embedded in their environment'. In presenting naturalistic drama, as in social and organizational life, the relationship between settings, costumes and performances is the crucial one. We cannot believe in stage maids who do not, in their every gesture, conform to our expectation of maids in that kind of setting, just as we find it difficult to believe in, say, a gynaecologist whose conduct and setting are not all of a piece. White coats, medical props, clean, well-scrubbed settings, nurses in crisp uniforms, a distinguished, somewhat distant mien all serve to induce the appropriate atmosphere.

The importance of setting in inducing behaviour, however, is a piece of commercial wisdom. The retail revolution in the United Kingdom has been spearheaded by designers who know the power of the image:

> You might think High-Tech or at least clinical minimalism would be *the* style to sell real technology, but at First Computers, a chain selling home and business computers on the high street, the 'user friendly' attitude dominates. The oversized logo of triangular blocks smacks of primary school. Digital typography is eschewed in favour of giant hand-written signs. The interior is homely — warm purples and patterned carpets — the staff high profile and the hardware relegated to workstations. (*The Face*, April 1985)

The impact is immediate and probably subconscious, just as the impact of a well-designed stage set is immediate and probably subconscious. The bare metal, the cold steel and the wire of the set for *Edward II* presages the brutal imprisonment and death of the king in a way which no imitation of a real castle or a real dungeon could do. The boardroom of the Heseltines, with its founders peering down upon the occupants, provides a context for their activity which it would take volumes to document.

Chapter 8

The Characterization of Action

ROSINA: Sir, I fear you mock me, when the wealthy and beloved son of the Mendons declares his love for Rosina Meadows, the humble farmer's daughter.

MENDON: There are those in the city to whom innocence and beauty such as these are incentives to wicked and unholy thoughts. I look with shame and pity upon the thousands who sacrifice all the purest feelings of nature upon the altar of sensuality.

ROSINA: I believe you, Mr Mendon, and will rely upon you.

MENDON: You may, Rosina: let me have your confidence and you will attain all you desire. (*Aside*) And so will I!

(*Rosina Meadows, The Village Maiden*, or, *Temptations Unveiled*)

In the theatre, having assimilated the sets, the properties and the costumes, we turn our attention to the plot which is necessarily carried forward by characters:

A tragedy is a *mimesis* of an action; action implies people engaged in it; these people must have some definite moral and intellectual qualities, since it is through a man's qualities that we characterize his actions and it is of course with reference to this action that men are said to succeed or fail. (Aristotle, *Poetics*, 6, 5)

Aristotle recognized that man is a social animal but appears in this passage to be positing a notion that character exists independently of action. At the outset, we would challenge this and assert that the notion of 'character' is nothing more (nor less) than a convenient reification for what it is that someone does. It is not the essence of someone in the sense of being *in* him or her, but is rather an attitude towards or a knowledge of him or her. As Lotman (1973) puts it: 'The "character" of a character is the sum total of the binary combinations with other characters (or other groups) . . . the sum total of their inclusions in groups of other characters — it is, in other words, a whole made up of differentiated counter-signs.' On the stage, the sum total of all of the scenes and each of the *interactions* provides us with the data needed to identify and define a character.

As on the stage, so in social life, the notion of character enables us to summarize what we know of a person's conduct and predict (however crudely) how it is that person will behave. What we know of Derek, for example, or Barry, how we see them as characters, is a product of *our* observation of their conduct and of our expectations of consistency which may well be ill-founded. Character is a simplification of accumulated observations and can only be adduced after the event, when all of the scenes are complete. In life, as in theatre, a character is the totality of actions and responses. Who Falstaff is can only be determined as a series of hypotheses arising from and elaborated through the action in which he engages. Who Derek is arises from the context, from his actions and from those of others towards him. Character and action are inextricably intertwined. Derek's refusal to arbitrate is an action performed by a sort of person, but at the same time, Derek's character is a precipitate of that way of behaving.

What is more, that precipitate exists in our minds as auditors or readers; it says nothing about the *essence* of Derek except in so far as he responds to our view of him. Bodkin (1958) describes the interplay well:

> In projecting the figure of a man of a certain disposition and analysing the forces behind his behaviour, the critic is inevitably using the emotional experience which he himself undergoes in living through the play. Having experienced, as communicated by the speeches of Hamlet, a certain psychological movement in which a strong impulse to action is aroused . . . a movement which, while imaginatively experiencing it, the reader imputes to the fictitious speaker — afterwards, in reviewing the total impression so received, with analysis and synthesis of its successive movements, the critic discerns . . . within the personality of Hamlet, the reflected pattern of the emotional forces that have operated within *his own* imaginative activity. (emphasis added)

We make and remake people from our own experiences; the aptness of a particular composition depends crucially upon our range of emotional life and our flexibility. To be sure, characters such as Mendon and Rosina with whom we began this chapter are relatively easy to construct; within the space of a few words and even fewer actions (we can all discern Mendon's intent, but the aside confirms it), we are aware of them as types: distressed heroine and villain. In many circumstances we construct our reification out of such thin material, in some we suspend judgement for some time and in a few we are quite unable readily to categorize those who appear before us on-stage or off.

As we have argued earlier, in order to exist, we all need to husband attention; living in a constant state of monitoring, of assessing and of constructing would be so energy-sapping that most of us would take to our beds and stay there. We move through social and organizational life with but few moments when we are fully attentive. For the most part, we engage in ritual performances with characters we take to be as stock as Rosina and Mendon; characters which have sometimes been referred to in the theatre as 'flat'.[1] Flat characters — be they heroes, villains or fools — are one-dimensional; they create no surprises, they can only do what they are destined to do and the audience knows what this is in advance. The make-up, costume, gestures and delivery of the actors reveals all. Instantly. Lest the audience fail to cotton on, another character or, as below, a group of them will ram the message home:

VILLAGE CHORUS: Farewell to Rosina, the sweet village maiden!
The word must be spoken, farewell, O, farewell!
She goes with our prayers and our best wishes laden,
While sorrow behind her, behind her shall dwell!
God bless the sweet maid, may her pathway be fair!
God bless the sweet maid, may her pathway be fair!

Not a dry eye in the house. Rosina is a standard, off-the-shelf, melodramatic heroine, and Mendon a standard villain. They are their actions and are defined by their interactions with the other characters and with the audience; note the aside '. . . let me have your confidence and you will obtain all you desire. (*Aside*) And so will I!' The hiss rises almost spontaneously when confronted with such blatant types. Playwrights of the nineteenth century were just as skilled as writers of soap in the twentieth are in producing the formulae which precipitate these characters. So, in fact, are organizational dramaturges — those who peddle sub-texts for efficiency and effectiveness to anyone who will buy. Unlike their theatrical and television counterparts, however, they begin with characters and trust that the inculcation of their tenets will result in action. Books purporting to deal with training and development are replete with character analyses which are redolent of the stock character approach to theatre.[2]

Kakabadse and Parker (1984), for example, identify 'four stereotypic characters' in their somewhat superficial look at the politics of organizations: the traditionalist, the team coach, the company baron and the visionary. The melodramatic nature of their effort is captured well in their character sketches. The traditionalists are 'concerned with maintaining the status quo', he or she 'accepts and maintains the power dependencies and resource allocation processes within the organization'. The team coach is 'flexible to the extent that he is stimulated by interacting with those who think and feel differently to them' and the company baron is 'able to recognize power dependencies' and will 'check the field before making his play'. The visionary operates in 'relative isolation' and may be 'considered' the 'saviour' or 'hit-man' brought into an ailing organization.

Somewhat more advanced is the kind of character analysis afforded by Blake and Mouton (1978) who, as is well known, provide managers with an opportunity to assess their managerial styles through a technique known as grid analysis. The grid affords one the opportunity to discover one's assumptions about 'people' and 'production'. High concern for 'people' and low for 'production', for example, will result in one being categorized as a 1,9 manager, whereas high concern for both will result in one being designated 9,9 — a hero. Needless to say, villains score 1,1 and are shown to exert minimum effort. One example of the character sketch provided by Blake and Mouton will be sufficient to make the point:

> A 9,1-oriented manager strives to be powerful, to control and to dominate. He is driven to win and to prove himself capable of mastering all, submitting to nothing and no one. . . .
> His greatest dread is to falter, to be beaten, to lose control, and to be defeated. . . .
> Anger is typically experienced as a reaction to the frustration of his will. He focuses on overcoming the outside source that triggered his anger rather than studying the cause of his lack of inner composure in dealing with a problem.
> . . . If a subordinate should question a 9,1-oriented boss about how work is to be performed, he might get an answer such as 'These are your instructions. They tell you who, what, where, when and how. Do them and don't give me any lip. If there's anything I don't like, it's insubordination.' (Blake and Mouton, 1978)

The latter could be transferred almost word for word to *The Mill Owner* or to an episode of *Dallas*. We could go on and fill the rest of these pages with descriptions of the kind of 'flat' characters urged upon us by theorists and practitioners. Like the writers of melodramas (ancient and modern), they seek to determine the essence of a particular style or character and present it to us with little or no qualification, though to be fair to Blake and Mouton, they are aware of the importance of situation upon conduct. They, like others, however, are only too ready to provide diagnostic instruments to enable us to determine our current character and training programmes to enable us to assume other equally flat but, from the point of view of the organization, more desirable characters:

> A 9,9-oriented manager desires to make a contribution to corporate success, coupled with a commitment to involve others with and through who he works. These values promote voluntarism, spontaneity, openness and responsibility shared with others in accomplishing clear and challenging goals.

Wright and Taylor (1984), in a more recent and considerably more sophisticated work in this genre, provide detailed guidance to those who wish to become effective leaders. They urge, for example, that he or she who would be recognized as a good manager must make every attempt to 'diminish or dispel adverse emotional reactions, such as anger, frustration, dissatisfaction, anxiety, despair and so on'. They give clear advice on how to comport oneself and offer actual words and phrases, stopping short of stage directions:

SUBORDINATE: That's typical. I try to do my job effectively and all you can do is criticize me for some minor infringement of company regulations. That's the final straw. From now on you can worry about maintenance problems. If the machine breaks down and we have to wait two months for spares, that's your problem, not mine. I don't see why I should worry. No one else does!

MANAGER:	You seem to be very upset about this.
SUBORDINATE:	Of course I'm upset. I do my best for the company. I get no thanks when things go right, but as soon as I ignore one petty rule, I get criticized out of all proportion.
MANAGER:	You feel that you don't get enough recognition for the work you do.
SUBORDINATE:	No I don't. You look at the other people. They do the bare minimum. If a machine breaks down, they just call in Maintenance. They don't care how long it takes to put right. I try to run things efficiently. I try to be prepared for emergencies, and what happens? Instead of thanking me for all the extra work I put in, all you can do is criticize.
MANAGER:	And you find that demoralizing because it seems unfair.
SUBORDINATE:	Yes, it does. I think the company should give more recognition to the people who have the company's interests at heart. I'm not saying I'm the only one — there are others — but. . . .

The character of the subordinate is, perhaps, the more interesting of the two; he seems to us less 'wet' than the manager, but Wright and Taylor are intent upon modelling and training stereotypic or 'flat' executives. Those of us who have been around training programmes can recognize instantly the kind of manager generations of dramaturges such as Blake and Mouton, Wright and Taylor wish to see in place.

It is clear that the human race is not constituted only of stock characters; there is more to most of us than there is to Mendon and Rosina, just as there is more to managers than is dreamt of by the kind of writers highlighted in the discussion to date. None the less, such stereotypes are useful; as we have argued earlier, our daily round is one of ritual and stereotypic interaction. We need the predictability that characters such as those addressed above afford us. Nor should we overlook that types such as the 9,1 manager or the company baron distil much of our experience into their formulae. They may simplify, they may even be slightly or, occasionally, hugely comic, but they are not totally unreal. What they are not, of course, is *individual*.

'All art', says Bergson, 'aims at what is individual.' What we see and hear in reacting to Derek and Philip, Barry and Tony, is, depending upon our approach, individuals or types. Derek may be seen as a ditherer, Barry as a blusterer, Philip as a querulous pedant, or each may be seen as something more, much more than these labels. Each may be seen as examples of 'rounded' characters, or what Bentley (1964) terms 'open' individuals. Consider the following passage:

You see, what I find amazing is, yes, I'm a terrier in one sense. Whether the issue is important or not. I'll hang onto it only because I'm going to say to people it's going to be looked at. And not just shuffled under the carpet and we'll forget it next month. Because I won't. And because I happen to have a very retentive memory, I can remember all sorts of obscure facts and figures and things, and dates of meetings and whatever, that I'll say to people, 'Well, I did actually raise that on such-and-such a date at such-and-such a meeting — what's happened?' Shuffle, shuffle, 'Well, nothing.' Partly it's because people are under too much pressure, partly because, other than the top 20 people, there is no one else to raise the issue. 'Why should I? I must be bloody daft.' It's true. If I wanted to live the life of Riley . . . so I am well paid, I'm on a reasonable contract and however good or bad I am, the company is going to make money with this product, at least until the end of the decade. Will I be here then? I don't know. I could say, sod it, 'Look, chaps, the order of the day is to do the best you can and keep quiet, don't bother me. . . .' I could do that. But it's not in my character to do it — I could do it, I really could and there are others in this industry doing it, and here. People who have worked here a long time and are still here and say 'He must be bloody barmy. It isn't our problem.' Of course there's that reaction and I know I could make life a lot easier for myself and for others. . . . But as Managing Director, the one thing I have to try to do is to look forward, seven years, ten years, that far. Lots of people here, I mean the bulk of the people here, do not want to know. They just carry on in the way that it has always been. If I were to do that, I may as well pack my bags and go. I can't say that I am actually enjoying it. I always enjoy a challenge but I can't say I'm exactly enjoying the pressure and the isolation of the job that I do. Because the things that are suffering, in a strictly personal sense, are my wife and my children, who I don't see much of, and my health. And my enjoyment of life. From the moment I get up in the morning till the moment I go to bed . . . but it's not happening here as it should do, it's not happening yet. . . .

Of course, it's difficult for you to see this man. In putting down what was said, we can see the individual in his splendid office, surrounded by all the symbols of status and power. We can feel his presence, meet his eyes, sit forward in our seats as we did when he spoke directly to us. Then as now, however, we were able to be involved with him in his struggle to present himself to himself as well as to us and simultaneously to reflect upon what he was saying. The characterization he offered us was both him and not him, it was an enacted image between us because in a very real sense he was both performing and commenting upon his performance. Even without the setting and the immediacy, we trust that what we have offered suggests a complex character, not an abstract type; someone who cannot be simply fatuously labelled 9,1, a company baron or whatever. Someone whose richness, whose ambiguity, whose qualities unknown even to himself at this stage of the exploration, is such as to hold the promise of making the consideration of conduct in organizations at least as interesting as an evening with Falstaff or Mother Courage. Certainly far more interesting than an evening with Rosina or Mendon, Kakabadse or Blake.

Such a character is not instantly accessible, nor is he predictable. He is not fully explained and yet he, like many characters upon the stage, manifests an immediacy, a reality, a humanity that is palpable. Hamlet, Dr Faustus, Falstaff, Mrs Malaprop, Don Juan, Galileo, Mother Courage, Peer Gynt, Estragon and Vladimir — the list is not endless, nor is it substantial, but it is capable of being constructed. As Bentley reminds us, great characters are enigmatic, beyond simple definition. 'A mysterious character is one with an open definition — not completely open, or there will be no character at all, and the mystery will dwindle to a muddle, but open as, say, a circle is open when most of the circumference has been drawn' (Bentley, 1964).

As in the theatre, so in life. Some members of some organizations, perhaps most members of most organizations, may be seen as types, predictable and controllable. A great deal of the writings on conduct in organizations is concerned to identify and classify such types. It takes the form of texts on organizational behaviour, and of biography or autobiography.

My Years with General Motors (Sloan, 1972) and *Back from the Brink* (Edwardes, 1983) offer us more idiosyncratic but no less complete views of men of action in action. Little room for the enigmatic here, no circles left not enclosed. And yet who can pretend that all life is here: the painful and the contradictory, the luminous and the dark, the groping and the realization. Great characters present the enigma of life, they do not resolve it; characters on the organizational stage may indeed seek to reduce ambiguity, no doubt a measure of the esteem in which they are held is related to the degree to which they are successful in reducing equivocality. They can never eliminate it entirely and accounts which neglect to mention the muddle and the unresolvable do less than a service to us all. The theatre reminds us of the essential mystery of life and invites us to think about it. Would that many of our texts on conduct in organizations did the same.

Part of that penultimate sentence may not be in accord with your experience. We do not simply think in the theatre. It will be even less in accord if your experience has been in theatres (or, for that matter, in front of screens), where actors schooled in 'the method' (or derivations of it) have performed. For Stanislavski, remember, the actor must become the role he or she is playing. The better the actor, the greater your identification with the part he or she is playing and the less your opportunity for conscious reflection. It is with Brecht rather than Stanislavski that the enacted image may be separated from the performer. Brecht had very different ideas about the nature of the theatre and about acting. Given his interest in oriental forms of drama, he was able to evolve a performance theory whereby the audience is invited to stand apart from the character depicted upon the stage. Galileo, the character, is, as it were, not one with the actor; we are not invited to empathize with him. Rather the enacted image of Galileo is distanced both from the audience and from the performer. It is offered as *a* definition, but not *the* definition. It is placed between the actor and the audience and communally constructed by both. The character invites both intellectual and emotional consideration. It is distanced. Not distanced in the same manner as 'flat' characters are distanced — abstract and predetermined. Rather a complex being but one presented in such a way that there is space to view, to feel and to think, to be open to alternative possibilities. Brecht, like Shakespeare, does not close the circle — indeed he draws attention to the opening and invites us all to offer our own interpretations.

We need to spend a little time on this self-conscious approach to theatre. Brecht purposefully breaks the dramatic mystification, as do a great number of contemporary dramatists. Not that this is a radically new departure: medieval drama is non-illusory (the audience knew the performers as butchers, bakers, candlestick-makers) and the conventions of Elizabethan and Jacobean theatre include asides, direct address, plays-within-plays and the like. The audience is reminded that it is watching a play which, while purporting to present reality, is a fiction.

What is different about the twentieth century and hence of particular interest to us is that in the theatre (as, we shall argue, elsewhere), self-consciousness is a persistent and pervasive theme.[3] Indeed, the emphasis upon self and awareness of self, upon reality and appearance, are symptoms of our age. There are no longer any absolutes, 'there is no outer reality, there is only human consciousness, constantly building, modifying, rebuilding new worlds out of its own creativity' (Irving Howe, 1967). Modern man, we are told, creates his own reality. 'If there are no meanings, no values, no source of sustenance or help, then man as creator must invent, conjure up meanings and values, sustenance and succour out of nothing. He is a magician' (Laing, 1967).

Perhaps the best manifestation within a play of the relationship of reality and appearances is the character, for it (as Brecht is quick to illustrate) embodies the great paradox of theatre: Hamlet (or whoever) is an artificial reality. A product of the author's imagination but one with a multiplicity of selves — almost as many as there are of us in the audience. Not that most of us respond to Hamlet with innocence — we 'know' about Hamlet just as we know about autocratic and democratic managers. Many characters — on the social as well as the theatrical stage — as it were pre-exist in our imaginations fed by personal and social preconceptions. On the theatrical stage, what we observe when we go to *Hamlet* is not only a product of our imaginations and that of the author, but also a product of our response to a third party, the actor. This is what makes the analogy so powerful: an author, an actor, members of the audience between them create the character. As in the theatre, so in social and organizational life: every one of us is not simply the product of our 'onli begetters', our parents, but are formed by the responses of others to us and ourselves to them. As characters we are the result — and only the result — of a process of creating, presenting, interpreting and being interpreted.

As characters within an organization, we may well approach the condition of theatricality. Elizabeth Burns (1972), in her book *Theatricality*, argues that the special relationship between audience and actors is one which does not exist in real life. In the theatre, she states, there exists a 'double occasion' consisting of 'two distinct but related modes of interaction — interaction between performers and spectators, and interaction between the characters is the play. . . .' She further argues that in the theatre 'composed behaviour' in the norm, whereas in real life such 'composed behaviour' is equated with role playing for an occasion and hence 'put on', artificial and insincere.

The purpose of this comparison will emerge in a moment when we have introduced one further important difference between the dramatic characters and real flesh and blood individuals. You and I, it is argued, have an existence apart from our actions; Hamlet does not, nor did Dan Archer (whatever his fans may believe). A dramatic character is no more than the sum of its actions:

> A character is shaped and determined towards a given end; that is, the character is what it is because of its function in a specific kind of action. A playwright assigns qualities and traits to a character in a play in order to make probable the actions which he must perform in the play and the words which he must say. The function of the character in the whole action determines the traits and characteristics he must have. . . . (Heffner, 1957)

The real-life individual, on the other hand, is not so determined:

> In the beginning of a human personality, the totality of his life cannot be known in the way in which a playwright knows the totality of action which a character must perform in a play. (Heffner, 1957)

The argument appears to be that in social life the individual possesses attributes that are separate from his action and constitute the essence of his being — his individuality. Hamlet is nothing, in the final analysis, but his actions as realized by an actor, an individual who has his own existence, his own essence. In real life, character precedes action; in the theatre, action illustrates and determines character.

Each of these arguments is specious. Elizabeth Burns's 'double occasion' exists in many areas of social and organizational life as clearly as it does in the theatre. One can readily observe occasions in organizations where performers perform before audiences; indeed, it is difficult to think of circumstances where they do not. Meetings may be seen to involve 'interaction between performers and spectators, and interaction between the characters . . .', with the complication that who is audience, who is performer and character tends to switch around more than is common in the theatre. The extracts with which we opened Chapter 6 of the book illustrate clearly the 'double' nature of the occasion. Michael is almost permanently audience (which, of course, may be seen as his performance) while Tony is audience to the first scene and lead performer in the others. Philip and Barry occupy the stage a great deal of the time, performing in a real and important sense for Derek, who is both star and potential critic.

144

Equally, the distinction Burns seeks to draw between 'composed' behaviour on the stage and the equation of such activity in social/organizational life with artifice is not capable of being sustained. The skill in the theatre, as in social life, is presenting oneself and one's interactions as though they are not 'put on'. A poor performance on the organizational stage, leading to accusations of insincerity and 'play-acting', has its parallels in the theatre. This is not to hold that controlled or composed behaviour does not occur on both kinds of stage: the skill lies in not giving the impression of control and distance. As we have argued earlier, rehearsal enables managers to shape and control their performance in a manner which appears 'natural'.

Finally, the points made by Heffner bring us full circle. Much of modern drama is about 'the dissolution of the ego'. Many of the plays of Pirandello and those who followed him are about the fluid nature of the individual, the inescapable relativity of man's existence. The theme of role playing is as common in the theatre as it has become in commentaries on social life. It is arguable that the social/organizational being is nothing more than a functional being; books on organizational behaviour suggest that it is only an individual's 'specific technical abilities' that matter. To the industrial psychologist and sociologist, we are answerable only to social contracts. There are no moral imperatives. We are what others make of us and they are what we make of them. If, therefore, identity is defined in terms of actions and roles and we deny ourselves essential selves, then we do approach the condition of Hamlet. Like him or like Miss Julie, we become no more than the sum of our actions. The theatrical character, from this perspective, becomes an almost exact representation of its real-life counterpart.

Back to Brecht. If, as we have argued, the condition of the individual is that he is no longer sure of an identity, no longer a character determining action but, as in the drama, a character determined by action but aware, however dimly, of an alternative conception of self, we have a condition which approaches that of the theatre. The metaphor is powerful because the circumstances of the social actor in the twentieth century find an exact parallel in those of the stage actor throughout history. As we have said, the dramatic character is twofold: both an actor and a character. We are or can be intellectually aware of this duality but in the theatre we normally are invited to suspend our knowledge. We are seeing Hamlet, not Stephen Williams. Miss Julie, not Gracie Fields. Now, and here we get to the point at last, some modern playwrights and some directors specifically wish us not to suspend our knowledge and actively invite us to remain aware (or to intermittently become aware) of the duality. By insisting on bifocal vision, the playwright seeks to illustrate the human condition; by emphasizing the distinction between the actor (the essential self) and the character (our role-playing activities). The moment you or I assume a social or organizational role, a duality emerges which is precisely the duality that is present in a dramatic character. Brechtian theatre celebrates theatrical awareness which, we have argued earlier, is the essence of human being.[4]

It is difficult to point to a Brecht in the literature of conduct in organizations, let alone a Shakespeare. We are all too schooled in rational approaches of one kind or another. It is not difficult, on the other hand, to point to characters in organizations who are not entirely circumscribed, who by their actions invite us both to identify with them and reflect upon the events that involve both them and ourselves. True we may, and frequently do, seek to explain their actions by reference to this or that motivation, this or that label: he is a megalomaniac, a workaholic, an idle jack or whatever. Given our education and the range of explanations available to us (we live in a rationalizing era), we may depict ourselves according to a limited number of labels, but occasionally we may just glimpse their inadequacy.

What else needs to be said? Here we are in the theatre observing the setting, taking stock of the properties, the costume, the make-up and the use of space and considering the characters who appear before us. The analogy serves to draw our attention to such things in social life. Interesting, but hardly worthy of so much space. A novel does as much, although it is less concretely realized in front of us. Drama is properly dominated by plot:

> In the drama, all human happiness and misery does and must take the form of action. Otherwise its existence remains unknown, and this is the great difference between the drama and the novel. (Bentley, 1964)

The theatre is not simply about character, flat or open. It is about living. It is about human beings walking, and standing, sitting, talking, shouting, arguing, fighting and *doing*. Santayana puts clearly the issue we are trying to come to terms with:

> Plot is the synthesis of actions, and is a reproduction of those experiences from which our notions of men and things is originally derived; for character can never be observed in the world except as manifested in action. . . . The acts are the data, and the character the inferred principle. (Bentley, 1964)

The theatre presents human relationships — the things men and women do to each other and to themselves. It depicts life as a process, a doing. Not, other than in its least successful forms, as a series of stereotypes but as a set of dynamics. The novel *Lord Jim*, for example, can run to several score of pages focusing on a single character revealing in exhaustive (and, on occasion, exhausting) detail every aspect of an isolated being. Drama is about action and interaction. As Fergusson (1949) notes in *The Idea of a Theater*, in drama 'we seek to grasp the quality of a man's life, by an imaginative effort, *through* his appearance, his words and his deeds'. He quotes the words of Virgil with respect to character: 'it is not perceived save in operation, nor manifested except by its effects, as life (is manifested) in a plant by the green leaves'. Even such a static piece as *Waiting for Godot* is constructed around the principle of relationships while denying that very possibility. We learn about Estragon not only from what he says about himself, but from what others say about him (principally Vladimir), to him (and how he responds) and about what he does (or fails to do).

As in the theatre, so too in life. What we know of Tom, the person whose soliloquy we presented earlier, is inferred not only from what he has to say, it is also constructed from what others say and do in his presence (as well as what he says and does in theirs) and in the actions that he takes. How many times have earnest students of conduct in organizations heard managers declare themselves as firm decision-makers only to witness them crumble in the face of opposition from their colleagues? Again, how often have we received a different slant on a particular character from situation to situation? The theatre reminds us that conduct in organizations is a matter of talking, shouting, persuading, manipulating, fighting, politicking — doing. Not a matter of traits and esoteric pronouncements but of actions, interactions, relationships and dialogue — the essence of conduct. Here is Tom, in a meeting, exercising his memory:

TOM: What about the issue of payment to the electricians?

DICK: What about if?

TOM: I need to know what they get paid. If they are going to play fast and loose with us on this sort of issue, then I propose we respond in kind.

HARRY: I don't follow.

TOM: This may well turn out dirty. If they go on strike, and it looks as though they might, then we must fight back. Telling the press what they earn for doing next to nothing will undercut any sympathy they may have.

HARRY: I see.

TOM: To do that, I need to know exactly what they do earn. I don't have that information.

DICK: I have.

TOM: I know you have and I've been asking for it for some months now. Since August 28th, to be precise. In a meeting in this very room. Still not got it.

DICK: I know.

TOM: Why not, Dick? I've reminded you on at least four occasions. On the 10th of September, on the 18th. . . .

DICK: OK, OK. I know. No need to enumerate each and every occasion.

TOM: But I still do not have the information. Why not, Dick? Why not?

DICK: Because I'm not sure what you will do with it. That's why.
There is a silence. Both look directly at each other. The others present study their papers or otherwise avoid contact with either of the protagonists.

TOM (*in measured tones*): I see. Well, we need to talk about that, don't we. . . .

Our picture of Tom is filled out by the exchange which is shot through with theatrical consciousness. Tom and Dick here are being unusually open with each other and are aware that they are so being. They proceed with caution to confront each other in a manner which is relatively common on stage and in books purporting to deal with training (see the exchange depicted by Wright and Taylor), but is much less common elsewhere. In so exposing aspects of his character, Tom enables us and others to see him more fully and to fill out our picture of him. We discern more of what we take to be him from his talk about himself, events such as the one reproduced above and comments about him made by other characters:

> Tom? He's alright, really . . . his bark is worse than his bite but you've got to hand it to him, he's really turned this place around . . . put a bit of go in it, stirred everyone up a bit. Needed it. No complaints, really . . . except he gets his nose in everywhere. Where he doesn't need to, as well. . . . Can't keep out of the detail, you know. Wants to know the ins and outs of everything. Good example. I'll give you a good example. Drinks cabinets. Hospitality is the name of the game in this game, as you can imagine. Tom's not been here five minutes before he is demanding an inventory from each of us — how much booze have we in our cupboards. Not just the whisky and the brandy — the expensive stuff. The lot. Orange juice, mineral water, bloody tonic. Every last drop of bloody tonic to be accounted for. . . . Stupid, isn't it? Man is fundamentally a puritan. Doesn't like the drinking and tries to control it but won't come out and say he's against it. . . .

Who is Tom, what is he? Those of us who interact with him and those who simply observe construct him in the light of his actions, his interactions and the myriad of statements which occur around him. Sometimes we think we have him, we can pin him down, label him and stick him in the collection; at other times, he eludes us and, no doubt, himself.

In conclusion, we need to say a word or two more about the nature of self and role playing. We have implied in this chapter and elsewhere throughout the book that there are actors and that there are roles to be assumed both on and off the stage. Such an approach is likely to raise issues of authenticity much more quickly than virtually any other we could imagine. The systems metaphor, to be sure, makes us little more than cogs in the wheels but cogs with a degree of integrity. Stating that life is like theatre and character is something constructed out of performance appears to deprive us of essence. Acting is, after all, in the common view feigning and dissembling. As Shaw (1889) puts it:

> In English, acting means shamming. The critic, then, despises the stage as a sham, and the actor as a wretched impostor, disguised in the toga of Caesar, and spouting the words of Shakespeare — a creature with the trappings and the language of a hero, but with the will of a vain mummer. . . .

This is a view which has a long pedigree in literature concerned with theatre and has been at the heart of much of the criticism directed at plays and players and at the use of the theatrical analogy in describing social and organizational conduct (Barish, 1983).[5] Acting, it is maintained, betrays the self and presents false personality; actors pretend to be what they are not and in so doing create problems for us all if such behaviour leaves the stage and becomes common on the streets.

It is, of course, possible to argue that stage actors only fully realize themselves when they assume a part or parts, when they become a character. A point which Shaw (1889) makes with reference to a star performer of the time, Salvini: '. . . he throws himself into them (particular parts) because in them he realizes himself as he never could realize himself in the prosaic parts that are played off the stage. . .'. For the actor, Shaw argues, 'the best part will be that which shows all sides of him and realizes him wholly to us and to himself'. Such a point of view, although expressed in much leaner and more elegant prose, is not a long way from the attitudes of writers such as Blake and Mouton, Wright and Taylor. They consider that there is no lack of authenticity in managers or executives being coached to assume what they, the dramaturges, take to be more effective characters since — they hold — only through effective performance can the managers fully realize themselves.

Stanislavski, perhaps the most influential figure in the area of modern acting practice, was concerned that there be no division between actor and part, self and role. His goal was to teach the actor to experience both himself and his character during rehearsal and performance. To ground the character in the self and the self in the character. What a Stanislavski-trained actor does is to express his own desires and aspects of his own identity in the character he plays on the stage; having done the preliminary work, the actor is free to express himself in the part:

> The difficulty of this aspect of emotional perception is that the actor is now coming to his part not through the text, the words of his role, nor by intellectual analysis or other conscious means of knowledge, but through his own sensations, his own real emotions, his personal life experience. . . . (Stanislavski, 1961)

Difficult, yes, but an approach which does not separate self from role, actor from character, and an approach which has its parallels in the training of managers for organizations. Encounter groups may be characterized as settings in which social actors can explore the nature of themselves and their performance and learn to put more of the former into the latter. Opportunities, that is, for the mask to become the face, for the individual to *be* his or her parts and the actor to become more at ease with the characters performed. Such theories and practices afford us all the chance to claim our actions as authentic or to rejoice in our alienation.

We cannot avoid some comment upon alienation since we ourselves have introduced it here and in our comments upon Brecht. In Brechtian theatre, the actor stands aside from his own emotions and from the character he is seeking to perform; he draws attention to the fact that he is acting, proclaims that what he presents is not an aspect of himself. Actor as observer and critic. By distancing himself from the role played, the Brechtian actor can hold characters up for examination, as it were, draw attention to their stereotypic nature and invite the audience to adopt a highly theatrical consciousness.

The closest organization literature gets to Brecht is, of course, the work of Erving Goffman. His view of us all as performers depicts each of us as not committed to any role but manifest in every role; like the Brechtian actor, we perform and simultaneously hold our performance up for inspection. In *Frame Analysis* (1974), Goffman appears to state that to be recognized as a role or character, the role or characterization must embrace its very theatricality; to do this we must — as audience to particular performances — recognize an actor behind the parts, a face beneath the mask:

> It is hardly possible to talk about the anchoring of doings in the world without seeming to support the notion that a person's acts are in part an expression and outcome of his perduring self, and that this self will be present behind the particular role he plays at any moment. After all, from any and all of our dealings with an individual we acquire a sense of his personality, his character, his quality as a human being. We come to expect that all his acts will exhibit the same style, be stamped in a unique way. . . . (Goffman, 1974)

In considering Tom, for example, as we have been doing in this chapter, we try to catch a glimpse behind his performance as reflective manager, decisive explorer of issues and his apparent obsessive concern with detail of who he really is. Like the Brechtian actor, he allows us to glimpse his face (or so we believe) and it is the face rather than the mask that we take to be him; the self behind the roles, the actor beyond the part. But, says Goffman, such an occasional glimpse is part of the performance — a Brechtian one, to be sure — but

> no reason to think that all these gleanings about himself that an individual makes available, all these pointings from his current situation to the way he is in his other occasions, have anything very much in common. Gleanings about an individual point beyond the situation to what presently will be found in all other gleanings of him, but one cannot say that they point in the same direction, for it is their very nature to make themselves felt as pointing in the same direction. (Goffman, 1974)

When we listen to Tom, what we see is what he wants us to glimpse of the face that lies behind the mask of, say, Tom the workaholic: the face revealed in the talk of personal problems, for example, is actuated by the character he presents to us of himself as hard-working executive; he signals his possession but allows us to infer that he is aware of its consequences, that it is not all there is to him. He allows us to 'glean' something of that which we take to lie beyond the character, to see the alienated actor holding up his role for inspection. It is, of course, entirely possible that this is but another mask, or part of the same one. Thus a head surgeon may play at being just an ordinary, jolly chap — one of the boys — to make his juniors relax and thus perform more effectively. Tom may allow us to see the overworked aspect of his character as part of that character. As Berger puts it:

> This view tells us that man plays dramatic parts in the grand play of society, and that, speaking sociologically, he *is* the masks that he must wear to do so. The human person also appears now in a dramatic context, true to its etymology (persona, the technical term given to the actor's masks in a classical theatre). The person is perceived as a repertoire of roles, each one properly equipped with a certain identity (Berger, 1966)

In the same way that we never really see a Brechtian actor, we never see the real Tom. The Brechtian actor playing Galileo or whoever is, in fact, doubly distant from us; he performs the character and performs the role of commentator upon it. We do not see Simon Callow the person but Simon Callow playing an alienated actor playing Galileo.

Our position is somewhat different from that of Goffman. If, as he and others who think like him appear to assume, we as individuals perform in line with the roles which are made available to us, then it appears necessary to posit our actor beyond these roles; a capacity which enables us to recognize and learn to play roles. Beyond Simon Callow playing an alienated actor playing Galileo, there is Simon Callow, the actor. Beyond Tom playing and embodying in his performance some glimpse of a worried, family-orientated man, there is Tom. Who he really is beyond the roles assumed is not open for exploration utilizing this model; we are simply asserting that there is an actor beyond the repertoire. We are not claiming that the repertoire does not impinge upon the actor.

Stanislavski argued, for instance, that type-casting led to actors being severely restricted, pigeon-holed and ending up in life behaving in line with the parts they play in the theatre. 'That is why even off stage the tragedian looks morose, the comedian cracks jokes, the ingenue goes round being charming, the tragic actress is forever suffering and the dandy talks trivialities' (Stanislavski, 1961). So too with performers on the organizational stage. Here are a couple of conversations we overheard after a training course:

'What kind of a manager are you?'
'9,1 — high on production, low on people. A hard man! (*Laughs*) And you?'
'5,5, me. Neither one nor the other!'
'Bullshit! You are a 10,0 — you're off the bloody scale!'
'My back-up style is to be too soft on people, a bit too *laissez-faire.*'
'You need to do something about that. If anything, I'm too hard. . . .'

Such conversations are intended to have consequences; the analysis of character — superficial as it may be — is part of a process whereby the actors are encouraged to become more 'effective', more 9,9, more production *and* people orientated. To learn the roles and become them.

Acting, assuming a character, be that a flat or an open one, is not radically different from the art of living and working in organizations, but it is not all there is to life and work. Simmel (1973) puts it well:

> To play a part, not just a hypocrisy or as deceit, but in terms of the involvement of the individual's life in a single expressive form which is entered upon in some pre-exisiting, pre-determined way, is part and parcel of the way in which our everyday life is constituted. Such a role may be appropriate to our individual self, but it is nevertheless something other than this individuality and not an intrinsic part of its external and unitary being.

We would differ only in detail, but significant detail. For us the actor, the individuality, is bound up with the roles; the unitary being that is Tom, Dick, Harry, Frank or whatever is a unity of actor and performance — who he *is* and what he *does*. Persons play roles and have a degree of freedom in choosing them. To be a person is not itself to play a role, just as to be an actor is not to be a particular character. Each, however, person and actor, is affected by what they do and doing always involves the assumption of roles. It does not follow that particular characterizations and performances are somehow not authentic, not expressive of some true self. It is probable that we are, in fact, most fully ourselves when we fully realize a character, even where that character signals a degree of distance from the performances he or she undertakes.

The theatrical metaphor, in allowing us to explore the nature of others and their roles, enables us to comment upon performance everywhere. It enables us to ask questions about the nature of our commitment; do we play roles on both the social and organizational stages which are representations of our real selves, expressive, in Cicourel's terms, of some 'deep structure', or are we simply role players simulating some sense of self? Is the actor an empty creature attuning himself to the winds of situations or is there something more to us than that? In the literature of both the stage and social life, the actor is seen as both authentic performer and as empty vessel.

Chapter 9

More than Words can Witness

Many years ago Goethe declared that a performance, any performance, must be considered as a collaboration between actors and audience: 'The stage and the auditorium, the actors and the spectators, together constitute the whole' (see *Poetics Today*, Spring 1981). Recently a number of writers have taken up this point and elaborated upon it. Steinbeck (1970), for example, notes that 'theatre does not exist as a "thing" with a fixed locus, but rather as a progression with the character of an event. Theatre is dependent upon the spectator and his presence and intentional collaboration.' Lazarowicz (1977) goes even further and talks of a 'triadic collusion': 'Actors, authors and playgoers all participate in their own way in creating the fictional world on the stage.' The *author* drafts a unique system of literary signs, normally a play, which is not addressed to readers, but to playgoers and actors. The *actors*, normally under the guidance and supervision of a director, transpose all this system of literary signs into a system of theatre-signs which comprise verbal and non-verbal elements. The *playgoers'* activity, however, consists in their observing the dramatic information in an attitude of 'external concentration, of apperceiving and structuring it, in understanding, experiencing and finally making it part of their fund of aesthetic knowledge. Such sensory, imaginative and rational playgoing activities are an essential part of what constitutes theatre. They are understood as a specific manifestation of "work in progress". That is a triadic collusion' (Lazarowicz, 1977).

In this chapter we wish to concentrate upon the playgoers' activity; furthermore, we wish to draw the parallel between that activity and that of the student of behaviour in organizations who also must adopt an attitude of 'external concentration', must apperceive and structure, must understand and experience and make what he observes part of his own knowledge if he is to be reckoned literate in such matters. Moving between stage and social life (as throughout) we will try to capture the more holistic nature of that which transpires between actors and audience, those who behave in organizations and those, having witnessed what transpires, seek to set it down.

We actually know very little about the nature of performance, either on-stage or off. The reasons for this ignorance are straightforward: a theatrical performance takes place over, say, a couple of hours, is usually complex in its structure and employs a great variety of means of expression — stage design, costumes, properties, make-up, lighting, music, mime, gesture, speech.[1] A 'scene' in an organization, such as any of those we have discussed in this book, is often part of a nested set of scenes, as it were, stretching back and forward in time and it too relies upon a great variety of means of transmission of its message or messages (assuming, for the moment, that it has one). To analyse, let alone synthesize, such presentations is an enormous undertaking; what follows is folly. This is an attempt to present first an extract from a play followed by a more holistic analysis than we have attempted up until now, and then a similar effort directed towards a fuller understanding of an episode deriving from within an organization.

Scene III of *Betrayal* by Harold Pinter.[2] Jerry and Emma are in the flat they have shared as lovers for some years. As audience, we know from Scene I that Emma has told Jerry that she has informed Robert, her husband (and Jerry's best friend), of the affair. We know from Scene II that Robert and Jerry have discussed the matter and Robert has told Jerry that he has known of it for years. This information confuses Jerry who was told in the previous scene that the confession was very recent. Scene III is set three years *before* these events and, given what we have heard in the previous scenes, we, as audience, are aware that was when the affair came to an end. They talk about the difficulties of meeting and then:

EMMA: It's a waste. Nobody comes here. I just can't bear to think about it, actually. Just . . . empty. All day and night. Day after day and night after night. I mean the crockery and the curtains and the bedspread and everything. And the tablecloth I brought from Venice. (*Laughs*) It's ridiculous.

Pause

It's just . . . an empty home.

JERRY: It's not a home.

Pause

I know . . . I know what you wanted . . . but it could never . . . actually be a home. You have a home. I have a home. With curtains, etcetera. And children. Two children in two homes. There are no children here, so it's not the same kind of home.

EMMA: It was never intended to be the same kind of home. Was it?

Pause

You didn't even see it as a home, in any sense, did you?

JERRY: No, I saw it as a flat . . . you know.

EMMA: For fucking.

JERRY: No, for loving.

EMMA: Well, there's not much of that left, is there?

154

Silence

JERRY: I don't think we don't love each other.

Pause

EMMA: Ah well.

Pause

What will you do about the . . . furniture?

JERRY: What?

EMMA: The contents.

Silence

JERRY: You know we can do something very simple, if we want to do it.

EMMA: You mean sell it to Mrs Banks for a small sum and . . . and she can let it as a furnished flat?

JERRY: That's right. Wasn't the bed here?

EMMA: What?

JERRY: Wasn't it?

EMMA: We bought the bed. We bought everything. We bought the bed together.

JERRY: Ah. Yes.

Emma stands.

EMMA: You'll make all the arrangements, then? With Mrs Banks?

Pause

I don't want anything. Nowhere I can put it, you see. I have a home, with tablecloths and all the rest of it.

JERRY: I'll go into it, with Mrs Banks. There'll be a few quid, you know, so . . .

EMMA: No, I don't want any *cash*, thank you very much.

Silence. She puts coat on.

I'm going now.

He turns, looks at her.

Oh here's my key.

Takes out keyring, tries to take key from ring.

Oh Christ.

Struggles to take key from ring. Throws him the ring.

You take it off.

He catches it, looks at her.

Can you do it, please? I'm picking up Charlotte from school. I'm taking her shopping.

He takes key off.

Do you realize this is an afternoon? It's the Gallery's afternoon off. That's why I'm here. We close every Thursday afternoon. Can I have my keyring?

He gives it to her.

Thanks. Listen. I think we've made absolutely the right decision.

She goes.

He stands.

(*From* Betrayal, *by* Harold Pinter, *Published by* Methuen, London, *and reprinted with permission.*)

The first thing to be noted is that Pinter's plays (as everyone else's) play better than they read. In the hands of competent actors and given some willingness to work on the part of the audience, each one of them should experience the kind of objectification of feeling we talked about in Chapter 6. We will return to what this may be in a moment, for the present we wish to emphasize the obvious. As we have indicated earlier, appearances on stage are important; it is likely that in the theatre we will focus closely upon the setting and upon the costumes worn by the performers. This may well tell us something about what is going on. They may not. The bed on the set is always something more than that: a bed. In fact it is referred to by Emma as something they bought together — a symbol of their sharing, forgotten or denied by Jerry. The tablecloth brought from Venice is also singled out and possibly also has some importance. No one says anything about the carpet, however, or the pictures on the wall. We do not wish to labour the point; as audience we recognize the objects on stage and are prepared to consider them as real-life functional objects and wherever it is signalled to us that it is appropriate (by lighting, gesture, reference or whatever), we are prepared to invest them with meaning. We are, that is, attentive to such possibilities.

This much we have already presented earlier. A further important feature of our attention is the nature of the actors. Actors, like each of us, have certain relatively stable features such as age, sex, physique and voice. To be sure, in the theatre these features can be and are altered but with very few exceptions, some aspects of the person remain visible through the character. We are aware at one level that it is Jeremy Irons who is playing Jerry and Patricia Routledge playing Emma. To be sure, we accept them as characters but are also aware of them as persons. They have attributes, often but not exclusively physical, that we admire or dislike; the late Sir Michael Redgrave's support for left-wing causes may have presented a problem to us in his role as Tory landowner, Elizabeth Taylor's physical characteristics may be a good reason for going to the theatre whatever part she is playing. What is clear is that the notion of a person playing a part is a powerful feature of the stage. Despite the injunctions of theoreticians such as Edward Gordon Craig, we do not flock to witness marionettes or puppets enact dramas. What we go to see are 'live' performers whose characteristics penetrate and interact with the fictitious parts they present. As audience, we are aware of the precarious nature of the theatrical event and physically, experientially aware of the personality of the performer as he tackles the part: 'The means and techniques of the theatre are too deeply rooted in life to let the natural signs be completely eliminated. In an actor's diction and mime, the strictly personal habits go with the voluntarily created shades of meaning, the conscious gestures are intermingled with reflexes' (Passow, 1981).

Going to the theatre is not like reading a book; the stage is a place — like life — where warm bodies contribute to the rhetoric largely by design, but occasionally and unavoidably by accident. The physical presence of actors is an important feature of the theatre, they create a focus for our attention and they respond to that attention in a manner which has a number of parallels in social life.

None of this is available to you as reader of this book. You are not privy to the setting and no amount of descriptive prose from us can fully make up for that, nor are you in the presence of the actors. Still less are you witness to the non-verbal communication that undoubtedly is an important feature of both social and theatrical presentation. Again, this is not a feature that we wish to dwell upon at great length, since there exists a substantial amount of literature. It is perhaps sufficient to note that a great deal of time is spent in interactions with others at a non-verbal level and that the evaluation of many spoken statements is dependent to a great degree on the behaviour of the person making it. For, taking into account the more limited possibilities for consciously influencing non-verbal behaviour, the recipient of contradictory information will, first and foremost, believe the information conveyed through non-verbal channels. Jerry may declare, as he does, that 'I don't think that we don't love each other', convoluted though that expression is, we as audience, will scrutinize his face, his body, his every gesture, to see whether or not they strengthen, refine or deny that message. The actor is aware, just as the rest of us are aware, that control of messages 'given off' is as important as control of the messages 'given'.

The notion that gesture has a value deeper than words has a long theatrical pedigree. In early theories of acting, the view was taken that gesture and facial expression were the direct consequence of feeling one of the key dramatic passions. There were thought to be ten: joy, grief, fear, anger, pity, scorn, hatred, jealousy, wonder and love, each distinguished 'by their outward marks in action'. John Hill (1755), for example, sees such gestures as the essence of man, well beyond words in their ability to put people in direct contact with each other. Gestures, he holds, have been 'dictated by nature's self, and are common to all mankind. The language of signs we all speak without having been taught it. . . .'[3]

As audience, we watch, we scrutinize, we listen. The words are, of course, important. What we apperceive is indeed 'more than words can witness', but without the words it would certainly be less. We selected Pinter as our example because the words are, on the surface, banal and the dialogue apparently aimless. Some refer to it as inane, even absurd. Deprived of the setting, the costumes, the corporal presence of the actors, the average reader finds it difficult to make sense of his meanderings. But the words are important.

'I am pretty well obsessed with words when they get going. . . . It is a matter of tying the words to the image of the character standing on the stage. The two things go very closely together. . . .' (Kennedy, 1975). Pinter plays are always concerned with the fumbling attempts of two or more characters to mark out contested territory with words: Emma seeks to have her reading of the affair and its present state prevail, Jerry to have his.

157

To appreciate Pinter, one has to recognize a couple of things. The first and the more commonplace is that we experience and can only experience his work through *listening* to the way that everyday language (such as he employs) is deflected by and alienates those who use it. In Boulton's words:

> Evocative or disturbing speech, language which is an accurate reflection of colloquial English and yet reflects the mystery that Pinter sees as an inevitable feature of human relationships: this is a starting point for a consideration of his vision. It leads directly to what is perhaps the chief irony in his plays: the discrepancy between the implicit claim in any *patois* that it is the currency accepted and understood by all its users, and the dramatic fact that all such language in actual usage reveals not complete communication between man and man but their essential apartness. (Boulton, 1963)

For all the apparent banality of the exchange between Emma and Jerry, there is real communication. Less obvious and more important in the present context is the stress Pinter lays upon the ambiguity of dialogue, on the growth of language out of what is 'unexpressive, elusive, evasive, obstructive, unwilling' in his characters. He is also concerned with the conscious exploration of a 'language where under what is said, another thing is being said' (Brown, 1965).

In Pinter, as in few other playwrights, there is nearly always a clear separation between the surface dialogue and the deeper structure of the play. In melodrama, it is all surface — Rosina says what she means and Mendon declares his evil nature for all of us to witness. Even in Shakespeare and Ibsen, for the most part things are what they are announced to be. There is something rotten in the state of Denmark and we are explicitly told so, and even where we are not told directly, the undertow of the play is matched to the surface current. Not so in Pinter. Emma and Jerry talk of furniture, of tablecloths, children and keys, but in so doing not only do they drive a deeper wedge between themselves, but also conceal, or seek to conceal, their feelings from each other. The sub-text of the play is about 'betrayal', who has been and is deceiving whom. The surface words evoke and provoke and yet shut off discussion around the issue. Emma implies that Jerry's betrayal consists in not having accepted the apartment as a 'home', he replies that there is no deceit since 'No, I saw it as a flat . . . you know.' Conflicts do rise to the surface in Pinter, often with the force of an eruption as they do here: 'For fucking.' All the talk of crockery and bedspreads, tablecloths, homes and children and, suddenly, the shocking. A couple of exchanges later, we are back to apparent inanity, but we are left in no doubt that something significant has been addressed, however inadequately, however temporarily:

EMMA: For fucking.
JERRY: No, for loving.
EMMA: Well, there's not much of that left, is there?
Silence.

158

JERRY: I don't think that we don't love each other.
Pause
EMMA: Ah well.
Pause
        What will you do about all the . . . furniture?

In Pinter as, we shall argue, in life, such moments of encounter are few, brief and unresolved. They are compressed, while the trivia are extended almost to the point of pain. Matters of great import to us all, of great pitch and moment, are often beyond words; we can but approach them in brief and with understatement. The silences and the pauses, the looks and the gestures, the set of the body, the stillness of the set all contribute to such moments. Pinter knows it, so too — we shall argue — at a deep, non-reflective level, do Tom and Dick in their encounter which we shall consider in some detail shortly.

Before so doing, one or two other points about Pinter need to be made. To do so, we need to address the final few lines of the scene.

JERRY: I'll go into it with Mrs Banks. There will be a few quid, you know,
        so . . .
EMMA: No, I don't want any *cash*, thank you very much.
Silence. She puts coat on.
        I'm going now.
He turns, looks at her.
        Oh here's my key.
Takes out keyring, tries to take key from ring.
        Oh Christ.
Struggles to take key from ring. Throws him the ring.
        You take it off.
He catches it, looks at her.
        Can you do it, please? I'm picking up Charlotte from school. I'm
        taking her shopping.
He takes key off.
        Do you realize this is an afternoon? It's the Gallery's afternoon off.
        That's why I'm here. We close every Thursday afternoon. Can I
        have my keyring?
He gives it to her.
        Thanks. Listen. I think we've made absolutely the right decision.
She goes.
He stands.

Echoes of the relationship abound. Emma's reaction to the notion of *cash* is, at a sub-textual level, a matter of relationship. She is affronted by the notion of *cash* being associated with what they have shared, Jerry less so. Payment makes her a whore; the offer, whatever its intent, divides and distresses. Another brief, illuminating eruption. And then the business with the keyring. There can be no doubt about the symbolic nature of this particular property: the means of entrance to their shared 'home'. Emma cannot remove the key from the ring but nor can she betray her feelings:

EMMA: You take it off.
He catches it and looks at her.

The actors must know what they are seeking to communicate to each other and to us, it is not a matter of any old look, the fumbling with the keyring, the attempt to communicate at a level beyond words, will tell each of them and us something about the relationship. Seven years of afternoons are coming to an end in this brief, isolated piece of action, the removal of a key from a ring. It is unbearable for Emma, who feels betrayed and used, but to protect herself she must deceive Jerry as to her present feelings.

EMMA: Can you do it please? (*Straight into the banal.*) I'm picking up Charlotte from school. I'm taking her shopping. (*The notion of afternoons and their previous association none the less breaks through.*) Do you realize this is an afternoon? It's the Gallery's afternoon off. That's why I'm here. We close every Thursday afternoon. Can I have my keyring? (words in parentheses are supplied)
He gives it to her.

One final deceit is necessary, one more betrayal:

EMMA: Thanks. Listen. I think we've made absolutely the right decision.'
She goes.
He stands.

Our contention is that by eschewing the exchange of accusation, by avoiding high-flown language about the nature of love and the pain of the ending of an affair, by enshrining the deep emotions within the surface banality, Pinter (in the hands of good performers) communicates with us powerfully. His work has an intricate dynamic pattern; the words, the faces, the simple actions, the pauses and the inactions, the tensions and the resolutions form a pattern which resonates with our own experiences. The form, the pattern and shape of his work match and evoke the content. What he has to say cannot be said in any other way, as our own struggles to express his 'meaning' cannot fail to have demonstrated.

The exchange between Tom and Dick which we introduced in Chapter 8 will serve as an example from conduct in organizations. It too plays better than it reads, certainly in the hands of performers as skilled as these two. To save unnecessary skipping back and forth between chapters, here is the exchange once more:

TOM:	What about the issue of payment to the electricians?
DICK:	What about it?
TOM:	I need to know what they get paid. If they are going to play fast and loose with us on this sort of issue, then I propose we respond in kind.
HARRY:	I don't follow.
TOM:	This may well turn out dirty. If they go on strike, and it looks as though they might, then we must fight back. Telling the press what they earn for doing next to nothing will undercut any sympathy they may have.
HARRY:	I see.
TOM:	To do that, I need to know exactly what they do earn. *I* don't have that information. (*He looks at Dick.*)
DICK:	I have.
TOM:	I know you have and I've been asking for it for some months now. Since August 28th, to be precise. In a meeting in this very room. Still not got it.
DICK:	I know. (*Pause*)
TOM:	Why not, Dick? (*Pause*) I've reminded you on at least four occasions. (*Pause*) On the 10th of September, on the 18th. . . .
DICK:	OK, OK. I know. No need to enumerate each and every occasion. (*Pause*)
TOM:	But I still do not have the information. Why not, Dick? Why not?
DICK:	Because I'm not sure what you will do with it. That's why. *There is a silence. Both look directly at each other. The others present study their papers or otherwise avoid contact with either of the protagonists.*
TOM	(*in measured tones*): I see. Well, we need to talk about that, don't we. . . .

In considering this passage, as with the one drawn from Pinter, we wish to extend an invitation to treat it in terms of its performance potential. The passage does not exist outside space and time, like a poem or a song, but is embedded in them, replete with spatial and temporal implications. Tom and Dick have a history, have a relationship which goes back a long way and here, as elsewhere, whatever they say will affect the future of that relationship. The sequence is intensely dramatic in the sense that Langer sees the essence of drama as the future always unfolding in the action shown:

> Drama, though it implies past action (the 'situation'), moves not towards the present, as narrative does, but towards something beyond; it deals essentially with commitments and consequences. Persons, too, in drama are purely agents — whether consciously or blindly, masters of the future. This future, which is made before our eyes, given importance to the very beginnings of dramatic acts, i.e. to the motives from which the acts arise, and the situations in which they develop; . . . It has been said repeatedly that the theatre creates

a perpetual present moment; but it is only a present filled with its own future that is really dramatic. (Langer, 1957)

Commitments and consequences; the very beginnings of dramatic acts, a present filled with its own future. . . . One can almost sense the temporal aspects of what we see occurring before us; the duration of the sequence, although in terms of actual time brief, seems almost painfully long; in a two-hour meeting perhaps, what, two minutes at most spent on this interaction but two minutes that they and we will remember. Like Pinter's comments about love, it flickers and dies, but while it burns, it burns fiercely and brightly. There is a rhythm to the passage: the introduction, the build (to the question 'Why not, Dick? Why not?') and the communication ('Because I'm not sure what you will do with it. That's why.'). With the silence that follows, the tension is gradually allowed to diminish, but a new build is implied in Tom's 'I see. Well, we need to talk to each other about that, don't we. . . .'

The scene also has a tempo, in this case a relatively slow one. Tempo is clearly related to duration but refers specifically to the number of incidents occurring per unit of time. The sequence lasts two minutes but has but a couple of incidents: a challenge to Dick by Tom and a denial of information to Tom by Dick. One can imagine a sequence lasting two minutes but full of incidents which would give the impression of a great deal happening very quickly. Here something significant happens in what appears to be a very measured space of time. The very lack of incident slows the tempo and dramatizes the denial in a singular and startling fashion.

In terms of the space, we must imagine it, since where this happened is as important as when (in terms of time) it happened. 'In this very room. . . .' The meeting room adjacent to the managing director's office. A place where management meetings take place, where the integrative activity of the organization is meant to be realized. What happens in private offices, in cars or aeroplanes, in lifts or canteens, is qualitatively different from the setting which, in Burke's (1969b) terms, 'both *realistically reflects* the course of action and *symbolizes* it'. For Dick to deny Tom the information he demands in the privacy of his own office is a very different matter from doing it here in this room in the presence of his colleagues. The setting in social life, no less than on the stage, is not just some piece of decoration to be ignored but is part of the process of apprehension, embodying meaning. The fact that the challenge and the denial occur in this room with the people around has specific and telling attributes. In effect, Tom is asking, 'Dare you, Dick, take me on in public in a circumstance and setting where my management authority is evident?' and Dick slowly but ineluctably answers: 'Yes'.

In a sequence such as this (as with the extract from Pinter), every detail is important. Tom, for example, displays his character in all its glory; he is controlled, he is calm and he is precise: 'I've reminded you on at least four occasions. (*Pause*) On the 10th September, on the 18th. . . .' He is also careful to explain to the audience, Harry, just why he needs the information. The scene, however, is not about getting the information. Or rather *in our view* the scene is not a matter of Tom getting Dick to give him the figures. The explanation that we would hazard is that the 'objective', the 'sub-text' of what is happening here may be expressed as Tom seeking to find out why Dick will not give the figures. In a sense, whatever Tom says to the contrary to Harry, he does not want the figures, he wants to know why he does not have and cannot get them. If there is a unifying principle to this sequence, this is it; to be sure, there may be other things going on but for us the complexity of the sequence is underpinned by Tom's wish to explore his relations with Dick. 'Why will he not provide me with the information? What is going on between us that he will deny me in this setting?'

Having produced the answer, Tom must consider the implications of it. He must determine whether or not he proceeds to explore the issue of trust that is now on the table. The electricians have served their purpose, a new and possibly more fraught sequence may be about to occur; whether it does or not (and it does not), the relationship has undergone a change and all concerned are aware of it. There is a silence. Both look directly at each other. The others present study their papers or otherwise avoid contact with either of the protagonists. Feeling has been emblematized. A relationship has been expressed.

It should be clear that recourse to the theatre as a source of analogy provides us with space not usually found in other analogies. It affords us, for example, with the opportunity to introduce naturally and readily into our analyses non-verbal means of expression. As in the theatre, so in social life. Many appear to adopt a posture somewhat similar to Hill's (1961) in that they believe that which is 'given off' to be more telling than that which is 'given' or said. Our good friends Wright and Taylor (1984) are somewhat ambivalent about it, claiming on the one hand that 'there is evidence that the less obvious non-verbal clues, such as body posture, provide a more accurate indication of an individual's true feelings', but on the other hand noting 'the fact that someone is displaying an emotion need not necessarily indicate that they are *genuinely* experiencing it'. As closet dramaturgists, however, they recognize the importance of performance: '. . . being a nice person is not a skill. But success at showing you are a nice person so convincingly does reflect a skill.' Ensuring that there is no inconsistency between verbal and non-verbal messages is for them, and many others, the essence of the skill.[4] Human communication does not take place simply or even often through the medium of words. None the less, it would be quite silly to believe that since 'vocalization' occupies a relatively small part of our time, it is relatively unimportant. We in no way wish to deny the physical effect of non-vocal signs in the theatre or elsewhere, but we do not wish to claim, Artaud-like, that there is nothing but direct sensory experience. To be sure, characters on the stage command our attention by the space they occupy, the settings in which they appear and the costumes in which they are clothed. They do so in life also. The chancellor of the university addressing the graduands in the Assembly Rooms at Bath is an imposing figure, but what he *says* can either maintain, enhance or diminish his authority. Should he stammer his way through some ill-conceived address, the occasion, however splendid the trappings, however high the expectations, will be rendered nugatory. One of us many years ago attended a poetry reading by T. S. Eliot which may serve to reinforce this point. Eliot was introduced by Empson, a famous critic and writer, who, rather than confirming expectations for such an event and briefly but cogently making way for the great poet, instead used the occasion to ramble on about his (Empson's) tax problems on returning to the United Kingdom from sojourn abroad. His speech, and indeed his language, stuck as it were in the banalities of his relations with the revenue, was clearly out of joint with the occasion.

The management of organizations is a performing art, an important aspect of that is the shaping of direction and the marshalling of support through appropriate rhetoric. Anthony's famous 'Friends, Romans, countrymen' speech has many a resonance in organizations where a high premium is put upon speaking intelligibly and persuasively.

To understand this issue of language or rhetoric, we can rewrite the extract in which Tom, Dick and Harry figure so prominently; the setting remains the same, and the context, but the kind of verbal display may radically alter our view of the interaction:

TOM: What about the issue of payment to the electricians?

DICK: What about it? It does not seem that the matter of payment to the electricians is a matter of concern to this group here and now. It seems to me that matters of industrial relations — amongst which I include payment systems — are within my brief and no more open to debate here than what kind of programmes Harry does or should make.

TOM: Well, I do believe that is a matter of more general concern and I am very disturbed that despite repeated attempts to discover what the electricians are paid, I have not been successful. You, Dick, are with-holding the information and I do not understand why.

DICK: Quite simple, really. I do not trust you with that information. I believe that you will misuse it and cause us further problems which I will have to spend time and energy dealing with. . . .

It is evident that such a passage, although ostensibly about the same issue, is qualitatively different from the version we offered previously. We can infer that the relations between Tom and Dick are much less tense in this passage than in the earlier one, that both can be relatively open and direct and that neither needs recourse to the procedure of 'by indirections finding directions out'. Dick denies Tom the information but requires little prompting to explain his denial. The words and phrases reveal differences clearly and unambiguously, just as in the earlier extract they also revealed tensions and uncertainties. None the less, the words must be seen in context; even this image of an open and frank relationship may be vitiated by a setting and a series of non-verbal clues that undercut or fail to reinforce the words. What is said must always be placed in context. Tom and Dick may, for example, be modelling a degree of openness for the purpose of forcing Harry to do the same with regard to his programme-making activities, or they may be acting out this version of their relationship for the benefit of an audience (some other executive or, say, a consultant). The words and phrases used may give us a clue, but the action is always and inevitably embedded in a context which has dimension stretching backward and forward in time, just as in the theatre a scene may both echo and foreshadow that which has been and is to be.

A further example may serve to confirm this crucial point. Here is another senior manager, Tony, talking to a number of his executives about objectives:

TONY: It seems appropriate to bring up the matter of objectives at this juncture. I've been working on mine — the company's, really — what we are to do over the next six months, and I would like to share them with you. OK?

BOB: Yes. Sounds like a good idea.

ERIC: Yes. I'd be interested to see them.
(John says nothing, neither does Michael.)

TONY: Just a flavour . . . we can look at them in detail on another occasion. (*He goes to the overhead projector with a slide and flashes a list of objectives up.*) You can see I've organized them so as to reflect what is to be done overall and — on the right — who is to be involved in it.

BOB: And that's supposed to match up with what we spell out as our objectives, is it? That on the right links in with what we spell out separately and individually?

TONY: Yes. I've identified what are key issues to me — to the company overall — what I need to be paying attention to, and flagged up what that means to you.

BOB: Means to each of us?

TONY: Yes.

ERIC: Each of us has to have a set of objectives?

TONY: Well, it doesn't make sense if we don't. . . .

ERIC: I agree, but you are expecting something like this from each of us in this room?

TONY: Yes.

BOB: Presumably linked to yours and the strategies for our separate areas of responsibility?

TONY: Yes.

BOB: So we will need to have agreed our strategy documents before this can be implemented? Seems like a good plan to me.

ERIC: Yes. First rate.

TONY: Well, it's a step forward, isn't it? A step in the right direction.

BOB:	You seem pleased with yourself.
TONY:	I am, I am. It's been a struggle but we're all getting there.
BOB:	All we need now is a strategic document for every area and we are off and running.
TONY:	Yes. (*Pause*) Yes, that's the case.
ERIC	(*innocently*): Who has to provide that? I've seen Bob's and you have mine. . . .
TONY:	Michael's I've seen and he is about to go public.
MICHAEL:	Yes. (*Pause. John does not look up, does not volunteer anything.*)
BOB:	So we all have to have something? By when, Tony?
TONY:	Oh. Well, within the next couple of weeks, I would suggest. (*Pause*)
BOB:	Are we agreeing to do that, then? Each one of us to follow that format up there?
ERIC:	Within our respective strategy documents.
BOB:	Within our strategy. . . .
ERIC:	Those of us who have done them. . . . (*All eyes are upon John, who eventually looks up.*)
JOHN:	Yes. Yes. If someone will tell me what is expected of me in terms of a strategy document — yes. . . .

The exchanges continue. The point about the extract is not the resolution but the fact that the interaction cannot be understood without regard to the context. Were we to be an audience to previous exchanges, we would know that Tony's objectives were influenced by both Bob and Eric working through a third party. We would know that without this influence, Tony would not have got himself organized enough to talk of strategy and objectives. We would know that some of the words and phrases flashed up on the screen are words and phrases they supplied. This approval of the process, therefore, and their pretence that what they see is new and fresh to them takes on a different meaning when we are aware of this than when we are not aware. Furthermore, we would also know from previous exchanges that they, Bob and Eric, are aware that John has not prepared a strategy document and is hostile to the idea that he should. Bob and Eric (and we as audience) consider from what they know of Tony that he is unlikely to instruct John to prepare such a document, so they manœuvre the present circumstances so as to place both John and Tony in a corner. Clearly, therefore, this scene has aspects which tie it back to previous scenes and previous settings while containing within it the future. From the moment Bob says, 'Yes. Sounds like a good idea', and is supported by Eric, we as audience can see that the object is not only to reinforce Tony but also to flush out John. It could well be that he sees it also; it could also be conceivable that Tony does. By the end of the sequence, he is aware that he is being driven towards confronting John and avoids it.

There is, of course, a much greater richness to such exchanges than we have space or inclination to explore. Whether or not one finds such accounts interesting or credible is beside the point, what matters is the insight into the processes by which language *in context* defines action and character. We know what we do of Emma and Jerry in part because of what they say about themselves, about each other and to each other (we also learn something about them from what they say to Robert, but that is another variation on a similar theme). We know about Tom and Dick from their interactions, what they say and do not say, the hints and indiscretions, just as we know (or think we know) about Barry, Philip and Derek. We constitute ourselves and others through dialogue, but dialogue which always recurs in the context of that which precedes and succeeds it; that which has occurred and is about to happen.

By now, some of you will be protesting — and rightly so — that what we *read into* these extracts is a matter of *interpretation*. Some may regard our activities as unnecessary — the dialogue speaks for itself — or as illegitimate. Our position is that not only is the act of interpretation necessary and legitimate, it is inevitable. We 'apperceive' and we 'structure', we are part of the 'triadic collusion'. To explain why this should be so, we need to return briefly to Emma and Jerry. When they *speak* the lines, when they enunciate the little squiggles on the page, they interpret. There is no neutral way of pronouncing Pinter, since we as audience presume that if we are shown 'neutrality', it signifies. All of us in the theatre, *as elsewhere*, begin with what we find on the stage (theatre or social). The setting, the shape and size of the actor, the colour of her hair (Emma as a blonde signals something different from Emma as a brunette), whether or not the character wears a Fair Isle slip-over. Everything we perceive is interpretation, whether or not it is so intended. Everything. Including these squiggles on this page.

Return to the extracts quoted earlier for a moment. What is observable there is a mass of marks; an exercise in typography. As the passage is read, the reader relates the marks to past experience and, given a certain level of knowledge as to how people use words, discerns that the person(s) uttering the remarks signified by the squiggles on the page meant such and such. The inference *you* as reader make may or may not coincide with that *we* draw. Such a possibility confirms our position: there is no meaning inherent in the squiggles; rather, we *make sense*.

An actor playing Jerry, Emma or, for that matter, Tom or Dick, must decide what it is he or she is to seek to convey to an audience. There is no question of simply 'letting the words speak for themselves'; suppression of colour, emphasis or whatever is a choice and is, therefore, willy-nilly an interpretation. As we have shown in our discussion above, the speed at which something is said, as well as the context in which it is said, causes us to treat it in a manner which it would not warrant if delivered at a different pitch or pace. Actors — stage and social — choose to say things in a particular manner and with particular emphases. They may choose this way or that way. There is no non-way. Making sense is an interactive process and is constructed between playwright, performer and audience.

To this point we have avoided the third element of the triad: the playwright. In the theatre, more often than not there is a text which performers interpret and in so doing give us as audience some clues as to how to interpret ourselves. There are few such obvious texts in social and organizational life. In the next chapter we will address this issue; a fundamental one since the text strongly influences the action and limits the interpretation that may be put upon it.

We need, however, to reiterate a point in concluding this chapter. In a very real sense, we have been unable to demonstrate the strengths of the holistic approach recourse to the theatrical metaphor affords us. We have been reduced to presenting squiggles on paper. In presenting extracts from plays and from performances in real life, we do violence to the method of apprehension appropriate to either plays or real life. Reading involves us in a primarily cerebral activity; we look at the words on the pages and infer from them *imaginatively* and *indirectly* (mediated by vocabulary and experience) what it is that is going on. In practice the process is usually quite rapid and goes unnoticed; in extracts such as we have presented, the effort required is noticeable and the processes of inference markedly slower than we would find in responding to much of what we read. We have made it the more so by explicitly attending to the processes which produce understanding, highlighting particular words, phrases and pauses and asking, in effect, 'how do we know what this means?' Such analyses are slow but, we would maintain, necessary to further our understanding of conduct.

In the theatre as in normal social intercourse, 'understanding' or 'apprehension' of what is going on does not proceed in such a manner; the impact of words and actions is more immediate and sensory. We see, hear (perhaps even smell) and almost touch that which is occurring around us. Actors and performers render their transactions corporeal, and unless the bond between us and them is deliberately severed (in the manner of Brecht), our experience of the action is not primarily cerebral. We do not go to the theatre to think. Nor, however, do we go to the theatre to react in a ritual fashion. As we have argued earlier, the theatre drives an emotional wedge into the ritual process, it affords us the opportunity to be both engaged and distanced.[5] In witnessing and being party to the transactions which occur between Emma and Jerry, we are made aware that that which occurs between them is only one of several options, that Jerry has open to him (although he may not recognize it) the possibility of other courses of action. On the stage, the actors, if they are good actors, behave in a spontaneous, intuitive manner; in the auditorium we respond but we do not respond ritually. There is a framing to that which transpires before us which permits and encourages rapid reflection, which comes between — however momentarily — the action and the response to it.

Nor in what passes for real life do Tom and Dick respond ritually; their exchanges are marked by a degree of hesitation, a monitoring of self and performance. In considering their exchanges in real time, as it were — sitting with them not reading about them — we would be aware of the difference in the pace of their interaction. There is, however, no Brechtian separation of actor from character, agent from action; neither of these social performers is alienated from what he is about. Each is simply and importantly theatrically aware of themselves, each other and the consequences of their exchanges. For them, it does not take several pages to analyse and reflect upon their conduct; they both think and act. A process of the utmost complexity but one which both they and we accomplish several times a day; a process which it takes actors a lifetime to reproduce.

Chapter 10

Getting it Right on the Night

We began the previous chapter by talking about the 'triadic collusion' between playwright, actors and audience and we concluded it by speculating about the nature and importance of 'interpretations', arguing that we, as spectators to a play or to an event, attempt to 'make sense' of what we apperceive. We, however, are but one part of that 'triadic collusion'; we seek to structure and understand what is occurring but in the theatre, at least, the actors in realizing their parts and shaping their interactions, have also sought to make sense of the material with which they are presented. We shall need to say a word or two about the nature of their 'interpretations' before developing the ideas for use in the study of behaviour in organizations.

For the most part actors in the theatre work from a playscript. Somebody, somewhere, now living or dead, has sat down and written out a series of lines (plus the occasional stage direction). This is the basis for the play (the event) that we see in the theatre. There are important qualifications to this statement which we will return to shortly; for the moment, let us accept that there is a playscript and that it can and does form the basis for a performance. As we have hinted in the previous chapters, however, the playscript is but one part of the performance; we cannot just 'do' it. The Pinter performance we discussed in Chapter 9 is more than the words bought from a bookshop. There are, for example, half a dozen ways in which one can say 'Good morning'. No one of them is 'correct', each is an act of 'interpretation', of making a 'reading' and projecting that 'reading' so that we as audience may also be guided in our 'reading'. There is, of course, no guarantee of one-to-one accordance between what the actors intend to carry out and our 'reading' of it.

It is clear from all that we have written that we are not committed to the view that all there is to a play is a script.[1] What we see in front of us in the theatre is an embodiment of an interpretation, a filling out, a performance (literally 'a carrying through to completion'), a realization of a drama. The choice of a setting, the selection of costumes, the casting of actors, all imply interpretation because, willy-nilly, we will take each of these aspects to be of significance — to signify. To select Jeremy Irons instead of John Wayne for the part of Jerry says something about the way the director sees the character. On the page, the only thing that comes between us and the writer is our spectacle frame; in the theatre, intervention is inevitable. What is more, not only is it inevitable, it is wholly and totally necessary. Theatre is a performance art; it is beyond all else live beings doing something before us; it is the *material* act of story-telling, the 'semblance of events . . . virtual life'.

Performance involves selection and choice: of setting, of costumes, of actors, of rhythm, of colour, of pitch, emphasis and pace. Such choices must be made on what appear to be relevant grounds and the consideration of such grounds is a matter of interpretation. There is simply no way of creating in advance, as it were, a full 'score' for *Betrayal* (or any other play); such a score would have to specify moment by moment 'sizes, shapes, colours, inflections, tones of voice, word emphasis, rhythms, duration of pauses, placements of actors on stage, movements, tempos and so on and would require thousands of pages and would still be less precise than the score of Beethoven's Fifth Symphony' (Hornby, 1977). In seeking to understand what appears before us on the stage, however, we need someone, somewhere, to have made some choices about each and every one of these features of the performance. To simply 'do' the script without having considered and made such choices is not possible; a decision to render the activity unintelligible is, after all, a decision, an interpretation.

On what basis is the interpretation made? Given the difficulty of presenting *Betrayal*, what guides the director and his actors in realizing the performance? Fundamentally a belief that beyond the complexity there is simplicity, that the breaking down and analysis of the smallest of details can produce a fruitful synthesis. Our mentor, Kenneth Burke, captures well the point we are groping for (although, as will be seen, in a different context):

> In an exhibit of photographic murals (Road to Victory) at the Museum of Modern Art, there was an aerial photograph of two launches, proceeding side by side on a tranquil sea. Their wakes crossed and recrossed each other in almost an infinity of time. Yet despite the intricateness of this tracery, the picture gave an impression of great simplicity, because one could quickly perceive the generating principle of its design. (Burke, 1969b)

For Burke, as for Aristotle, there is simplicity beyond complexity, underlying a work of art or a performance is one whole action. An idea echoed by Brecht:

> Each single incident has its basic gestus: *Richard Gloster courts his victim's widow. The child's true mother is found by means of a chalk circle. God has a bet with the Devil for Dr Faustus's soul. Wozzeck buys a clasp knife in order to do his wife in, etc.* The grouping of the characters on the stage and the movements of the groups must be such that the necessary beauty is attained above all by the elegance with which the material conveying the gist is set out and laid bare to the understanding of the audience. (Brecht, 1964)

Performance for Brecht was holistic; words and actions set up and enacted to convey meaning. A view which parallels that of Stanislavski, who held that underlying not only every scene but underlying the whole performance were a series of 'objectives'. The actor's job is to discover this 'sub-text' of motives and make them manifest for the audience. The sub-text, it will be recalled, is that which 'lies behind and beneath the actual words of the part'. He describes this as that 'which makes us say the words we do in a play. . . . It is the manifest, the felt expression of a human being in a part, which flows uninterruptedly beneath the words of the text, giving them a life and a basis for existing' (Stanislavski, 1961).

The script is basic to the performance because it is completed first and, as we have implied above, it has form. It has a shape and a development, it is likely to be structurally coherent and it sets limits of purpose within which the other elements which go to make a play must function. The script is not neutral. Just as there can be no neutral performances, so there can be no neutral texts. Scripts help to set limits to performance; it is possible but perverse to play *Hamlet* as a farce; it would be even more perverse to play *Charley's Aunt* as a high tragedy. The script is not simply a matter of squiggles upon a page. It provides lines for the actors to speak, it affords them opportunities for display, but above all else it sets up the basic relationships and patterns which inform the performance. We wish to insist at this stage that the script does not simply consist of words; it is an arrangement of words which constitute patterns and structures. An interpretation from a Stanislavski perspective, for example, considers scenes within a play not as individual words and lines but as a series of 'objectives'. To perform a text, the actors and the director must agree on these objectives; they are not given, they must be constructed from a close reading of the script. What we see performed on the stage is an interpretation of a script, but one in which the script is embedded in the performance.[2] To be sure, a script is realized in performance only through interpretation, but that interpretation is itself influenced by the script. To put it another way: a script is a performance *in potentia*. The process by which the structure, pattern and relationships within it are emblematized (to return to a term we used earlier) is not one-to-one. The director and the actors, the set designers and the lighting crew, the costumiers and the make-up people, fill it out.

In the proper sense of the term, a performance is a *fulfilment*, a circumstance in which the potential of the script is filled out and made complete. A good production of *Betrayal*, for example, is one in which we as audience are not aware of the script as something separable from the performance. It is script-into-performance rather than script-and-performance. Pinter as playwright provides the director and actors with the potential which it takes their skill to actualize.

Performance in the theatre, therefore, is a matter of realizing the emergent focus. Even the most precise form of theatre — that, say, of the Kabuki — can only approximate the kind of detailed guidance available to a musician.

Most theatre is much looser. What we can say about it at best is that it 'fits' the author's intent or that it does not do violence to it. Does not violate what the director and actors take to be the author's ideas; a performance of *Hamlet* as farce is a 'travesty' simply because it is not consistent with what most would take to have been Shakespeare's intent. What presently we take to be the pattern and structure of the play is such that to play it for laughs is, quite simply, an unacceptable reading. Times, however, may change.

In the theatre, the script is, of course, very important but it is by no means the only source for the actors and the director. A performance of *Hamlet* is likely to be based upon the sediment of a considerable number of such performances; it would be a rare and unusual event to witness a naïve *Hamlet*. Generations of actors have wrestled with it and produced literally dozens, if not scores, of possible interpretations. With the obvious and unusual exceptions of premières, nearly all performances are influenced by previous performances. Not that a particular production of *Edward II* or whatever arises out of a specific prior performance (although all productions of *Richard III* have to reckon on Olivier's, and all of *Streetcar Named Desire* have to deal with Brando's interpretation),[3] but rather that at particular times and in particular places, there exists a consciousness of what has been and can be offered.

It is, of course, rare to find explicit scripts in organizations. Managers do not walk around with dog-eared wodges of paper, nor do they stand in corners carefully memorizing lines before coming in on cue. Managers and, for that matter, workers do, however, receive very careful guidance as to the general outline of the performance that is expected of them; indeed it is probably the norm to find that each and every organization one encounters is managed in accordance with some text or other. What we do today is often structured by the thoughts, words and actions of playwrights long dead. Choices made in previous generations of management may well affect current performance as in the illustration in Chapter 6 where the actions of Frank Tobias are acknowledged to have set the scene for Philip and Tony. Such is the form that he set up — the notion that the appropriate way to deal with each other is conflict, leaving arbitration in the hands of the family — that each and every actor follows it (up until the events we have recorded) without a moment's reflection. And this is the point we wish to stress; whatever precedes a particular action or sequence of actions heavily influences that action or sequence. Just as no theatre director can direct *Hamlet* without reference to the dozens of interpretations that have gone before, just as he or she cannot produce a naïve *Hamlet*, so no senior manager can realize a completely new interpretation of what he or she is about in running ICI, General Motors or the State Department. What has gone before and what persists in the actions and interactions of the actors and audience constitute the text which must be 'read', must be given meaning and cannot be ignored. It may not exist in dog-eared form, there may be no first editions to hand but the traditions of *commedia dell'arte* — improvisation around set scenes, with standard characters and skilled ensemble playing — persists more strongly in organizations than it does in the theatre.

Texts, however, like theatre scripts, do not speak for themselves, they have to be interpreted. There can be no neutral reading of an organization; the Heseltines have a text, a history, but what does it mean? ICI has a text, generations of actions and interactions which may, theoretically, be sampled at any point but what does it mean in 1985? What interpretations can be offered to guide current performance? There is no shortage of interpreters, just as in the theatre many critics consider themselves well able to advise the actors and the director what the play is really about and how the performance ought to be realized, so in organizational life there are many willing to advise. Effectively, all such souls are offering themselves as interpreters of the text, diviners of the sub-text; given that this is how your organization appears to be, this is what the underlying message is or ought to be.

An example will serve to illustrate the point. Many managers work long hours chasing their tails in an attempt to nail everything down. The text, the way things have happened over the years, the ritual performances the managers invoke and perform appear to require action not reflection. Many consultants and writers (the organizational equivalent of literary critics) claim and argue that such performances are, in effect, misreadings of the text; management, they proclaim, is about achieving objectives through people and this can be done by planning and articulating rather than by chasing one's tail. *The One-Minute Manager* is one such attempt to provide a sub-text for the majority of organization texts. Written by Blanchard and Johnson (1981), it has sold a million copies and has spawned many imitators. It is worth spending sixty seconds or so on considering its message.

The One-Minute Manager is difficult to categorize as an illustration of a dramatic genre. It is a melodrama without the villain, a pantomime without the dame; the closest we can get to anything remotely recognizable in the theatre would be to term it a parable. Unlike Brecht's parables for the theatre, however, the authors of this text offer no irony; everything they say is straight. The plot is simple, a young manager hears of an effective manager — a rather special person — and visits him to hear the secrets of the universe. The special manager initiates him into the three secrets of success: one-minute goals, one-minute praisings and one-minute reprimands. He does so in a manner which is highly dramatic. The one-minute praising, for example:

'What does that mean?' the young man wanted to know. 'Well, when he has seen that you have done something right, he comes over and makes contact with you. That often includes putting his hand on your shoulder or briefly touching you in a friendly way.'

'Doesn't it bother you when he touches you?' the young man wondered.

'No', Levy insisted. 'On the contrary, it helps. I know he really cares about me and he wants me to prosper. As he says. "The more consistently successful you people are, the higher you rise in the organization." '

'When he makes contact, it's brief, but it lets me know once again that we're really on the same side.'

'Anyway, after that', Levy continued, 'he looks you straight in the eye and tells you precisely what you did right. Then he shares with you how good he feels about what you did.'

'I don't think I've ever heard of a manager doing that', the young man broke in. 'That must make you feel pretty good.' (Blanchard and Johnson, 1981)

A little of this material goes a long way. A true and completely ingenuous parable: 'a fictitious narrative [. . . by which] moral or spiritual relations are typically set forth' (*Oxford English Dictionary*). Blanchard and Johnson set out (in about three lines, but repeat themselves for several hundred more) the sub-text for all who would be successful, all who would achieve 'very big results from people — in a very little time'. The theme of *The One-Minute Manager* is simply stated: 'look after the people and the rest will follow'. Explicitly stated by the hero:

'It's ironic', the manager said. 'Most companies spend 50 per cent to 70 per cent of their money on people's salaries. And yet they spend less than 1 per cent of their budget to train their people. Most companies, in fact, spend more time and money on maintaining their buildings and equipment than they do on maintaining and developing people.'

'I never thought of that', the young man admitted. 'But if people get results, then it certainly makes good sense to invest in people.' (Blanchard and Johnson, 1981)

It is easy to send up such material, but the sales indicate the demand for interpretations, for reach-me-down readings that will enable the manager to give some sense of direction to those for whom he feels himself responsible.[4] Without an interpretation, a clearly articulated set of beliefs about purpose and process, the performance is likely to be less than successful. Without some notion of what kind of play we are appearing in, it is very difficult to put on a convincing show. Without a sense of what we are about, we behave like characters in search of an author.

A less whimsical example than that of the one-minute manager is available to us in the comments of Hochschild (1983) in her study of Delta Airlines. She documents in considerable detail the attempts the management make to have prevail their current interpretation of what an airline is about — service with a smile.

The sub-text for Delta Airlines in the 1980s does not have to be 'service'; it could be, for example, 'safety' or 'quality', it could be 'speed', 'reliability', even 'exclusiveness' (as with the British Airways Concorde). In a sense, it does not matter as long as there is some interpretation, some sense of direction around which executives, employees and passengers can coalesce. Without such, the performance is likely to be less than satisfactory.

Within such organizations, much of the responsibility for the provision of a guiding interpretation, a 'reading' of the situation, lies with senior managers, often with the chief executive. Beyond all else, the leader in any environment is the person to whom others look for the provision of a sub-text; once provided, the individual structures and processes which support it can be put in place by lesser mortals (as in the stewardess training at Delta). The more successful leaders, however, leave little to chance. Here is Michael Edwardes seeking to have his vision of British Leyland (BL) held by a wide audience and intervening with comedians responsible for a widely networked programme to ensure that the appropriate image is projected:

> I said earlier that colleagues have described this period (mid 1978–mid 1979) as an illusion of progress, and so it was in the sense that ageing products and a rising cost base were about to catch up with us — exacerbated by a strong pound. Nevertheless, this was the time when we built up management resolution, and started to firm up attitudes for what was to come. . . . We were recognizing the need to stand up to extremist tactics and we were learning how best to do so. The company had been at great risk through the Bathgate strike, the deferment of parity payments, the disruptive militant leadership at Longbridge, and Roy Fraser's attempt to force us to recognize his élite craft union. But in none of these instances did the company compromise on principle. It mattered greatly that no concessions were contemplated or made and that *this did not go unnoticed. I drew this point to the attention of the two 'Ronnies' who generously offered to review the nature of their 'Leyland' jokes*, so that we heard less about workers clocking on by signing the visitors' book. (italics our own) (Edwardes, 1983)

As a performer, Edwardes is in the grand tradition of Beerbohm Tree and Sir Donald Wolfit. He writes his own parts, selects his cast and puts the show on the road (he also takes a percentage of the house, but that's another matter). 'There is no better way to achieve mobility of executive management than to change the structure sufficiently to create transparency — that is, to create a climate in which each and every job must automatically be subjected to a spotlight. . . .' Edwardes, in his tenure of the Leyland National Theatre, took great pains to select and cast each and every senior manager for his part. He was equally careful about sets and settings: '(on appointment as Chief Executive) I avoided going to the dark green monolithic headquarters, Leyland House, in Marylebone Road, and went instead to an unpretentious building not far from Piccadilly Circus, which was to be my base'. His own performance, however, holds it all together: here he is appearing at a factory where 'militants' are attempting to picket out 'loyal' workers:

> We arrived at 9.15 am and were let in to the factory by an astonished security guard. Past practice has been that the Chairman gave several weeks of advance warning before a factory visit, during which time, the stewards claimed, vast sums were spent getting everything shipshape. Ken Edwards briefed us on the current situation, and confirmed our hunch that what was needed was a quiet morale-boosting visit covering every corner of the factory.
> What a din! As the message spread ahead of us, the ladies of S.U. banged every piece of metal at hand, converting the visit into the biggest cacophony of metallic sound imaginable. Appreciation of the visit poured out. . . .

I must have shaken hands and talked to hundreds of these determined women, who were defying the pickets each day and insisting on keeping their plant and the rest of BL going. . . .

'Everyone was surprised when they saw him', one lady is reported as saying later. 'It cheered us all up tremendously.' (Edwardes, 1983)

A little touch of Michael in the dawn.

It is the Michael Edwardeses of the management world, the Watsons, the Proctors, the Gambles, the Hewletts, Sloans, Geneens and Fords who not only interpret the texts, but surpervise every detail of their realization. In the strictest sense, of course, few if any of these star actor-managers actually write the texts; the form arises from their actions, is a summation rather than a blueprint. Edwardes and others like him evolve their 'philosophies of management' over long periods of time and, for the most part, are masters of the art of improvisation; highly creative practitioners in the *art* of management. To be sure, they need something to improvise around and, possibly, within. Most of what Edwardes does, for example, can be encompassed within what may be termed the scientific or rationality sub-text well rehearsed in many an organization: analyse everything, control everything, get the costs right and productivity will follow, go for growth, select appropriate key managers and give them the authority to make decisions. A great deal of this kind of thinking lies behind what Edwardes enacted at BL. There is little of the *One-Minute Manager* about him, and his approach owes even less to those who would interpret the workplace as arenas for self-realization such as Mayo, McGregor, Argyris and the like. Edwardes is more in the tradition of practitioners such as Frederick 'Speedy' Taylor and seeks to realize many of his views in the performances he supervises. Other managers at other times in other places derive their interpretations from other sources; some, now in the UK, derive their ideas from Sir Michael himself.

Successful leaders, however, do not simply follow ideas slavishly. They take what is available, try it out and see whether or not it brings results. They are creative and what becomes known as their style is a product of their interaction with the text (that which precedes them) and how they interpret it. In a sense, BL is a finished work when and only when an interpreter such as Edwardes enacts it in a way that takes it beyond that which preceded him; BL is not simply a performance informed by a 'reading' of Taylor's *The Principles of Scientific Management* (1911); it goes beyond the text and in so doing becomes a text itself for others to use. As we discussed in Chapter 6, creativity and improvisation in the form with which we are concerned rests upon the notion of variation and selective retention. What we have added in our present discussion is that these processes occur within and around a text. There can be no 'correct' reading of BL by Michael Edwardes or anyone else, for that matter, but that is not to say that any reading, any interpretation is valid. A 'correct' reading of a text is one that realizes it so that what we see enacted we take to be coherent and complete. Taylor, for example, is explicit that those who would practise scientific management understand people as limited in their capabilities and therefore assignable to some parts or positions within the organization and not to others. It is unlikely that there can be a 'correct' enactment of *The Principles of Scientific Management* that violates this element. Sir Michael Edwardes knows this well and casts for each and every part within his new BL:

> Of the top 300 managers, 60 were recruited externally by selective search plus psychological assessment, and although the remainder were found within the company, they had to be assessed and appraised because there was the need for extensive redeployment and I could not be sure that internal appraisals were always objective. Of the other 240, no less than 150 managers found themselves in new positions, often because of the need to get 'line' people into 'managing' jobs and 'staff' people into basically advisory jobs. (Edwardes, 1983)

Such 'casting' is an essential element of the sub-text which has come to be known as scientific management and is a violation of the sub-text known as 'human relations'. Thus, to imply, as such assessment and assignment do, that abilities and capacities are limited, narrowly defined and not capable of development is beyond the tolerance of the later interpretation and those who have developed it.

Thus Sir Michael Edwardes is able to mount the performance he does because he is aware of the text — the nature of BL as evidenced in the actions and interactions of those who constitute it — and is able to bring to bear upon it a sub-text which can be utilized to shape a revised performance without doing violence to that text. It would, for example, be difficult for Sir Michael — or anyone else, for that matter — to 'read' a university in a scientific management fashion and secure a convincing performance from the staff. Such attempts, of course, have been made and are fundamentally unconvincing. Sir Michael at BL is, in the term used in our earlier comments upon creativity, in touch with the interpretations within which he is working (developed, in his case, during his years with Chloride and handed down to him by another great actor-manager), and proceeds through a process of trial and error to interpret what he sees around him and render it less ambiguous, more determinate, more manageable and quits at a point 'where a stage is reached which in the opinion of those involved represents an appropriate breaking off point':

> The across-the-board improvement in the outlook for BL influenced my decision to move on when the five years was up — to create space for others. I felt I had served my purpose: by mid-1982 the de-manning was almost completed — some 90,000 employees, staff and shop floor, had left the payroll. The new test facilities and the advanced technology centre at Gaydon were established and in operation. Modernisation at Longbridge, Cowley, Land Rover at Solihull, Leyland in Lancashire and Freight Rover in Birmingham had transformed old-fashioned factories into effective production units. Our fixed costs in all parts of the business had been severely pruned, partly by de-manning and partly by rationalisation of production; by closing factories we did not need to match production capacity so that it lined up with market demand for the products,

with sufficient headroom for expansion when the market recovered. Production time lost through disputes had been reduced to one-seventh the 1977 figure and productivity had soared ahead. Management had regained control of the business. (Edwardes, 1983)

(*From* Back from the Brink *by Michael Edwardes. Published by Collins and reproduced with permission.*)

What we are saying is that the text, the basic form, is laid down generation by generation and is rarely completely abandoned for something new and even more rarely are such abandonments successful. We have chosen to comment upon one relatively well-known interpretation, but organizational life is at once more complex and more simple than that. Donaldson and Lorsch (1983), in an interesting discussion of decision-making at the top, noted that of the twelve companies they studied, all had been founded by a 'dominant individual' and '. . . the personal values and beliefs of these founding fathers were an integral part of present day belief systems . . .' even though the founders were in many cases long dead. Echoes of Frank Tobias. In one company they studied, there had been only one departure from the firm's objectives in thirty years. In other words the change was incremental and well within the text laid down by the original authors. Incremental change is the product of experience and interpretation and there can be no better vindication of the process than that which Donaldson and Lorsch, writing out of quite a different tradition, adduce:

> . . . there is another aspect to the development of these beliefs that becomes evident as corporate managers search the external environment for opportunities that fit their beliefs about distinctive competence and appropriate risk (*a good performance*). If an opportunity fits these beliefs (*is within the text*), they will try it, often on a small scale with a limited commitment of human and financial resources (*rehearsal*). If the trial fails, the belief emerges that the activity is outside the firm's distinctive competence and that future activities in this direction would be too risky. If the trial succeeds, the conviction grows that further efforts in this direction are appropriate risks. (words in parentheses are supplied) (Donaldson and Lorsch, 1983)

We could hardly have produced a better description of creative endeavour had we written it ourselves. The performance of all within an organization is ultimately dependent upon the interpretation of the basic text. Some texts persist in relatively incorrupt forms, modified and amended by various interpretations and serve as the basis for still further attempts to realize the form for contemporary appraisal. Others are lost or corrupted beyond recognition and simply cannot be realized with the actors available. Still other organizations have a proliferation of competing interpretations and no clear sense of what it is they are trying jointly to present. What is obvious is that without some shared interpretations, the triadic collusion between audience, actors and playwright cannot be achieved.

We would stress once more that the key activity in the contemporary theatre and no less in contemporary social and organizational performance is that of direction. In the theatre, evidence of direction is present in each and every scene; none the less, theatre, as we have seen, is an actor's medium. The live actor, breathing, moving, speaking — an almost tangible presence to the audience — playing off his fellow actors, editing his performance in real time, is the stuff of theatre. To the extent that this is all the audience is aware of, the direction has become invisible; the choices exercised, which to a large extent govern what the actors do, are not evident to us.

Notwithstanding the overwhelming presence of the actors, of the set, the costumes and properties, the dialogue, the characters and the sense of spontaneous enactment, the absent factor — executive action — is the key to this entire realization. The direction is and has been the final authority on all artistic matters; fundamental decisions have been made about interpretation, creation and evaluation. Executive action will have been instrumental in 'pulling it all together', co-ordinating the activities of others in realizing the performance which we see. Without direction, even the most talented actors and designers, following their own uncoordinated impulses, will almost always produce chaos.

It is as well to remember that when we go to the theatre and derive satisfaction from our excursion (not necessarily a frequent experience), it is because the performance as a whole has been brought off successfully. The set has not been merely 'pretty' or 'nice'; the music not simply 'catchy' or 'effective'; the lighting not just 'evocative' or 'subtle'; the actors not only 'good' and 'audible'. The combined talents of all those involved have coalesced to produce a 'wholeness', a sense of unity, a perception (at whatever level) that what we have experienced is 'a play', not 'some acting' or some good set design or whatever. The many tasks of direction in the theatre may be reduced to this one, that of unifying the production — giving all concerned a sense of purposive action.

As in the theatre, so, we would maintain, in organizational life. We all know of organizations where the sense of direction is lacking, where co-ordinated effort is unusual and where the part appears more important than the whole. Where star performers fight to upstage each other and appear more concerned about their next role than the play in which they are currently performing. Where settings (My office is larger than yours) or properties (I'm entitled to a better car than you) predominate. Above all, where leadership, in its fullest sense, is absent. Some of us may also know of organizations where ensemble playing is the norm, where the whole enterprise exudes a sense of purpose and direction. Occasionally, particularly in our media-conscious times, we may be made aware of the name of the leaders, but the entire set of activities stimulated and co-ordinated is the true expression of that skill and most of us apprehend little of it in that which we observe directly. The paradox is similar to that which we pointed up in the theatre: the inverse ratio of the direction's importance to the enterprise and its lack of visibility to us, the audience.

The role of the direction in the theatre, we have asserted, is to be the unifying force.[5] There is dispute within the profession that this unity can be achieved through the activities of one central, dominating figure; some actors argue that companies controlled by the performers could and should dispense with the office of director — a feature of rhetoric about organizations not unfamiliar to those of us operating in other contexts. Co-ordination is to be achieved in such circumstances by the willing co-operation of all concerned; those party to decisions will implement them with more enthusiasm and commitment. After all, the case runs, the director is a relatively recent innovation. Shakespeare did not have one for his plays and what is good enough for him. . . . Leaving aside the quite bizarre notion of Shakespeare as a paragon of democratic leadership (just look at what Hamlet has to say to the players for an inference of Shakespeare's attitude), it is worth noting that actors' co-operatives have not been outstandingly successful. Left-wing actor/directors such as Chaikin found that trying not to be leader in co-operative groups resulted in compromises that satisfied no one:

> Somewhere along the line I realized that groups don't work democratically, and I wanted so much that they do. I had promised everybody I worked with that we would operate that way. I didn't want to betray the promise, or violate my own fundamental idea that they should. So it took a long time before I realized that they didn't and they weren't, and, in fact, I was really making a lot of choices I made-believe I wasn't making. And that was a very painful and arduously difficult period — and long period. Some of the people I worked with expressed to me a sense of violation when I started more and more openly and explicitly doing what I was doing anyway. (*Drama Review*, Fall 1981)

Theatre companies, of course, are in business to be creative, and enterprises devoted to such ends may well be different from other kinds of organized activity. In such circumstances one may well need a particular form of leadership:

> I have observed that no creative organization, whether it is a research laboratory, a magazine, a Paris kitchen, or an advertising agency, will produce a great body of work unless it is led by a *formidable* individual. (Steiner, 1965)

The director in the theatre is hired to realize upon the stage a particular playscript. The playwright has chosen the principal action and organized it into a plot (however rudimentary) and has suggested the lines along which the characters should develop. The director takes over the series of choices and continues them. The playwright's initial choices have constrained his subsequent ones and now narrow the scope of the director. Similarly, each choice the director makes influences his subsequent options and restricts those of the actors and designers. It follows that the initial choices made by the director are of considerable importance; Jonathan Miller's decision to perform *Rigoletto* as though it were set in a Mafia-dominated American city of the 1930s was a matter of consequence, as was Adrian Noble's decision to foreground the fool in Lear. Therefore, the director must carefully study the text (script and interpretations) to discover the limits of his creative freedom and to divine the possibilities for action open to him. In other words, the director is responsible for the interpretation of the playscript; not alone — others clearly have an input — but the director's function is that of chief interpreter:

> The interpreter directs his energies as exclusively as possible to one question: what is this thing, this script; how does it work; what play is latent here? Many factors intervene between interpretation and performance which dictate that the play be unlike what reading has 'revealed', but simple respect for the author and the selfish desire to find the most that can be found in the script lead us to begin the playmaking process with a selfless and painstaking act of interpretation. (Gross, 1974)

Not only has the director a primary responsibility for direction, he has the supervisory responsibility for the creation of the *mise-en-scène*. He begins by assigning roles to specific actors; choosing particular people to embody the conception of the role that the director has tentatively developed. Again a matter of consequence. Limitations are imposed by actors' bodies, voices, ranges and repertoires which influence particular conceptions. Olivier or Brando may well be the finest actors alive, but a resolve to cast either as Romeo signals a somewhat unusual perspective on young love. Since the director is concerned with the creation of an appearance that signals a particular conception, he must be concerned in casting with selecting the actor who can best embody the end he has in mind.

Once having done his interpretation and selected the cast, the director seeks to realize his ideas upon the stage. Such realizations are not impositions upon the material he is working with — playscript or actors. The movement and actions spring from the interpretation; the basic thing the director does is to create the life from which the lines spring. The initial interpretation, constraining though it is in that it informs the casting, constitutes the master plan. Like any manager, however, the director in the theatre needs other people.

In concluding his relatively sparse discussion of the manager as leader, Mintzberg (1973) notes that 'the key purpose of the leader role is to effect an integration between individual needs and organizational goals. The manager must concentrate his effort so as to bring subordinate and organizational needs into a common accord in order to promote efficient operations.' Nowhere is this more apparent than in organizations devoted to creative achievement; in a very real sense (as we have noted above), the director acts as an agent for the collective endeavour. If he cannot succed in bringing the piece together on the night, there are consequences for all.

The director needs the support of other key figures, but they need him; the relationship is symbiotic:

> As an actor, Mason has definite ideas about the kind of director that he enjoys

working with. He cites decisiveness as a key factor. 'I find the most difficult thing for me as an actor is when I experiment with something and a director says, "Oh, that is nice." And then, when I do something completely different, he says, "Oh, that was nice, too." There's no indication as to which direction one should go in. That's very frustrating. As an actor, I feel I need that guidance from the outside because, otherwise, I'd start to direct myself, and you'd get an intellectual performance. But *Twelfth Night* was complicated for me because certainly David knew what he wanted very strongly. In that respect he was a marvellous director for me because I really did not have to worry about being unsure what choices should be made. David was very, very definite about that.

'However, it was very frustrating because it was pretty much a dictatorial experience. That is, I didn't feel we actors got a chance to contribute very much. It was really filling in David's outline.

'As an actor I don't really think I would work very well with a director who was terribly critical without also being supportive. It's very important to know where you're at and to get some sense of what you're doing. And, as I said, some opinion is better than none at all, better than just, "Let's do it again."

'Imagination is also important. But trust is the most important thing, the feeling that the director is not going to let me make a fool out of myself or ask something of me that is really false.' (*Drama Review*, Fall 1981)

What is clear, notwithstanding the manic activities of people such as Quaal and Edwardes, is that leaders cannot be everywhere, cannot do everything; the performance, like that on the stage, is a live one but unlike it, may frequently have a cast of thousands and be occurring simultaneously in a number of locations. Theatre is live performance and as such is revealed only in the act of execution and for the duration of the performance; *Edward II* as performed appears, if the cast and director have worked well together, to be spontaneous, a matter of consequence to us all with a shape and feel to it which are encompassed within the space and the time that we devote to it.

What occurs in front of us on-stage has a finality; events occur and once apperceived are gone. This finality of performance, this rendering down of all interpretation and rehearsal into a series of consecutive exchanges makes the theatre such a powerful analogy. Professional actors, no less than professional managers, must exercise their skills in what appear to be spontaneous actions and responses under the pressure of time. As we have noted earlier, the successful performance is marked by this thinking and action. An executive working for BL, no less than an actor working at the Royal Shakespeare Company, must perform — must act and respond — so as to give the semblance of spontaneity and in so doing he or she produces events which are taken to be consequential. The social actors, no less than the stage actors, cannot easily edit or revise what they have done after it is done; theirs has the finality of performance.

Given that the actor in performance makes irrevocable decisions, it is easy to see why such a heavy emphasis is placed upon casting, pre-planning and rehearsal. What leaders or directors cannot realize themselves being present on-stage during the live performance, they build in.[6] Given that they cannot edit the work of performers, they seek to pre-edit it. The direction of Delta

Airlines is similarly concerned; they cannot be at every check-in desk nor on every flight, but they can and do seek to pre-edit. The trick is, of couse, as on the stage, to bring off such pre-editing without doing violence to the spontaneity of the performance; we have to believe in the smile of the hostess; what she does has to convey to us a sense of immediacy which denies all the training, rehearsal and direction.

The key to this pre-editing is the notion of interpretation which has figured so centrally in this book and the activity around which we will focus these final pages. We have, of course, discussed rehearsal earlier. We are not seeking simply to go over that ground again (although these aspects of activity are inextricably interwoven with those aspects of leadership to which we are also seeking to draw attention). What we are interested in here is the notion of 'interpretation' and the director's part in it. Interpretation, we have argued earlier in this chapter, is inevitable. There is no way of simply 'doing' *Edward II*, or any other play for that matter. Plays do not simply speak for themselves any more than social encounters do. The selection of a particular emphasis — to render Lightborn chilling, for example — implies choice. The director (as we have seen in consultation with his actors) chooses a particular emphasis and, through movement, gesture, action and reaction, points it up. Such a choice is a matter of consequence and, if it is to be credible to an audience, must be capable of being sustained. What we see the director doing in our extracts is trying out an interpretation, taking apart the text and putting it together again. Analysis and synthesis. Starting with the words that Marlowe wrote, the actors and the director relate them to their own experiences and categories or constructs for understanding and come up with what they take to be a reasonable inference about what may be going on between the characters they are presenting. That is, they do not *discover* meaning, they *construct* it.

This act — the act of interpretation, the act of constructing a guiding rationalization for the choices made — is of fundamental importance. Without it the actors cannot function, they cannot know who they are nor what they are about. We are back to the issue of possession:

> In truth, the part of Hermann in *Despair* was the nearest thing to a complete mental and physical take-over that I had endured since von Aschenbach had eased silently into my existence: it is an extraordinary experience in every way. The actor has to empty himself of *self* completely, and then encourage the stranger he is to be to come into the vacuum created.
> It is not easy. But once caught, and it takes time to do the catching, one's whole personality alters, and it is not at all understandable to 'civilians', as I call non-players, to comprehend. It is more of a mental alteration than a physical one, but sometimes in a bar, or in a shop, at the reception desk of an hotel, even talking to Forwood at a meal, I would find that I was speaking, and more than that behaving, exactly as my alter-ego would have done. This is not affectation: it is possession. . . . (Dirk Bogarde, 1983)

To achieve this possession an actor needs an interpretation, a powerful sense of control over his material which, paradoxically, allows him to perform in a spontaneous manner. Let us take this step by step. Assume that Bogarde (or any other actor, for that matter, though few are so good) wishes to put on this particular character. Given the nature of human behaviour, even were he to spend the rest of his life observing madmen (for such is the character he is to play), his analysis would never be complete enough to enable him to synthesize a performance that would pass muster. The complexity of conduct is such that he or she who wishes to reproduce it as an appearance on the stage can never approach it. What Bogarde needs is something that will generate spontaneous, intuitive behaviour in line with the part he is playing. Bogarde knows that he is convincing on the screen to the degree that his performance appears all of a piece, and further he knows that this integration comes not from specific words or actions attributed to him in the script but from the underlying sub-text that he and the director arrive at and share. This master interpretation (or set of interpretations) is a conscious device, an analytical tool for controlling the preconscious processes which make or break a performance. Our actors playing Lightborn and Mortimer do not have to name their relationship nor their feelings for each other, but (if they are to convey anything at all to us out in the stalls) they must feel who they are in relation to each other. Providing they share an interpretation, their spontaneous behaviour will tell us all we need to know. Without sub-text, the actor, however distinguished he or she is held to be, has great difficulty in controlling their attention and will become lost in the detail of their performances. The sub-text is not given in the script; Shakespeare, Shaw, Ibsen, Beckett do not provide handy guides to actors. The director and the actors must create their own maps, evolve their own directions. There is nothing beyond the subtext, no truth, no play as Shakespeare or anybody else 'really intended it'.

Interpretation is not a matter to be taken lightly nor is it something which can be undertaken by the unskilled. It is rarely a once-off flash of inspiration; the director of *Edward II* began with a notion that the play was about 'power', about 'political intrigue', but soon realized that to sustain such a clear interpretation he would have to do violence to some of the text. Edward's relations with Gaveston are difficult to play as 'power' and the former's violence at the death of his favourite almost impossible to view as anything other than a lover's vengeance. Like any company of performers, the actors had to meet the challenge of each line, each relationship, each new situation. The director and his cast were obliged to understand the play fully; to be sure, they can (as was done here) cut out passages which offend their interpretation, but there can be no question of leaving ambiguities and difficulties unresolved. Every issue must be resolved; it matters what the precise relationship is between Mortimer and Lightborn since, willy-nilly, in performance the actors must play it in one way or another. Choice has to be made and choice depends upon interpretation.

The director of a play exercises choice in a fundamental manner; the director in an organization is equally dominant. Michael Edwardes values a particular approach, interprets the circumstances in which he places himself and creates or stages the results of his interpretations. Directors interpret through acts of intellect and imagination. There are no blueprints in life or theatre. A successful director or manager seeks to reduce ambiguity, to provide shape and substance and to provide structure for the actors. Packard, a great interpreter of the 'human relations' sub-text, considers that innovation is central to understanding and hires 'really great people and creates an environment where people can make mistakes and grow'. To realize the performance, to emblematize the HP Way, the 'company makes specific point of its use of first names, managing by wandering around, and its feeling of being one big family. All three amount to explicit direction by the organization's top leadership that the chain of command should be avoided in order to keep communication flowing and encourage maximum fluidity and flexibility (Peters and Waterman, 1982).

In the theatre, as in social life, somebody, somewhere, sometime has to call a halt to the rehearsal and actually perform. For the triadic collusion to be successful, we as performers and audience need some interpretation around which we can focus. Edwardes chose to emblematize a united BL making cars at the levels of efficiency hitherto thought beyond the capacity of a British manufacturer. Such an interpretation is very different from one in which BL or, for that matter, the coal industry is emblematized as a social service, a community asset. It is perfectly possible to mount a performance of BL (or anywhere else, for that matter) not as efficient or productive, but as simply occupational (much of the Western world's training programmes for unemployed youth are currently of this ilk). All one needs to realize such performances and to regard them as worth while is a powerful leader, a willing cast and an empathetic audience. A triadic collusion, the stuff of the theatre and of organization.

Dominant though directors may be, they do not constitute the whole. They occupy a key role, to be sure — a link between the particular play or organization and the wider community, and they embody the standards against which a particular performance is likely to be judged — and their skill is crucial to the achievement of a degree of integration. As the quote from Mason reminds us, however, the performers need to develop trust in them if the performance is to be a good one. Ensemble playing is a product of players who are at once convinced and convincing; playscripts and texts in organizations are fully realized by the activities of intelligent, imaginative and creative directors and actors, executives and managers. Packard, Edwardes, Sloan, Watson and the rest provide direction, construct meaning and purpose for the enterprises with which they are associated, but they cannot act in isolation; construction occurs through and between people and is necessarily participative. Edwardes, in his initial responses to the offer of the job at BL, has some clear ideas about what he wishes to realize, but these are modified and elaborated in interaction with others to produce some approximation of ensemble playing. Iacocca at Chrysler goes through a similar process, as do Watson at IBM, Geneen at ITT and numerous other successful performers. The director working in the theatre, no less than the actor/manager working in his own organization, both shapes and is shaped; the theatre director knows that in the final analysis his production fails or triumphs to the extent that key performers (lighting, set, costumes and actors) co-operate enthusiastically in its realization.

We conclude as we began Chapter 6 with an extract from a meeting in the boardroom of the Heseltines. It is some eighteen months later in the same room with the same cast but, as will be readily discerned, playing somewhat different characters. Derek, the managing director, with some help from an itinerant dramaturge and extensive co-operation from his colleagues, has now realized a different kind of performance which appears to be settling in for a long run:

DEREK: OK. China next. Your baby, Philip. . . .

PHILIP: Yes. I circulated the papers about four or five days ago and I have been around and covered the basics with everyone, I think — except you, Derek. Couldn't get in your diary in time.

DEREK: That's OK. I've read it, in any event.

PHILIP: What I've done is to pull together the points raised by each of you on this slide (*flashes up overhead*) and, as you can see, there are about six or seven points we need some discussion on. (*All peruse the screen.*)

BARRY: I'm not sure my point about the competition is up there, Philip.

PHILIP: The competition?

BARRY: Yes. What are Morgans doing in China, if anything? What are Schpa-erpartz-AG up to in Düsseldorf, and so on, or are we going to be lone pioneers?

PHILIP: I thought that would be covered in Number Four — 'The Market' — but I'm happy to flag it up separately.
A great deal of animated and detailed discussion occurs around each point and the meeting concludes with the following exchange:

DEREK: Well, thanks very much for taking us through that, Philip, a good paper and a set of decisions I think we can all . . . er . . . agree on.

TONY: Far be it from me to be seen to slavishly follow the boss, but if this is the way we are going to work in the future, it gets my vote.

BARRY: Well, it always had mine.

PHILIP: I'm not sure I can take too much of this. . . . The big thing is most of the problems were ironed out before we got in here. . . .

DEREK: One to one . . . with everybody. That's the way it should be.

Individuality into ensemble.

Notes

Chapter 1

1. Strictly speaking, we are here dealing with 'tropes — figures of speech — only one of which is the metaphor; but the idea of titling this chapter 'The tropical organization' or 'Tropics of organization' seemed overly fanciful. In addition, we have adopted a view of language as a creative enterprise which is at odds with more widely recognized positions on the relationship of language and reality. (For a fuller exposition, see particularly T. Hawkes, 1972). There is enough potential confusion in all that without adding to it; thus, we use 'metaphor' as a more recognizable shorthand that is meant to stand for any figure of speech.

The conventional view of language which treats 'factual', non-fanciful statements as necessary conditions for meaningful speech has been widely accepted among philosophers of science and social scientists alike. Of course, such a viewpoint has a history; but it suffices here if we merely indicate the broad dimensions of this position against which we are tacitly arguing. Logical positivism had its origins in an effort to provide an unequivocal philosophical view of the form of scientific theories in the face of the challenges presented by quantum physics and the theory of relativity. Most importantly, this view sought to give definitive meaning to all scientific terms through explicit links to the empirical world; as an early slogan of this approach claimed: 'The meaning of a term is its method of verification' (Suppé, 1977). This link between linguistic expressions and their meaning as actual, physically observable realities has become the hallmark of what we have learned to call the verificationist theory of meaning. Yet somehow in this philosophical effort, language became more important than any observable reality. It is the *form* of acceptable scientific statements which has been at issue — whether that be treated as verified, verifiable, falsified, falsifiable or merely acceptable to an appropriate scientific community — more than any particular observables.

Moreover, the vast respect which has been rendered to scientific discourse led to the extension of its formal standards to all kinds of statements that one would want to claim as meaningful. The only meaningful form which statements could take, then, became the form which was acceptable for meaningful scientific statements. No matter that for one reason or another the logical positivist effort failed as a *rigorous* philosophical endeavour, it has managed to chill thinking about the forms of meaningful expressions. Beneath the surface of much contemporary work in the philosophy of language, one can still find the remnants of the empirical criterion of meaning and its determination to separate linguistic expressions into the verifiable and the meaningless.

Fortunately, this criterion no longer dominates discussions of linguistic meaning and conceptual analysis proceeds without its dogmatism. Yet the inability of most of this work to find an honoured place for indeterminate expressions, such as metaphors, does testify to a survival of standards that accept some human statements as meaningless because of their form. Philosophers do prefer clear language which is literal in the sense of excluding multiple interpretations, even if this is not the usual character of human speech. An insistence on the normalcy of quite special kinds of linguistic usage — philosophical reconstructions of how language *can* be meaningful — is often juxtaposed against the problematics of everyday speech to the pronounced advantage of the former. Indeed, an imagined view of scientific discourse as clear and unequivocal still floats in such philosophers' talk as a tacit standard of acceptable linguistic expressions.

Against this background, it is easier to grasp the continuing importance of the notion of scientific practice as an activity which seeks to match its theories with an external, objective reality — to give precise empirical meaning to mere words. In fact, the idea that language is meaningless without some real, objective referent has been more difficult to eliminate than the formal rigour of the verificationist theory of meaning. Yet, it is precisely this lingering understanding of language as the formal link between concepts and the real world which contains the limits of any effort to grasp language as creative of our reality, to formulate words as inventive of the world as we know it. But surely, one might say, we cannot abandon the idea of a real, empirical world without losing all claim to be engaged in scientific inquiry. And one would be correct. It is, however, not the case that we have to accept this 'real, empirical world' as an objective reality with inherent properties which are *independent of our experience*. Rather, we can decide to treat experience as constitutive of reality, its properties and relationships. Such as approach is *not* to be mistaken for an idealist's claim that mind creates reality; it is the much more recognizable sociological assertion that experience is an interpretative activity.

Of course, this view is not without philosophical justification — notably among the American pragmatists, such as G. H. Mead, John Dewey and Charles S. Peirce — but it is more importantly an understanding of human experience that is rooted in studies of how this is accomplished in different societies and communities. Experience has to be interpreted if it is to become meaningful. It is this process of interpretation through metaphoric concepts which constitutes the real world as we know it, whether as scientists, philosophers or people waiting for our bus in the morning.

2. We could fill a number of pages here with a bibliographic note which suggested classic books and articles in which the various metaphors for organization, about which we are talking, are explored in great detail. But this is not close to our objectives in this volume: we are not concerned to offer an even-handed survey of the field of organizational analysis; other volumes do that. However, readers interested in the issues which surround various approaches to organizations — assumptions about the nature of human life in organizations, about appropriate strategies for studying them, about the consequences of adopting particular images of the organization and so on — would be fascinated by Gareth Morgan's (1983) edited collection of original essays by practitioners of the many divergent approaches to organizational analysis.

3. In the last portion of the chapter we have adopted a view of science, both natural and social, that is — predictably — at odds with some widely recognized accounts of science. Our approach here continues to emphasize the continuities between scientific activity and all other forms of organized human life. Unlike more conventional views which have been influenced by positivism and have treated science as *the* standard form of rational inquiry and knowledge, we would assert a more sociological position and take science as one among many institutionalized practices, none of which can serve as a privileged yardstick of rational knowledge. This viewpoint, which can loosely be described as the 'social construction of scientific knowledge', has risen in importance in the past few years and bids fair to challenge conventional positions. A delightful introduction to this approach can be found in the recent collection of original

essays that has appeared under the editorial authority of Karin Knorr-Cetina and Michael Mulkay (1983).

Chapter 2.

1. We have deliberately ironized the 'tradition' to which we claim to be making some contribution. Not only are we unaware of the extent to which the theatrical metaphor has been used by various writers, we are ignorant of the range of everyday theatricality in the history of human·cultures. In that sense, then, it is not anything like a tradition to which we hope to speak. Indeed, the scholarly effort which would be involved in tracing the many uses of a dramatic trope, even as a key image and not simply as a commonplace, is simply daunting. Perhaps it is sufficient to mention two distinct themes in the Western employment of the metaphor (the use in non-Western civilizations would be quite another issue) in order to give some idea of the work there entailed.

In Plato's *The Laws*, we find an image of humans as puppets of the gods and it is something like this which informs the medieval view of the world as a stage on which people act for God's pleasure. This fatalistic vision crops up again and again, even surfacing in the manipulative social dramas of twentieth-century totalitarian rulers who saw the masses as *their* puppets (for this latter usage we would recommend George Mosse's fine book *The Nationalization of the Masses* (1975), even if he restricts himself to Germany). Counterpointed to this we can locate another theme, that may have its origins in the thinking of Posidonius of Apamea, but which flowered in the work of the Roman Stoics who followed him. In the writings of Seneca and Marcus Aurelius we find an impression of the human as actor, playing out public parts, but reserving the expression of an inner being to private moments. It is this notion of human as actor, an image of *active* performing, which is woven against the manipulated human as puppet across the many centuries. Of course, in our own times, the role-playing human, alienated from self, has become a commonplace against which thinkers have worried in search for true human identity (the most profound treatment of identity and the dramatic trope is Bruce Wilshire, 1982).

The recently 'discovered' theatricality of pre-literate people (Gregor, 1977) only emphasizes how little we know about the 'theatrical consciousness' in other cultures and in earlier historical periods. We do not know to what extent, in fact, our common understanding of the identification of persons with their role in simpler societies is a result of researchers' assumptions or is a marker of the variation of theatricality across cultures. Plainly, there are volumes to be written exploring these issues: they are, however, not central to our efforts in this book.

Chapter 3

1. 'Ritual' is a concept that is often applied to *parts* of interaction that seem to have no instrumental outcomes. We think of ritual as forms of interaction with little content — greetings, table manners, inspecting guards of honour; we think of them as religious, liturgical activities; we think of them as customs whose purpose is buried deep in history; we often equate ritual with ceremonial. Certainly, these restrictive uses of this concept among social scientists have been most common (yet do compare Collins, 1981); but there is little enough uniformity in even this limited employment to allow us to stretch the concept and yet lean comfortably on Edmund Leach's comment that:

> . . . even among those specialized in this field there is the widest possible disagreement as to how the word ritual should be used and how the performance of ritual should be understood. (Leach, 1965)

'Performance', on the other hand, has had nothing like this widespread employment and often has been used as if it were simply descriptive of conduct — carrying no implications of theatricality. Moreover, when this concept has been employed in an explicitly metaphoric fashion it has been to distinguish modes of conduct that are performed from those which are not. This might have been done in a stipulative way as did Austin (1962), noting that language in an actor's performance is somehow void of its normal functions, or simply as a way of highlighting *particular* kinds of conduct as *like* the audience-attentive mode of the 'performer'. *Our* usage of the concept is an efffort to grasp *all* conduct as audience-attentive, if not audience-aware.

However, to talk about social life as *ritual performance* is to work with a phrase that contains an inner contradiction. Rituals have no audiences only participants: performances, on the other hand, are audience-attentive forms of conduct. To talk about ritual performance, then, is to discuss something that does not *literally* exist. Fine, that is the point of metaphor; they are not literal. We can have it both ways. We can grasp social life both as being performed as if before audiences, *and* as ritual as if it were a serious, taken-for-granted activity that contained only participants. The contradiction here only sharpens our appreciation of the complexity of the human world: it never allows us to fall into the trap of taking our metaphor as reality.

2. With this view of rituals as *stable solutions to repetitive problems*, we rely on the philosophical foundations provided by G. H. Mead. For those who know his work, our writing here and elsewhere will ring in the familiar tones of his understanding of human action. For those who do not know his work, and it is by no means widely read outside North America, it is hard to recommend any short introduction to his thought. His most widely recognized volume, *Mind, Self and Society* (1934), was a posthumous publication of a course of lectures on social psychology given in the latter part of his career at the University of Chicago. Yet for all the deserved attention this volume has received, we still believe that the collection of his papers called *The Philosophy of the Act* (1938) is a more fundamental text. Naturally, there are a number of secondary works on Mead. The classic commentaries by Herbert Blumer can be found in his volume *Symbolic Interactionism* (1969); David Miller's philosophical appreciation *George Herbert Mead* (1973) contains a very full bibliography of work by and about his old teacher; recently, David Lewis and Richard Smith have published *American Sociology and Pragmatism* (1980) offering a controversial re-evaluation both of the unity of pragmatism as a philosophical movement and of the position of George Mead as an influential figure among sociologists; finally, a complete issue of *Symbolic Interaction* (Fall, 1981) was given over to essays on Mead varied enough for all tastes.

3. We think of attention as some kind of focusing which involves both a narrowing and directing of awareness. The effect of such direction of our awareness is to highlight, to give the foreground some things and to consign others to the background. Yet, this gives an overly visual metaphoric account of a process that is no more visual than it is olfactory or aural. Attention can be directed to any of the sensations which we have in order to construct a perceptual object from them; at the same time, attention might equally well be directed to an object that we locate completely within our own mental processes.

However, although we pay attention to aspects of our environment which 'interest' us (as the pragmatists noted), there are limits to attention. Not the least would be the physiological limits to the amount of information which we can deal with at any one time. As Miller (1956) suggests in a classic paper, we do not seem to be able to pay attention to more than seven items, give or take two, at a time. Yet, whether that number is seven or seventeen, what is beyond question is the experience-based and limited character of attention. Given that attention is limited, we find two basic approaches in the social sciences to understanding how people get around their social worlds. After all, we cannot direct our attention to everything that happens: some things must be treated as taken for granted if others are to get our focused awareness.

How is that accomplished? Most simply, the answer here would be that routines are accomplished through patterned forms of conduct. What separates the two approaches is where they locate these patterns. Typically, psychologists will find them in mental, cognitive processes in the form of plans, schemas, tendencies to respond and the like: equally typically, sociologists will locate these same regularities in institutional conduct. Crudely, one approach finds order in an inner, cognitive world; the other finds such order in the outer world of social action. By extension, and again over-simply, one approach would take social order to be an externalization of mental order; the other would find the structures of thought in the structures of action.

Where in all of this, then, does our notion of 'ritual' stand? The ritual process of everyday life is the non-reflective performance of routine solutions to routine prob-lems, as we have said. Contained in this definition is the assumption that the process of mind which is involved in such routines is to be found in the way the environment is shown to be ordered by those ritual actions. For us, as for anyone who follows George Herbert Mead, mind is not some 'inner' mental activity; it is always available naturalistically in the world where organisms and environment intersect in ordered forms. Rituals, therefore, display a mental process in the only form in which that is available. Action can no more give order to mind than can mind form action: human conduct is mindful. This is not to say that all conduct involves that form of mental activity which we would call self-reflection; it is only to assert that the ritual process exhibits a mindful organization of the world which requires no postulate of a separate and inner mental realm.

4. We have formulated 'reality' in pragmatic terms as that which is taken for granted in any kind of encounter with the social world. In the context of this pragmatic understanding, our task is to say what we mean by 'appearance' as a concept in opposition to 'reality'. Most generally, appearances have to be construed as perceptions whose meaning is problematic. In everyday life, such perceptions occur when we are unable to accomplish what we set out to do and have to reconstruct our perceptual field in order to represent the conditions under which we *can* finish what we started. How, then, does this apply to the theatre? In what way is theatre to be understood as 'appearance' — a perception or set of perceptions whose meaning is problematic? Obviously, for the regular theatre-goer, the process of getting to the theatre, obtaining tickets, finding a seat and buying a drink at the bar presents no great problem. These activities are as real as any other that one routinely carries out. What constitutes appearance, then, has to be that action which we frame as the performance. Oh, yes, conventions about what is and what is not performance will vary and the boundary will always be somewhat vague between performance and life in the theatre, but in most instances it is the play itself which constitutes the theatrical appearance. The theatre-goers' problem is to construct what and how this means. What is *not* problem-atic within conventions of theatre are that it is actors who play characters, sets which communicate locale and acting that presents the drama — these matters are taken for granted, they are real in the sense in which we are using that concept. What constitutes appearance in the theatre is the *meaning* of characters, sets and acting; this is the problem that is presented to the audience.

5. Of course, we are not about to claim that theatre always arises from rituals; that would be nonsense. Our point is somewhat more limited. Drama is a transformation of aspects of the social process that depends on the capacity of individuals to distinguish between the characters in rituals and those who perform them, between those taking part and those watching, between symbolic and instrumental action, between appear-ance and reality. Yet such transformations do not occur in all rituals. They occur, and this does not and has not happened in all societies by any means, in those areas of social life which are specially framed and elaborated in order to tell stories about a society and its people to those same people.

We do not have to go far afield to exotic locales for illustrations of story-telling;

they too easily distract us from the more familiar, commonplace telling of tales that is all around us. So much of what we are calling 'story-telling' has been thought of as folklore that we should try and indicate to what extent we have an interest in using this concept. The answer, briefly, is that we have none. Formal interest in story-telling has seen it as a practice *marked off* from the everyday by a number of 'keying' devices which vary from culture to culture. Whether one then thinks about such keyed activities as folk 'lore' or as a kind of performed verbal art — an oral literature — is a matter of choice (although we should much prefer, for obvious reasons, an approach via performance, see for example Bauman, 1975). Our notion of story-telling is broader than either of these approaches, even if we should be prepared to see story-telling as a keyed segment of interactive processes. Indeed, we are almost prepared to consider narrative accounts as the crucial form of most speaking which is not simply instrumental; or, more modestly, be willing to consider what it would be to treat much verbal communication as a narration and consequently find the *significance* of life in what is told and retold, rather than what is merely lived. But here we only want to alert readers to the prevalence of narrative forms in speaking, among which particular kinds — those which tell stories about people to those same persons as an audience — are the basis for drama. Think about the family gatherings at birthdays and weddings, at wedding anniversaries and over major festivals and all the stories that are told. About Uncle Joe and the time he lost his watch, about Grandad being arrested and executed for murder in Los Angeles, about Auntie Jane getting drunk and being covered up by a flag as she lay groaning in her armchair, about the year that Henry came back from the war and told his story of it once and never again. Sit two or more men down over a bottle of rum in Nova Scotia and they will immediately fall to telling stories about the worthies and unworthies of their community, creating and re-creating its past and present in vignetted character sketches that often capture the accents, expressions, gestures of those discussed in what is an incipient drama. Indeed, what is gossiping but stories of reputation won and lost?

In fact, to stretch the point just a little, if we listen carefully to the talk around, it is not difficult to think that story-telling goes on almost non-stop. People transform their lives and their experiences into stories with practised ease. The day at work thus becomes two stories; one relates the accident in the morning rush hour, the other presents the story-teller as victim of an unfair decision by her boss. A long and difficult day spent moving an old house to its new site as a workshop — a day with hard work, great skill in manœuvring the house by means of a bulldozer and some rum — becomes transformed into an account of the man who stuck his head between a tree and the house in order to tell the people on the other side that the house would not get past! A near tragedy in a windy harbour where a man in a dinghy was being swept out to sea by tide and wind is transformed into a comedy of errors where his resourcefulness at reaching and scaling the sea wall becomes a farcical clinging to the rocks which is capped — after rescuers have brought him the oars which the inflatable lacked — by his realization as he casts off from the sea wall that he does not know how to row. Indeed, we tell each other stories in order to provide ways of talking about some aspects of persons and relationships that we can not or do not want to speak of more directly.

Story-telling is a common feature of life in all societies, therefore, and can be as mundane as the illustrations which we have offered or as elaborate as the costumed performances which accompany status passages or important times in social calendars. Not long after the Nigerian Civil War an important horse-race, the High Commissioner's Stakes, was scheduled on the track in the capital city. At the end of a divisive conflict, the outcome of such a horse-race could tell a significant story to the nation. So, in the presence of various dignitaries, with the high commissioner's staff in their finest clothes, it was no surprise to find that the winning horse was called 'Keep Nigeria One'. It was a good story to tell, even if the race had to give a suspicion of being fixed to tell it. Similar performances which present stories about a people to that people can be found in the initiation rituals of aboriginals in Australia, in the chuck-wagon races of the Calgary Stampede, in the public ceremonials of the Santa Fe Fiesta, in the Trooping of the Colour which marks the monarch's official birthday in Great Britain. It is from performed rituals like these that there has emerged in a myriad of intermediate forms (and some of these are part way between rituals and theatre) what we can recognize as the performance of theatre. From story-telling *ritual* in which there is no distinction between actors and characters, audiences and performers, reality and appearance, we find emerging story-telling *theatre* in which all these distinctions can and have to be made.

The development of the Greek theatre serves as an illustration of the point we are trying to make. (As with any area of scholarship, there is a dispute about the origins of Greek theatre; it is not within our skill or knowledge to resolve the many issues raised by specialists in the area. We have chosen to take the line which appears in more popular texts which seek to chart the development of the theatre. In what we outline we rely heavily upon works such as Kitto (1956) and Pickhard-Cambridge (1968). Francis Fergusson's *The Idea of a Theater* (1949) here, as elsewhere in this book, has been an important influence upon our thinking.) It is arguable that the form of classical tragedy owes much to, and is ultimately derived from, a very ancient ritual, that of the seasonal god, the Enniatos-Daimon. Somewhere in the dim and exceedingly distant past early inhabitants of Attica joined in these ceremonies to celebrate or propitiate the non-human forces which, presumably, they took to surround them; such rites involved widespread participation rather than, as later became the case, the possession of the few on behalf of the many. By the tenth century BC or so, the epic poem had emerged as a form of mythic story-telling that became part of their religious ceremonials. In understanding the transformation of ritual to drama these poems provide a clear bridge from the rites which may have occasioned, say, the original Festival of Dionysus and the sophisticated works of Euripides, Aeschylus and Sophocles.

Thus, before the emergence of Greek tragedy, there was a body of poems, highly dramatic in content though not in form, for the most part recounting the prowess of a god or hero. At a festival, it is probable that these poems were sung by a narrative chorus who, at least initially, did not seek to identify with the characters of whom they sang. To transform the poems into drama, it was necessary for one member of the chorus to take it upon himself (the chorus was entirely male) to speak or sing the words attributed to the god or hero in the poem. Tradition ascribes this innovation to a performer called Thespis and even gives him a date; he is said to have taken this monumental step in Athens around 534 BC.

Although the use of a masked soloist speaking the verse to help illustrate the story was a significant development, it did not represent an interest in characterization. The plays of Sophocles, Aeschylus and Euripides are not plays of character. Characterization is subordinated to the general pattern. The purpose of the tragic poets was didactic; they were concerned to show the way in which a person should live and the limits of human power; they were especially concerned with life in contemporary society and they used their drama to illustrate what could and ought to be. Their method was to relate stories which had ritualistic origins, to use poetry, dancing and singing to illustrate how the world had been ordered in the past as a way of learning how it ought to work in the present. These dramas were put on at a festival for the entire population; no longer a rite directly involving the community as participants but one in which they, as represented by the centrality of the chorus in what was presented, could participate indirectly. From what we know, it was an all-singing, all-dancing show with processions, religious ceremonials, verse-speaking and slapstick succeeding each other throughout the day. But at the centre of the events and at the centre of the dramas themselves was an 'image of the community' — a dancing, singing chorus of citizens. The Festival of Dionysus at this time was a means for everyone to discuss and ponder the important issues of human relations with the gods and of life and death. At the same time, and perhaps equally important, it represented a bonding, a bringing together of the community in a significant social activity.

It is clear that by the time of Sophocles some of the distinctions which we have argued are critical to the development of theatre *qua* theatre are being made. The performances are crafted by agents, playwrights and actors; there is an increasing distancing of the audience, a separation of performers and spectators, a greater use of effects and machinery and so on. None the less, there is no sharp dividing line to be drawn between story-telling rituals in a religious genre and theatre proper; rather, we find a gradual secularization of theme accompanied by a developing professionalization of performers.

By the fourth century the link between the community and what it saw in the theatres had become much weaker. The plays did not deal with issues of substance, entertainment prevailed rather than instruction (moral or otherwise) and the chorus — the key symbol of communal participation — had virtually disappeared. This development — or decline, as some would see it — is concurrent with a change in religious outlook and is paralleled by an emphasis upon a growing professionalism in the theatre. For some, this decay set in with Thespis — a professional actor effecting a rudimentary characterization — but it is worth noting that for nearly 100 years the change did not precipitate a significant move towards characterization by the playwrights. The function of the actors — and for a long time there were no more than three of them in any performance — remained to illustrate a central pattern and it was accepted that they spoke in narrative rather than dramatic form. At the same time, the audience continued more as participators with the chorus and actors than as mere spectators. By the fourth century, however, this had changed. Direct address that summoned audiences to be participants had been much reduced, other than in comedy, the number of characters portrayed by professional actors had increased and, perhaps most significantly, the most sought after prize at the festival was that of best performer.

Remarkably similar things could be said about the development of mystery plays in medieval Europe. The original cycles were clearly informed by a didactic purpose; they used myth and story; they grew out of religious ceremonial and chorus presentation. The plays were presented as part of a festival, and combined processions, ceremonials, slapstick, dancing and spectacle. For the most part, they were popular and community oriented and provided a means for reflecting about humans, their place in the universe and their relations with God. The strong links to a communal tradition of ritual story-telling are still discernible in present-day performances of these cycles at York, Chester and Oberammergau.

It is equally the case that not all story-telling rituals develop into full-blown theatre; there are many forms of ritual dramatic action in which the distinctions necessary for theatre — the separation of actors and characters, audience and performers, and so on — are blurred and ambiguous. One particularly delightful illustration of such intermediate forms is to be found in the British tradition of mumming that takes place in many places, but is nowhere more interesting than in the Cotswold village of Marshfield where we have observed it for several years. Mumming has survived through several centuries. An early description is available dating from 1377 (not of the Marshfield performance) and it is possible to discern a line through from that period into the masques of the seventeenth century. In the early work we are told the mummers assumed 'the disguise of popes, cardinals and African princes carrying gifts . . . an obvious association with the Calendar Festival of the Epiphany'. By the time we reach the type of performances put on by the Marshfield Paper Boys, the link with Christianity is weaker, although the theme of death and resurrection is clear. To be strictly accurate, since the Marshfield ceremony involves a presenter and a text, it should be called a disguising. Later, in the transition from disguising to masque, the

195

ritual or religious aspect of the performance almost completely disappears (Chambers, 1903; Hardison, 1965; Wickham, 1963; Brody, 1970).

In Marshfield, which has a dramatic ceremony going back centuries, the performances take place the day after Christmas, but neither the time nor the precise locations are given beforehand. In effect, the audience does not go to the play but rather it congregates in a likely location and waits for the play to come to them. The play is short and does not usually last more than twenty minutes, even with the collection of money which succeeds it. The troupe does not move from house to house but from station to station within the village; some, particularly the locals, know most of these locations but there remains an air of mystery about the troupe's perambulations and a definite feeling that to reveal the exact times and places of the ceremonies will 'break their luck'.

Since there is no theatre building to house the event, its stage must be created anew with every performance; this is a far from haphazard business. Indeed, the marking out of the stage, the clearing of the area by the performers in procession, set it apart from seasonal ceremonies such as the hobby-horse processions at Padstow in Cornwall. Here there is a procession just as in the mummers' performance, but there is no clear separation between the audience and the actors. It is only in the mummers' ceremony that the action is set apart from the spectators when, led by the presenter dressed in black and sounding a handbell, the performers form the circumference of their acting area, each, in turn, entering the circle as and when he has occasion to speak.

The men dress in a mass of shredded paper (often newspaper) which begins at the top of the crude, conical hat and falls all the way down the body until nothing can be distinguished beneath it but a pair of boots. The identities of the 'Paper Boys', as they are called, other than that of the presenter, are thoroughly indistinguishable. The costume is non-representative, nothing more, nor less, than primitive, ceremonial disguise.

The play itself is relatively short and to those unversed in the dialect of the region almost totally incomprehensible. The 'actors' (roles handed down within families) narrate and illustrate the action rather than display it and do so on behalf of the community rather than performing in front of it, although some rudimentary histrionics are evident. The 'performance' ends abruptly and the participants move on to their next 'station' to repeat it.

None the less, for all those societies in which a theatre has emerged from story-telling ritual, there are many more where this has not happened. In that sense, mumming represents a kind of story-telling that is somewhere between ritual and theatre, somewhere between playing to audiences and having only particpants, between people acting parts and being themselves, somewhere between dramatic appearance and mundane reality. Even though these distinctions between actors and characters, audience and performers, reality and appearance are the necessary conditions for the emergence of theatre, they do not determine such a change in rituals; most do not and will not.

Chapter 4

1. However, not all dramaturgically relevant work is disposed to offer this focus on performance and action, this sense of innovative, fluid life in which people act out their characters with an artist's feeling for placement and timing. Among anthropologically interested writers another powerful image which fits within a dramaturgical approach to social life is that of 'the text'. This image suggests a documentary basis to life that makes our action far less important than the scripts which prescribe its form. The idea of 'the text' comes from the way in which one might look at a written document as a thing in itself, to be understood separate from the intentions of its author, or the circumstances under which it was produced, or whatever. It elevates 'that which was

performed' or 'that which will be performed' to a more crucial analytic status than any performance itself. To that extent, then, an image of text has been most comfortable in application to written or oral expressions, and most analyses employing this image have been directed to material which has been rendered as literally textual. Greetings, speeches, songs, stories, recitations of genealogies and so on have all been transcribed and analysed; more widely, the everyday speech of many pre-literate people has been turned into a grammar of their language.

Perhaps this distinction between the many concrete episodes of speaking a language and the grammatical form of that language as a whole has been the most influential in developing an approach through text. Plainly, although we speak grammatically none of us has a complete and explicit knowledge of the grammar of our language. Nor, indeed, do we refer to grammatical rules when we are talking with each other in order to make up sensible statements. We follow a grammatical script without being consciously aware that we do so. It is this image of subterranean patterning deep beneath the surface of conduct which has accompanied the extension of the notion of 'the text' not only into documents derived from verbal interaction but also into all aspects of social life conceived of as analogous to texts.

A structuralist concern for universal patterns in language, myths, rituals or whatever is only one form of the *explication de texte*. Another form — the hermeneutic, broadly considered — allows for an interpretative spinning out of possible meanings without sense of closure or certainty. One might even want to include here ethnomethodological attempts to locate the ordering procedures which people employ to experience their world as sensible. However, we shall save our readers the effort of trying to make sense of the many, often arcane, approaches to life as text. Whatever the many differences among these approaches, they can be simply sorted into those which approach texts to locate specific *universal* features, whether those be thought of as rules, structures or patterns, in opposition to those which approach texts in order to make an *interpretation* of them, to speak about what they mean.

The first orientation tends to be strongly linguistic in its approach to texts and one finds oneself looking at well-crafted, often extremely technical discussions of written texts that have been transcribed from the performance of situated interaction. Generally, the analytic effort is to disentangle the text from whatever it might have meant to those who produced it in order to examine it for formal patterns that are considered to be at a level deeper than any person's intentional conduct. The content of any text, here, is no more than a surface feature which is generated by deeper patterns that shape the way in which anything can be said or done. In this sense, texts require no interpretation, they 'mean' only what formal structures of language and action allow them to mean. In the theatre, this analytic impulse can be traced among those who insist that a script be played as written; that such texts require no interpretation since they already contain their meaning in the form of the script itself, with words, speeches, stage directions and all.

One illustration of this style of work on texts is a pioneering work on the rationality of politeness behaviour. At the beginning, as is typical, the authors offer an orientation which enables us to dissolve any specific interest we might have in the meaning of expressions of politeness in order to focus on an aspect of their form:

. . . one recognizes what people are doing in verbal exchanges (e.g. requesting, offering, criticizing, complaining, suggesting) not so much by what they overtly claim to be doing as in the fine linguistic detail of their utterances (together with kinesic clues). (Brown and Levinson, 1978)

In the body of this long peper, they display linguistic parallelisms in the forms of politeness across three different languages where even the details of 'negatives, subjunctives, hedging particles and tags . . . of plurality, tense and person' afford a unity of formal expression which they explain with a model of persons as rational actors desiring to protect their public self-image. In other words, the patterns of politeness expression in the various texts which they examine are 'found' to be explicable by 'universal' rational strategies for maintaining public self-images. It is, however, the texts which display these strategies and not the performers of the texts.

The other approach to an *explication de texte* offers as broad a range of analytic strategies that are unified by a concern to *interpret* texts and action treated textually without presuming the universal applicability of any result. It is the issue of meaning which is central to such efforts at interpretation and the particular technique employed to reach a conclusion about the meaning of a text — literary criticism, psychoanalysis, linguistics — is much less important than the purpose for which it is used. In the theatre, clearly, this understanding of scripts presents itself among those who require an interpretation of the play, who seek out a sub-text within it to give unifying life to their reading.

One of the most rewarding of the anthropological exponents of textual *interpretation* is Clifford Geertz. In one wry image he tries to express the way in which social life is like a text:

> Doing ethnography is like trying to read (in the sense of "construct a reading of") a manuscript — foreign, faded, full of ellipses, incoherencies, suspicious emendations, and tendentious commentaries, but written not in conventionalized graphs of sound but in transient examples of shaped behaviour. (Geertz, 1973)

If one combines this evocative picture with his notion of interpretation as 'intrinsically incomplete [such that] . . . interpretive anthropology is a science whose progress is marked less by a perfection of consensus than by a refinement of debate', we have a remarkably accurate exemplar for this whole interpretative stance towards texts.

Despite the well-deserved attention that has been given to his essay 'Deep play: notes on the Balinese cockfight' (1973), it is difficult not to mention it once more as a very accessible illustration of his style. In this paper, he combines the tools of traditional ethnography with a series of analytic probes that use sources as diverse as a Freudian notion of the identification of 'penis' and 'cockerel', a Benthamite concept of 'deep play' for irrational betting, a theatrical understanding of the cockfight as a status dramatization and a literary critic's vision of universal events which allows both *Macbeth* and a cockfight to serve as key texts of a culture. These probings of the Balinese fascination with the cockfight allows him to conclude:

> . . . that it provides a metasocial commentary upon the whole matter of assorting human beings into fixed hierarchical ranks and then organizing the major part of collective existence around that assortment. Its function, if you want to call it that, is interpretive: it is a Balinese reading of Balinese experience, a story they tell themselves about themselves. (Geertz, 1973)

Yet, 'text' as an approach to understanding social life, even in Geertz's humane version, is difficult for dramaturgical analysis to embrace wholeheartedly as a resource. In the theatre, texts have a special place, most importantly in the selection of a play to be performed, in the decision about which version of that play is to become the text, and in the whole rehearsal process. Outside that, and certainly in performance, there will rarely be a sense of text either for actors or audience. The text is only a factor in *some* aspects of theatrical productions. To treat 'text' as *the* metaphor of all conduct, therefore, is to elevate rehearsal above performance and treat what is plainly a special case — the sense of textuality in a performance — as the general instance.

We need the perspective of the literary critic, the actor in rehearsal, the actor in the play which has run forever; we do need the resources of an approach through text.

We have to remember, however, that this perspective is a limited slant within a theatrical approach. Performances are always open to improvisation, to disruption, to success and failure, to change; they are open to considerations of actors and their characters, to settings and their expression; they are open to the nature and conduct of audiences. Textuality, as a particular sense about performances, exists precisely *as a result* of performance. The very nature of theatre is to give texts their vitality when performed by actors before audiences. The theatrical metaphor, then, allows us to affirm a key point of the symbolic interactionist tradition within which we work; it is interaction which creates social order and disorder, it is not rules, norms and principles of order which give social interaction its form.

2. This is not to say that we have run out of dramaturgical resources in the mainstream that relate to this 'thread'. Not at all; there are materials in social psychology written and read by sociologists which unexpectedly reveal themselves as relevant here. To take only one illustration, the so-called 'expectation states' approach (for a summary see Meeker, 1981) that seeks to offer a highly formalized treatment of task group process wherein expectations for others determine the structure of power and prestige. In the absence of a researcher establishing a group in which all 'appear' as status equals, the theory assumes that individuals' expectations will be influenced by whatever status people bring to the group. In other words, the dramaturgical communication of status — race, age, gender, occupation, education — becomes the basis for the expectations of performance that people will hold of each other in such task groups.

3. We do not intend to be dismissive either of G. H. Mead or Sigmund Freud. We rely, as do most interactionists, on Mead's work for our basic assumptions and have so indicated earlier: nor are we unaware of Freud's germinal work on symbolism and the theatre of the mind. However, in this volume we have avoided an effort to discuss the nature of the 'actor's' mind and have treated the concept of 'actor' as a primitive and undefined notion with which to explicate the playing of 'characters'. To have discussed Mead's and Freud's dramaturgic understanding of mind would have essayed a sketch of the nature of the actor's mind about which we do not wish to speculate here. To have done so would lead to one of two possibilities. Either we should have turned our dramaturgical model back on itself and found that actors themselves are only social actors playing characters (and where does that kind of regress end?); or we should have looked at the common-sense views of personality which critics, actors and directors hold about the nature of actors (and found that they all derive from various social scientific notions of mind and the person). Neither of these possibilities recommends itself to us. Working within a theatrical model we can only 'know' lay theories of mind and people as they operate in the motive talk of the everyday. All models have their limits: we cannot 'know' what people really are using in this approach.

4. This has its roots in Burke and travels from him to C. Wright Mills (1940). The pace picks up a little after this and we find that Foote (1951) is followed by an increasing number of essays, Scott and Lyman (1968), Hall and Hewitt (1970), Hewitt and Hall (1973), Hewitt and Stokes (1975), Stokes and Hewitt (1976), Perinbanayagam (1977), and very recently is treated in monographic length by Semin and Manstead (1983). Naturally, there is other work relevant to a concern for verbal motives (whatever these might be called), but these pieces are held together by both a conceptual and citational awareness in a way that other work is not.

Chapter 5

1. Data acquired during extensive non-participant observation of Bristol Old Vic Theatre Company rehearsing and performing *Edward II* by Christopher Marlowe — Spring 1981.

2. There are too many books to list, many either of too general a nature or too

specialized for the kind of reader approaching this work from a social science perspective such as we take much of our audience to be. For the very interested we would suggest *The Revels History of Drama in English* (available in paperback) and, while scholarly, not so densely written as to be off-putting. Less specialized but valuable are Styan (1975) and Fergusson (1949). For those interested in the illumination shed on normal interaction through study of rehearsal, we would suggest Hiley (1981), Heilpern (1977), Callow (1984) and Sher (1985).

3. Oddly enough, techniques such as those adopted by Brecht — causing the actors to stand away from their parts and signal their distance from them — appears to be readily accepted as yet another convention. The net result is that the audience appears to identify even more strongly with the character than had no such alienation effect been attempted.

4. Of course, this is not a hard-and-fast rule; actors and audiences occasionally collude to break the conventions and then continue as if nothing had happened: 'An excellent show. There has been a queue for returns all day, so the audience are even more enthusiastic than normal; their hysteria is quite thrilling and occasionally catching. During the rape-on-the-dining-table scene (or inter-course intercourse), everything just stops for about thirty seconds while Ali and I join in the audience screaming with laughter. A most peculiar event, breaking all the rules. The more we laugh, the more they do. At last we struggle back on to the text and the audience seems as shame faced as we are for having misbehaved so badly . . .' (Sher, 1985).

5. The discussion of creativity here owes much to a working paper 'Blueprints for anarchy' (Mangham, 1983), which in turn is informed by Briskman's (1981) important discussion of scientific and artistic creativity.

6. Our ideas here derive in part from Fergusson (1949), but primarily from Cole (1975). The notion of possession, being taken over by an alien spirit or personality, may seem to deny the sort of control an actor manifests in performance. This, as Cole points out, is to misunderstand the nature of possession; it is not that persons possessed simply throw themselves about in an idiosyncratic and unpredictable manner. The possessions anthropologists witness have often turned out to be very much like stock characters that may be found in the drama of any country at any time. Those possessed learn possessions which depict 'the traditional conception of some mythical personage'. In some situations, particular possessions are assigned to particular cult members just like casting at the Royal Shakespeare Company.

Interestingly enough, certain personality traits are thought in a number of cultures to fit one for particular shamanistic performances: 'Frequent fainting-fits, excitable and sensitive disposition, taciturnity, moroseness, love of solitude and other symptoms of a susceptible nervous system' (Oestereich, 1930). Characteristics, as Cole notes, of the 'star' in any era.

Travers (1981) uses the idea of possession in a persuasive and powerful analysis of aspects of social life, linking this closely with a dramaturgical perspective deriving in part from, but going beyond the work of, Erving Goffman.

7. The categorization of actors into those of the 'method' and the 'classical' schools is crude and simplistic. It serves our purpose here, but we would not wish anyone to believe that we put great store on such categories. Actors throughout the years have been concerned to understand their art — though not necessarily to share that understanding with others — and can be broadly divided into those who work from externals inwards (the 'classical') and those who work from internal states outwards (the 'method'). Many actors fluctuate somewhere between the two, few are clearly in one group exclusively. Wiles (1980) is a valuable commentary on acting theory and style, as is Funke and Booth (1961); Billington (1973) is the work of a journalist but serves as an adequate introduction.

Chapter 6

1. Data drawn from participant observation of group 1982–84. The material has been presented without the inevitable overlaps of statement, the background noise of conversations pursued simultaneously and the hesitations and false starts characteristic of such meetings. Thus, as presented, it appears more similar to dialogue in the theatre than is the case. The decision to present it in this manner was taken primarily on the basis that it was less confusing so to do.

2. The question of what is and is not a performance has become a matter of importance in recent years with some theatre companies experimenting with street theatre and others deliberately attempting to break down the separation of performers and audience. The crucial point lies not in physical distance, costume or whatever, but in the stance of the member of the audience. As Wilshire (1982) puts it as someone going to the theatre: 'One is not just a being in the world but becomes aware *that* one is a being in the world. One becomes aware of oneself as aware, interpreting, and free.' A state which approximates to that which we termed the specific theatrical consciousness.

3. Some hazards are less easy to negotiate successfully. Actors do not like appearing with children or animals; the former because they frequently upstage the professionals, the latter because they are simply too real: 'The trouble with bringing on a real horse is that it distracts an audience. They sit there thinking, "There's a real horse which might shit any moment" instead of listening to the lines' (Sher, 1985).

4. The key feature of theatre is that of engagement or involvement. In attending properly in the theatre we are caught up within the activities of the beings who appear before us; we recognize the types represented and we identify with them. They may be heroes, villains or fools but they have a vitality and presence which invites us to empathize with them, to put ourselves, as it were, in their shoes. We identify in this scene with Edward II, with Mortimer and with Edward's lover, Gaveston. We are moved by what happens to them because we are not completely detached from them. Even where we do not approve of their actions — the violent death visited upon Edward by Mortimer — we are involved with the character. If we are not, either the performance is a poor one or we are not properly attending; theatrical consciousness in the sense that we are interested in it requires a form of distancing, to be sure, but distancing which allows us contact at an emotional level with what occurs on the stage. We grasp what is going on and are carried along by it; we do not labour our way through *Edward II*, we apprehend it at a much less conscious level but remain sufficiently distanced as to be not totally overwhelmed by that which we experience (Gross, 1974). The activity is akin to, but not directly the same as, intuition (Bastick, 1982).

5. There is, for example, little evidence that Goffman ever went near a theatre; his understanding of actors, rehearsals, performance and the like does not appear to be informed by actual contact with plays and players.

6. Schank and Abelson (1977). This notion of script has been used by Mangham (1978, 1979) to examine interactions in organizations. It is, however, worth noting that in this form it does not derive from the theatre but from studies of computing.

7. Kemper (1978) is an important work in the literature concerned with the sociology of emotions. Here we can do no more than sketch in some ideas, but in his work and that of Mangham (1986) the way particular emotions are aroused by particular 'readings' of circumstances is examined in detail. With the recent publication of articles and books taking a similar perspective on emotion and affect, we would forecast that this is an area likely to yield greater insights into the dynamics of relationships over the next few years. See, in particular, Collins (1981), Hochschild (1983), Denzin (1978), Averill (1982), Malatesta and Izard (1984), Plutchik and Kellerman (1980).

8. This passage derives from Mangham and Overington (1983a). The special issue on

dramaturgy in which this occurs contains important papers by Haas and Shaffir, Manning, Perinbanayagam, Travers, Watson and Wilshire.

Chapter 7

1. 'All that is on the stage is a sign' (Veltrusky, 1940). Here we draw upon another literature but one which has been and is clearly involved with the theatre: that of semiotics — the study of the production of meaning in society. As such it is concerned with the means whereby meanings are generated (the process of signification) and exchanged (the process of communication). Possibly the more accessible texts are Eco (1977) and Elam (1980). *Poetics Today* (Spring 1981) devotes an entire issue to the semiotics of drama, theatre and performance. The 1983 Special Issue on Organization Culture of the *Administrative Science Quarterly* attempts in part to apply semiotics to conduct in organizations and is distinguished only by the poor quality of most of the contributions.

2. Again a vast literature, but one with which students of organizations are likely to be familiar. We would draw attention in particular to the work of Birdwhistell (1973) and Argyle (1975) and Argyle and Henderson (1985).

3. One of us has been professionally associated with the design of office settings and on more than one occasion has been buttonholed by individual executives who have complained about their space allocation. On one occasion, the executive concerned refused to move into an office which he claimed was eighteen inches shorter than that of a peer.

4. This discussion relies heavily upon the work of Rapaport (1982). The point about all of this, of course, is that settings are more than physical adjuncts to scenes. The setting provides the cue to action; the kind of building indicates that this is a church, this kind a bank, this kind a supermarket or whatever. Settings help in the running off of routine performance; when one enters a certain kind of building (in England, stone and often imposing) and sees serried ranks of wooden benches facing towards a raised stone table lit by light filtered through stained glass windows and are greeted (or ignored) by male officials in robes, one is keyed into being in church and one acts accordingly. Settings in part constitute a mnemonic device for guiding our words and actions. People such as those at Columbia Records believe that the setting not only stimulates appropriate behaviour but actually constrains it; without the proper setting they are unable to realize their performance. They are clearly not alone in their belief that getting the scene/agent ratio right is the key to good performance. See also Levy-Leboyer (1982) and Canter (1975).

5. Clothing alerts the public by identifying the wearer's background to his social audience. Sennett (1974) provides a clear illustration of the function of dress as identity:

> The following is the reaction of one middle-class husband, an oil merchant, to his wife's dressing above herself, reported in the *Lady's Magazine* of a slightly later period, 1784:

> When down dances my rib in white, but so bepuckered and plaited, I could not tell what to make of her; so turning about, I cried, 'Hey, Sally, my dear, what new frock is this: it is like none of the gowns you used to wear.' 'No, my dear,' crieth she, 'it is no gown, it is the *chemise de la reine*.' 'My dear,' replied I, hurt at this gibberish . . . 'let us have the name of your new dress in downright English.' 'Why then,' said she, 'if you must have it, it is the queen's shift.' Mercy on me, thought I, what will the world come to, when an oilman's wife comes down to serve in the shop, not only in her own shift but that of a queen.

> If the oil merchant's wife or anyone else could wear a *chemise de la reine*, if imitation was exact, how could people know whom they were dealing with?

Again, the issue was, not being sure of a rank, but being able to act with assurance. (Sennett, 1974)

See also Robeiro (1984) *Dress in Eighteenth Century Europe.*
6. In conversation with one of us, these very fine performers were intensely aware that clothes signalled different things to them and to an audience. One cannot, they maintained, perform a serious piece, even one designed to amuse the audience, in casual clothes. In part the comedy depends upon musicians in tailcoats playing Berio with straight faces. Corpsing ruins the effect as much as jeans do.

Chapter 8

1. Our discussion of characters and characterization in the theatre owes much to Bentley's (1964) seminal work, *The Life of the Drama.* We have also made use of ideas contained in Gross's (1974) *Understanding Playscripts: Theory and Method.* A good introduction may be found in Dawson (1970) *Drama and the Dramatic,* particularly Chapter 5.
2. The library shelves groan under the weight of such tomes. We appear to live in an age when direction in the most minute detail is not only offered but actively sought out. What manuals of etiquette were to previous centuries, training manuals are to the twentieth.
3. Here our discussion owes something to Styan (1975), particularly to his excellent chapter on 'Acting and role playing', and to Schlueter (1979); it also owes something — as does much of what we write — to Barish (1983). Needless to say, we do not agree with every conclusion drawn by these distinguished commentators.
4. This duality is, of course, at the heart of theatre; an actor takes on a role and creates a character (in association with other performers and the audience). He or she is physically present before us playing someone we take he or she not to be. Any character presented to us on the stage is inherently dramatic in a way in which they are not in a poem or a novel. As we have said, Brecht, in his epic theatre, urges the actors to emphasize the distinction between themselves and the characters they assume on the stage. In part this is an effective device for pointing up the alienation of modern man, but we should not delude ourselves into thinking that in this or any other examples where the inherent duality of staged performances are concerned that we approach the so-called 'condition of modern man'. What we see before us in the theatre is an actor assuming a role of someone (an actor) who is distanced from the character he is purporting to present. We do not see a duality, rather we glimpse a splitting into three. As audience, we soon recognize the implied duality as but one more convention.
5. Barish's text is a must for anyone interested in the long and quite undistinguished hostility manifested towards theatres and those who frequent them. He documents each and every kind of prejudice, but particularly apposite to the points we are making here are those who have taken play-acting to be hypocrisy. The Puritans, for example, held that there was a true self 'in whom there is no variableness, no shadow of change, no feining, no hypocrisie'. They maintained that God had declared that there are bounds to each and every creature, 'the bounds of which may not be exceeded'; consequently 'he requires that the actions of every creature should be honest and sincere, devoyde of all hypocrisie'. Further, God, it is argued, 'enjoynes all men at all times to be such in show, as they are in truth: to seeme that outwardly which they are inwardly; to act themselves, not others . . .' (Prynne, quoted Barish, 1983). Players are evil because they are hypocrites, they seek to substitute a self of their own devising for one given them by God.
Such views have a long provenance; we should be what we seem to be. The duality implied by the model of life as theatre, man as actor, is profoundly disturbing to this

day. Hence we would argue — and go on so to do — the complex signalling that occurs in organizations and elsewhere in social life around self, character and performance.

Chapter 9

1. Theatre is above all forms of art (save opera) a visual and auditory experience; we see and hear what is performed. Eliot sums up what we are about in this chapter rather well in an essay on Seneca and the Elizabethan stage:

> Behind the dialogue of Greek drama we are always conscious of a concrete visual actuality, and behind that of a specific emotional actuality. Behind the drama of words is the drama of action, the timbre of voice and voice, the uplifted hand or tense muscle, and the particular emotion. The spoken play, the words which we read, are symbols, a shorthand, and often, as in the best of Shakespeare, a very abbreviated shorthand indeed, for the actual and felt play, which is always the real thing. (Eliot, 1951)

The play is only fully realized in the theatre; the conduct of members of an organization can likewise be only fully recognized and interpreted in context.
2. In what follows we rely heavily upon writers such as Gross (1974) and Hornby (1977) for the general approach of script into performance and upon Kennedy (1975) and Quigley (1975) for a background to Pinter's language. The comments upon the play derive from the experience of one of us in seeing the original production and his subsequent analysis of the film starring Patricia Routledge and Jeremy Irons.
3. It is as well to remember that other commentators upon acting, while agreeing that gesture complements words in realizing complex dramatic situations, differ as to its nature. For Diderot (1978), what is realized 'depends not, as you think, upon feeling, but upon rendering so exactly the outward signs of feeling, that you fall into the trap'. Actual feelings for Diderot are irrelevant, it matters not a jot to him whether the actor playing Macbeth actually feels remorse, guilt, anger or whatever; what matters is the representation of the appropriate emotion he is able to signal through his gestures. There is a fascinating study of Shakespeare's language of gesture in Bevington's (1984) book, *Action in Eloquence*.
4. We cannot resist commenting upon the kind of advice to managers offered by Wright and Taylor (1984). 'An appearance of friendliness, warmth and attention can be evinced by such cues as smiling, greater eye contact, standing or sitting closer, etc.' Precisely so, 'an appearance'; so schooled are we nowadays in the tricks of the trade that we seek to discern what lies beyond them. Aha, we are inclined to think, he is smiling and making eye contact with me to make me think that he is sincere but really he is. . . . Our model does not deny that such displays are possible, but holds that the relationship between actor and the part he plays is much more complex and consequential, not something to be assumed with the kind of Goffmanesque cynicism implied in such passages.
5. Richards (1925) notes that there is more to the arts than: 'the quality of momentary consciousness which they occasion. . . . The after-effects, the permanent modification in the structure of the mind, which works of art can produce, have been overlooked. No one is ever quite the same again after any experience; his possibilities have altered in some degree. . . .' Mental life goes on round the clock throughout life; thinking — obvious mental activity — is but a small part of it. We argue for a continuum from the pre-conscious through to the hyper-conscious rationalizing activities we each of us undertake from time to time. Theatrical consciousness operates at many levels but not primarily the latter.

Chapter 10

1. Shakespeare, for example, seems to have shown very little interest in having plays published. All of his drive seems to have been devoted to realizing them in performance.

2. The discussion here owes much to Hornby (1977), Gross (1974), Styan (1975) and Natchkirk (1976). In particular we would stress yet again that there is no meaning inherent in the script, it cannot be simply discovered, it is created through a long process of suck-it-and-see.

3. A performer such as Olivier leaves his stamp on a part in such a way that he becomes a difficult person to follow:

> 'Now is the winter. . . .' God, it seems terribly unfair of Shakespeare to begin his play with such a famous speech. You don't like to put your mouth to it, so many other mouths have been there. Or to be more honest, one particularly distinctive mouth. His poised, staccato delivery is imprinted on those words like teeth marks. (Sher, 1985)

In the same way Henry Ford leaves his indentation upon his company, Watson on IBM, Geneen on ITT, Reith on the BBC are difficult acts to follow.

4. As our good friends Wright and Taylor (1984) put it, 'All organizations face the problem of how to influence their members to work effectively towards the achievement of organizational objectives'; once you have bought this you can be sold anything. It is an interpretation, however popular a one, to declare that there are *organizational* objectives and that these constitute the purpose of such organization. If, to be perverse, one embraced a notion that the institution existed to facilitate the development of individual objectives, the kind of readings offered would be (and have been) very different.

5. The role of the director in the theatre, like that of leaders in any settings, has been written about extensively. The most useful from our perspective has been the work of Shank (1972) to whom we are indebted for the idea of the director as the person whose choices are key to the realization of particular interpretations. We differ from him in a number of respects but agree on the most important ones, viz.: the play is an emblematization or objectification of feeling and the director is a most important figure in both providing a preliminary interpretation and securing the climate in which other performers can co-operate.

The organizational literature has recently seen a reawakening of interest. Two good books are those of Schein (1985) and Sergiovanni and Corbally (1984), both purporting to deal with organizational culture and leadership.

6. We cannot resist quoting Sher (1985) on what can happen when the pre-editing has not been effected well, when actors go their own way: *Richard III* 'set in a lion's cage, everyone was in track suits (different colours for different factions) and had white faces. We all had to learn acrobatics, aiming for back-flips and eventually settling for forward rolls. . . . Anarchy ruled. After Tyrell reported the successful murder of the princes, Jonathan (playing Richard) used to slip in a "Nice one, Tyrell" between some immortal couplet. In his tent at Bosworth he used to bring the house down by referring a line about "soldiers" to the strips of toast on his breakfast tray. . . . In the hands of brilliant dangerous actors like Jonathan and Bernard Hill . . . the clowning was inspired, departing from the rehearsed scenes. . . .'

Parallel experience may be had in many an organization where what is severally enacted may be inconsistent and contradictory, even if inspired.

References

Administrative Science Quarterly (1983). Special Issue on Organization Culture, **28** (3).

Argelander, R. (1973). 'Scott Burton's behaviour tableaux', *Drama Review*, **17**, 107–113.

Argyle, M. (1975). *Bodily Communication*, New York: International University Press.

Argyle, M., and Henderson, M. (1985). *The Anatomy of Relationships*, London: Heinemann.

Aristotle, *Poetics* 6, 5, translated by M. E. Hubbard, in D. A. Russell and M. Winterbottom (eds.), *Ancient Literary Criticism*, Oxford: Oxford University Press.

Asch, S. (1951). 'Effects of group pressure upon the modification and distortion of judgements', in H. Guetzkov (ed.), *Groups, Leadership and Men*, Pittsburgh: Carnegie Press.

Austin, J. L. (1962). *How To Do Things With Words*, New York: Oxford University Press.

Averill, J. R. (1982). *Anger and Aggression: an Essay on Emotion*, New York: Springer-Verlag.

Back, K. W. (1981). 'Small groups', in M. Rosenberg and R. Turner (eds.), *Social Psychology: Sociological Perspectives*, New York: Basic Books.

Baker, G. P. (1925). *Theatre Arts Monthly*.

Barish, J. (1983). *The Anti-Theatrical Prejudice*, Berkeley: University of California Press.

Barthes, R. (1964). 'Rhetorique de l'image', *Communications*, **4**, 40–51.

Bassnett-McGuire, S. (1983). *Luigi Pirandello*, London: Macmillan.

Bastick, T. (1982). *Intuition*, Chichester: Wiley.

Bauman, R. (1975). 'Verbal art as performance', *American Anthropologist*, **77**, 290–311.

Becker, E. (1975). *Escape from Evil*, New York: The Free Press.

Becker, H. (1963). *Outsiders*, New York: The Free Press.

Benney, M., and Hughes, E. C. (1970). 'Of sociology and the interview', in N. Denzin (ed.), *Sociological Methods*, Chicago: Aldine.

Bentley, E. (1964). *The Life of the Drama*, London: Methuen.

Berger, P. (1966). *Invitation to Sociology: a Humanistic Perspective*, Harmondsworth: Penguin.

Bergson, H. cited in E. Bentley (1964).

Berkowitz, S. D. (1982). *An Introduction to Structural Analysis*, Toronto: Butterworths.

Bevington, D. (1984). *Action is Eloquence: Shakespeare's Language of Gesture*, Harvard: Harvard University Press.

Biddle, B. J. (1979). *Role Theory: Expectations, Identities and Behaviors*, New York: Academic Press.

Billington, M. (1973). *The Modern Actor*, London: Hamish Hamilton.

Birdwhistell, R. L. (1973). *Kinesics and Context: Essays*, Harmondsworth: Penguin.

Blake, R. R., and Mouton, J. S. (1978). *The New Managerial Grid*, Houston: Gulf Publishers.

Blanchard, K., and Johnson, S. (1981). *The One-Minute Manager*, London: Fontana/ Collins.

Blau, P., and Schoenherr, R. (1971). *The Structure of Organizations*, New York: Basic Books.

Blumer, H. (1969). *Symblic Interactionism*, Englewood Cliffs, New Jersey: Prentice-Hall.

Bodkin, M. (1958). *Archetypal Patterns in Poetry*, New York: Random House.

Bogarde, D. (1983). *An Orderly Man*, New York: Knopf.

Bogatyrev, P. (1971). 'Les Signes du Theatre', *Poetique*, **8**, 517–530.

Boulton, J. T. (1963). 'Harold Pinter: *The Caretaker* and other plays', *Modern Drama*, **1963** (September), 131–140.

Brecht, B. (1964). *Brecht on Theatre*, New York: Hill and Wang.

Briggs, J. (1983). *This Stage-Play World*, Oxford: Oxford University Press.

Briskman, L. (1981). 'Creative product and creative process', in D. Dutton and M. Krausz (eds.), *The Concept of Creativity in Science and Art*, The Hague: Nijhoff.

Brissett, D., and Edgley, C. (eds.) (1975). *Life as Theater: a Dramaturgical Sourcebook*, Chicago: Aldine.

Brody, A. (1970). *The English Mummers and their Plays*, London: Routledge and Kegan Paul.

Brook, P. (1969). *The Empty Space*, New York: Discov Books.

Brown, J. R. (1965). 'Dialogue in Pinter and others', *Critical Quarterly*, **1965** (Autumn).

Brown, P., and Levinson, S. (1978). 'Universals in language usage: politeness phenomena', in E. N. Goody (ed.), *Questions and Politeness*, Cambridge: University Press.

Brown, R. H. (1977). *A Poetic for Sociology*, Cambridge: Cambridge University Press.

Brusak, K. (1938). 'Signs in the Chinese theatre', in A. L. Matejka and R. Titunik (eds.), *Semiotics of Art*, Cambridge, Mass., MIT Press.

Burgon, B. (1982). *The Gramophone*, **60** (October).

Burke, K. (1957). *The Philosophy of Literary Form*, New York: Vintage Books.

Burke, K. (1959). *Attitudes towards History*, Boston: Beacon Press.

Burke, K. (1965). *Permanence and Change*, Indianapolis: Bobbs-Merrill.

Burke, K. (1966). *Language as Symbolic Action*. Berkeley: University of California Press.

Burke, K. (1968a). *Counterstatement*, Berkeley: University of California Press.

Burke, K. (1968b). 'Dramatism', in *International Encyclopaedia of the Social Sciences*, Vol. VII, New York: Macmillan.

Burke, K. (1969a). *A Grammar of Motives*, Berkeley: University of California Press.

Burke, K. (1969b). *A Rhetoric of Motives*, Berkeley: University of California Press.

Burke, K. (1970). *The Rhetoric of Religion*, Berkeley: University of California Press.

Burns, E. (1972). *Theatricality: a Study of Convention in the Theatre and Social Life*, New York: Harper Torchbooks.

Callow, S. (1984). *Being an Actor*, London: Methuen.

Canter, D. (1975). *Environmental Interaction*, London: Surrey University Press.

Carroll, W., Fox, J. and Ornstein, M. (1982). 'The network of directorate interlocks among the largest Canadian firms', *Canadian Review of Sociology and Anthropology*, **19** (1), 44–69.

Chambers, E. K. (1903). *The English Folk Play*, London: Oxford University Press.

Cicourel, A. V. (1964). *Method and Measurement in Sociology*, New York: Free Press.

Cicourel, A. V. (1982). 'Interviews, surveys, and the problem of ecological validity', *The American Sociologist*, **17**, 11–20.

Cohen, A. (1981). *The Politics of Elite Culture: Explorations in the Dramaturgy of Power in a Modern African Society*, Berkeley: University of California Press.

Cohen, S., and Taylor, L. (1976). *Escape Attempts: the Theory and Practice of Resistance to Everyday Life*, London: Allen Lane.

Cole, D. (1975). *The Theatrical Event*, Middletown: Wesleyan University Press.

Collins, R. (1981). 'On the microfoundations of macrosociology', *American Journal of Sociology*, **86**, 984–1014.

Combs, J. E., and Mansfield, M. W. (eds.) (1976). *Drama in Life: The Uses of Communication in Society*, New York: Hastings House.

Dawson, S. W. (1970). *Drama and the Dramatic*, London: Methuen.

Denzin, N. K. (ed.) (1978). *Studies in Symbolic Interaction*, Volume 1, Greenwich: JAI Press.

Denzin, N. and Keller, C. (1981). 'Frame analysis reconsidered', *Contemporary Sociology*, **10**, 52–60.

Diderot, D. (1978). 'The paradox of the actor', see A. Billy (ed.), *Oeuvres*, Paris: Gallimard.

Dion, K., Berscheid, E., and Walster, E. (1972). 'What is beautiful is good', *Journal of Personality and Social Psychology*, **24**, 285–290.

Donaldson, G., and Lorsch, J. W. (1983). *Decision Making at the Top*, New York: Basic Books.

Douglas, M. and Isherwood, B. (1979). *The World of Goods*, New York: Basic Books.

Drama Review (1981). Issue on Actor/Directors, **25** (3).

Duncan, H. (1953). *Language and Literature in Society*, Chicago: University of Chicago Press.

Duncan, H. (1962). *Communication and Social Order*, New York: Oxford University Press.

Duncan, H. (1964). *The Rise of Chicago as a Literary Center from 1885 to 1920*, Totowa, New Jersey: Bedminster Press.

Duncan, H. (1965). *Culture and Democracy*, Totowa, New Jersey: Bedminster Press.

Duncan, H. (1968a). *Symbols and Social Theory*, New York: Oxford University Press.

Duncan, H. (1968b). *Symbols in Society*, New York: Oxford University Press.

Eco, U. (1977). *Semiotics of Theatrical Performance*, Bloomington: Indiana University Press.

Edwardes, M. (1983). *Back from the Brink: an Apocalyptic Experience*, London: Pan Books.

Elam, K. (1980). *The Semiotics of Theatre and Drama*, London: Methuen.

Eliot, T. S. (1951). *Selected Essays*, London: Faber.

Face, The (1985).

Fergusson, F. (1949). *The Idea of a Theater*, Princeton, New Jersey: Princeton University Press.

Fieldman, A. (1966). *Collected Works of Oliver Goldsmith*, Oxford: Oxford University Press.

Foote, N. (1951). 'Identification as the basis for a theory of motivation', *American Sociological Review*, **46**, 14–21.

Fry, C. (1952). See R. W. Corrigan (1965), *Comedy: Meaning and Form*, San Francisco: Chandler.

Funke, L., and Booth, J. E. (1961). *Actors Talk about Acting*, New York: Avon Books.

Garrick, D. (1980). *The Plays of David Garrick*, Carbondale: Southern Illinois Press.

Geertz, C. (1973). *The Interpretation of Cultures*, New York: Basic Books.

Geertz, C. (1980). *Negara*, Princeton: Princeton University Press.

Goffman, E. (1959). *The Presentation of Self in Everyday Life*, Garden City, New Jersey: Anchor Books.

Goffman, E. (1961a). *Encounters*, Indianapolis: Bobbs-Merrill.

Goffman, E. (1961b). *Asylums*, Garden City, New Jersey: Anchor Books.

Goffman, E. (1963a). *Behavior in Public Places*, New York: The Free Press.

Goffman, E. (1963b). *Stigma*, Englewood Cliffs, New Jersey: Prentice-Hall.

Goffman, E. (1967). *Interaction Ritual*, Garden City, New Jersey: Anchor Books.

Goffman, E. (1969). *Strategic Interaction*, Philadelphia: University of Pennsylvania Press.

Goffman, E. (1971). *Relations in Public*, New York: Basic Books.

Goffman, E. (1974). *Frame Analysis*, New York: Harper and Row.

Goffman, E. (1983). 'The interaction order', *American Sociological Review*, **48**, 1–17.

Gregor, T. (1977). *Mehinaku: the Dramatization of Life in a Brazilian Indian Village*, Chicago; University of Chicago Press.

Gross, R. (1974). *Understanding Playscripts: Theory and Method*, Bowling Green: Bowling Green University Press.

Grunberger, R. (1974). *A Social History of the Third Reich*, Harmondsworth: Penguin.

Guardian, The (1981). 30 June.

Gusfield, J. R. (1963). *Symbolic Crusade: Status Politics and the American Temperance Movement*, Urbana, Illinois: University of Illinois Press.

Gusfield, J. R. (1981). *The Culture of Public Problems: Drinking-Driving and the Symbolic Order*, Chicago: University of Chicago Press.

Haas, J. and Shaffir, W. (eds.) (1978). *Shaping Identity in Canadian Society*, Scarborough: Prentice-Hall.

Hall, E. T. (1966). *The Hidden Dimension*, Garden City, New Jersey: Doubleday.

Hall, P. M., and Hewitt, J. P. (1970). 'The quasi-theory of communication and the management of dissent', *Social Problems*, **18**, 17–27.

Haney, C., Banks, C., and Zimbardo, P. (1973). 'Interpersonal dynamics in a simulated prison', *International Journal of Criminology and Penology*, **1**, 69–97.

Hardison, O. B. (1965). *Christian Rite and Christian Drama in the Middle Ages*, Baltimore: Johns Hopkins University Press.

Hare, A. P. (1985). *Social Interaction as Drama*, Beverly Hills: Sage.

Harré, R. (1979). *Social Being*, Oxford: Basil Blackwell.

Harré, R., and Secord, P. F. (1972). *The Explanation of Social Behaviour*, Oxford: Basil Blackwell.

Hawkes, T. (1972). *Metaphor*, London: Methuen.

Heffner, H. C. (1957). 'Pirandello and the nature of man', *Tulane Drama Review*, **1** (3), 23–40.

Heilman, S. (1976). *Synagogue Life: a Study in Symbolic Interaction*, Chicago: University of Chicago Press.

Heilpern, J. (1977). *Conference of the Birds*, London: Faber.

Heiss, J. (1981). 'Social roles', in M. Rosenberg and R. Turners (eds.), *Social Psychology: Sociological Perspectives*, New York: Basic Books.

Hewitt, J. P., and Hall, P. M. (1973). 'Social problems, problematic situations and quasi-theories', *American Sociological Review*, **38**, 367–374.

Hewitt, J. P., and Stokes, R. (1975). 'Disclaimers', *American Sociological Review*, **40**, 1–11.

Hiley, J. (1981). *Theatre at Work*, London: Routledge and Kegan Paul.

Hill, J. (1755). *The Actor*, London.

Hill, W. F. (ed.) (1961). *Collected Papers on Group Psychotherapy*, Provo, Utah: Utah State Hospital.

Hirsch, P. M., and Andrews, J. A. Y. (1983). 'Ambushes, shoot-outs, and knights of the Round Table: the language of corporate takeovers', in L. Pondy *et al.* (eds.), *Organizational Symbolism*, Greenwich, Connecticut: JAI Press.

Hochschild, A. R. (1983). *The Managed Heart: Commercialization of Human Feeling*, Berkeley: University of California Press.

Holland, P. (1979). *The Ornament of Action: Text and Performance in Restoration Comedy*, Cambridge: Cambridge University Press.

Hornby, R. (1977). *Script into Performance*, Austin: University of Texas Press.

Howe, I. (1967). *The Idea of the Modern in Literature and the Arts*, New York: Horizon Press.

Jonson, Ben (1617). *The Vision of Delight*.

Kakabadse, A., and Parker, C. (eds.) (1984). *Power, Politics and Organizations*, Chichester: Wiley.

Kemper, T. D. (1978). *A Social Interactional Theory of Emotions*, New York: Wiley.

Kennedy, A. (1975). *Six Dramatists in Search of a Language*, Cambridge: Cambridge University Press.

Kirby, M. (1976). 'Structural analysis/structural theory', *The Drama Review*, **20**, 51–86.

Kitto, H. D. F. (1956). *Form and Meaning in Drama*, London: Methuen.

Klapp, O. (1962). *Heroes, Villains and Fools*, Englewood Cliffs, New Jersey: Prentice-Hall.

Klapp, O. (1964). *Symbolic Leaders: Public Dramas and Public Men*, New York: Irvington.

Knorr-Cetina, K., and Mulkay, M. (eds.) (1983). *Science Observed: New Perspectives on the Social Study of Science*, Beverly Hills: Sage.

Kottack, C. P. (1979). 'Rituals at McDonald's', *Natural History*, **87**, 75–81.

Kuhn, T. H. (1970). *The Structure of Scientific Revolutions*, Chicago: University of Chicago Press.

Laing, R. D. (1967). *The Politics of Experience*, New York: Ballantine Books.

Lakoff, G., and Johnson, M. (1980). *Metaphors We Live By*, Chicago: University of Chicago Press.

Langer, S. (1957). *Problems of Art*, New York: Scribner.

Lazarowicz, K. (1977). 'Triadische Kollusion', in *Das Theater und Sein Publikum*, Vienna: Osterreichische Akademie der Wissenschaften.

Leach, E. (1965). 'Ritual', in *The Encyclopaedia of the Social Sciences*, London: Macmillan.

Levy-Leboyer, C. (1982). *Psychology and Environment*, Beverly Hills: Sage.

Lewis, D. J., and Smith, R. L. (1980). *American Sociology and Pragmatism*, Chicago: University of Chicago Press.

Lotman, Y. (1973). *La Structure du Texte Artistique*, Paris: Gallimard.

Lundberg, F. (1969). *The Rich and the Super-rich*, New York: Bantam Books.

Lyman, S. M., and Scott, M. B. (1970). *A Sociology of the Absurd*, New York: Appleton-Century-Crofts.

Lyman, S. M., and Scott, M. B. (1975). *The Drama of Social Reality*, New York: Oxford University Press.

Machiavelli, N. (1908). *The Prince* (trans. W. K. Marriott), London: Dent.

Malatesta, C. Z., and Izard, C. E. (1984). *Emotion in Adult Development*, Beverly Hills: Sage.

Mangham, I. L. (1973/74). 'Facilitating intraorganizational dialogue in a merger situation', *Interpersonal Development*, **4**, 133–147.

Mangham, I. L. (1978). *Interactions and Interventions in Organizations*, Chichester: Wiley.

Mangham, I. L. (1979). *The Politics of Organizational Change*, London: Associated Business Press.

Mangham, I. L. (1983). 'Blueprints for anarchy', unpublished paper, Centre for the Study of Organizational Change and Development, University of Bath.

Mangham, I. L. (1986). *Power and Performance in Organizations: an Exploration of Executive Process*, Oxford: Basil Blackwell.

Mangham, I. L., and Overington, M. A. (1983a). 'Performance and rehearsal: social order and organizational life', *Symbolic Interaction*, **5** (2), 205–222.

Mangham, I. L., and Overington, M. A. (1983b). 'Dramatism and the theatrical metaphor', in G. Morgan (ed.), *Beyond Method*, Beverly Hills: Sage.

Manning, P. (1980). 'Goffman's framing order: style as structure', in J. Ditton (ed.), *The View from Goffman*, New York: St Martin's Press.

March, J. G., and Simon, H. A. (1958). *Organizations*, New York: Wiley.

Marvell, Andrew, lines 53–64 from 'An Horatian Ode upon Cromwell's return from Ireland', quoted in S. Orgel (1975), *The Illusion of Power*, Berkeley: University of California Press.

Mead, G. H. (1934). *Mind, Self and Society*, Chicago: University of Chicago Press.

Mead, G. H. (1938). *The Philosophy of the Act*, Chicago: University of Chicago Press.

Meeker, B. F. (1981). 'Expectation states and interpersonal behavior', in M. Rosenberg and R. Turner (eds.), *Social Psychology: Sociological Perspectives*, New York: Basic Books.

Miller, D. L. (1973). *George Herbert Mead*, Austin: University of Texas Press.

Miller, G. A. (1956). 'The magical number 7 ± 2: some limits on our capacity for processing information', *Psychological Review*, **63**, 81–97.

Mills, C. Wright (1940). 'Situated actions and vocabularies of motive', *American Sociological Review*, **5**, 904–913.

Mintzberg, H. (1973). *The Nature of Managerial Work*, New York: Harper and Row.

Moreno, J. L. (1943). 'Sociometry and the cultural order', *Sociometry*, **6** (3), 299–344.

Morgan, G. (ed.) (1983). *Beyond Method*, Beverly Hills: Sage.

Mosse, G. L. (1975). *The Nationalization of the Masses: Political Symbolism and Mass Movements in Germany from the Napoleonic Wars through the Third Reich*, New York: Howard Fertig.

Muir, E. (1981). *Civic Ritual in Renaissance Venice*, Princeton: Princeton University Press.

Natchkirk, A. (1976). *Runes, Rhymes and Reasons*, Alice Springs: Aboriginal Press.

Neale, R. S. (1981). *Bath: a Social History 1680–1850*, London: Routledge and Kegan Paul.

Nye, R. (1982). *The Voyage of the Destiny*, London: Putnam Publishing Group.

Oestereich, T. (1930). *Possession, Demonical and Other*, London: Kegan Paul.

Orwell, G. (1933). *Down and Out in Paris and London*, London: Gollancz.

Parkinson, C. (1957). *Parkinson's Law and Other Studies in Administration*, London: Heinemann.

Passow, W. (1981). 'The analysis of theatrical performance', *Poetics Today*, **2** (3), 237–255.

Penrod, S. (1983). *Social Psychology*, Englewood Cliffs, New Jersey: Prentice-Hall.

Perinbanayagam, R. S. (1964). 'The definition of the situation: an analysis of the ethnomethodological and dramaturgical view', *Sociological Quarterly*, **15** (4), 521–541.

Perinbanayagam, R. S. (1977). 'The structure of motives', *Symbolic Interaction*, **1** (1), 104–120.

Perinbanayagam, R. S. (1982a). 'Dramas, metaphors and structures', *Symbolic Interaction*, **5** (2), 259–276.

Perinbanayagam, R. S. (1982b). *The Karmic Theater: Self, Society, and Astrology in Jaffna*, Amherst: University of Massachusetts Press.

Peters, T. J., and Waterman, R. H. (1982). *In Search of Excellence*, New York: Warner Books.

Pickhard-Cambridge, A. W. (1968). *The Dramatic Festivals of Athens*, Oxford: Oxford University Press.

Pinter, H. (1978). *The Betrayal*, in *Plays: Four*, London: Methuen.

Pirandello, L. (1923). *Each in his Own Way*, London: Dent.

Plutchik, R., and Kellerman, H. (1980). *Emotion: Theory, Research and Experience*, Orlando: Academic Press.

Poetics Today (1981). Issue on Drama, Theater, Performance, **2** (3).

Pospisil, L. (1965). *The Kapauku Papuans*, New York: Holt, Rinehart.

Prynne, W., quoted in Barish (1983).

Quigley, A. (1975). *The Pinter Problem*, Princeton: Princeton University Press.

Ranum, O., and Ranum, P. (1972). *Popular Attitudes towards Birth Control in Pre-industrial France and England*, New York: Harper Torchbooks.

Rapaport, A. (1982). *The Meaning of the Built Environment*, Beverly Hills: Sage.

Richards, I. A. (1925). *Principles of Literary Criticism*, New York: Harcourt Brace.

Righter, A. (1962). *Shakespeare and the Idea of the Play*, Oxford: Oxford University Press.

Robeiro, A. (1984). *Dress in Eighteenth Century Europe*, New York: Holmes and Meier.

Rosaldo, M. A. (1980). *Knowledge and Passion: Ilongot Notions of Self and Social Life*, New York: Cambridge University Press.

Rose, M. (ed.) (1961). *The Wakefield Mystery Plays*, New York: W. W. Norton.

Roy, W. (1983). 'The unfolding of the interlocking directorate structure in the United States', *American Sociological Review*, **48**, 248–257.

Saint-Simon, Duc de (1901), *Memoirs of Louis XIV and the Regency*, Washington, DC: M. W. Dunne.

Santayana, G. cited in Bentley (1964).

Schank, R., and Abelson, R. (1977). *Scripts, Plans, Goals and Understanding*, Hillsdale, New Jersey: Lawrence Erlbaum Associates.

Scheff, T. J. (ed.) (1975). *Labelling Madness*, Englewood Cliffs, New Jersey: Prentice-Hall.

Schein, E. (1985). *Organizational Culture and Leadership*, San Francisco: Jossey Bass.

Schlueter, J. (1979). *Metafictional Characters in Modern Drama*, New York: Columbia University Press.

Scott, M. B., and Lyman, M. (1968). 'Accounts', *American Sociological Review*, **33**, 46–62.

Schutz, A. (1967). *Collected Papers*, I, The Hague: Nijhoff.

Semin, G. R., and Manstead, A. S. R. (1983). *The Accountability of Conduct*, London: Academic Press.

Sennett, R. (1974). *The Fall of Public Man*, Cambridge: Cambridge University Press.

Sergiovanni, T. J., and Corbally, J. E. (eds.) (1984). *Leadership and Organizational Culture: New Perspectives on Administrative Theory and Practice*, Urbana: University of Illinois Press.

Shank, T. (1972). *The Art of Dramatic Art*, New York: Delta Books.

Shaw, G. Bernard (1889). See D. H. Lawrence (ed.) (1961). *Platform and Pulpit*, New York: Hill and Wang.

Sher, A. (1985). *Year of the King*, London: Chatto and Windus.

Shotland, R. L., and Goodstein, L. (1983). 'Just because she doesn't want to doesn't mean it's rape', *Social Psychology Quarterly*, **46**, 220–232.

Simmel, G. (1973). Cited in E. Burns and T. Burns, *Sociology of Literature and Drama*, Harmondsworth: Penguin.

Sitwell, E. (1932). *Bath*, London: Faber.

Sloan, S. (1972). 'Translating psycho-social criteria into design determinants', in W. Mitchell (ed.), *Proceedings of Environmental Design Research Association*, Los Angeles: University of California Los Angeles.

Sommer, R. (1979). Cited in A. Rapaport (1982).

Speer, A. (1970). *Inside the Third Reich*, London: Sphere Books.

Stairway to Success, Newsweek Inc., 24 Oct. 1966.

Stanislavski, C. (1961). *Creating a Role*, New York: Theatre Arts Books.

Steele, F. I. (1973). *Physical Settings and Organization Development*, Reading, Mass.: Addison-Wesley.

Steinbeck, D. (1970). *Einleitung in die Theorie und Systematik der Theater Wissenschaft*, Berlin: De Gruyter.

Steiner, G. (ed.) (1965). *The Creative Organisation*, Chicago: University of Chicago Press.

Stokes, R., and Hewitt, J. P. (1976). 'Aligning actions', *American Sociological Review*, **41**, 838–849.

Strachey, L. (1942). *Eminent Victorians*, Harmondsworth: Penguin.

Styan, J. L. (1975). *Drama, Stage and Audience*, Cambridge: Cambridge University Press.

Suppé, F. (ed.) (1977). *The Structure of Scientific Theories*, Urbana: University of Illinois Press.

Swift, G. (1983). *Waterlands*, London: Picador.

Symbolic Interaction (1981). Special Issue on G. H. Mead, **4** (2).

Taylor, F. W. (1911). *The Principles of Scientific Management*, New York: Harper an Brothers.

Terkel, S. (1975). *Working*, London: Wildwood House.

Thomas, E. M. (1965). *The Harmless People*, New York: Vintage Books.

Thourlby, W. (1978). *You Are What You Wear*, New York: Signet Books.

Townsend, R. (1978). *Up the Organization*, New York: Fawcett.

Travers, A. (1981). 'The stalking ground', Ph.D. thesis, University of Bath.

Tulane Drama Review, Spring 1985.

Veblen, T. (1953). *The Theory of the Leisure Class*, New York: Mentor Books.

Veltrusky, J. (1940). 'Man and object in the theater', in P. L. Garvin (ed.) (1964). *A Prague School Reader on Esthetics, Literary Structure and Style*, Washington: Georgetown University Press.

Wagner, J. (1975). 'The sex of time keeping', *International Journal of Symbology*, **6**, 23–30.

Walsh, E. J., and Warland, R. H. (1983). 'Social movement involvement in the wake of a nuclear accident', *American Sociological Review*, **48**, 764–780.

Weick, K. (1969). *The Social Psychology of Organizing*, Reading, Mass.: Addison-Wesley.

Wickham, G. (1963). *Early English Stages 1377–1660*, Volume 1, London: Routledge and Kegan Paul.

Wiles, T. J. (1980). *The Theater Event*, Chicago: University of Chicago Press.

Wilshire, B. (1982). *Role Playing and Identity: the Limits of the Theater as Metaphor*, Bloomington: University of Indiana Press.

Wood, P. (1981). Programme note, National Theatre, London.

Wright, P. L., and Taylor, D. S. (1984). *Improving Leadership Performance*, Englewood Cliffs, New Jersey: Prentice-Hall.

Young, F. (1965). *Initiation Ceremonies: a Cross-Cultural Study of Status Dramatization*, Indianapolis: Bobbs-Merrill.

Author Index

214

Subject Index

217

218